This Is Your Country on Drugs

This Is Your Country on Drugs

The Secret History of Getting High in America

RYAN GRIM

WILEY

John Wiley & Sons, Inc.

Published by John Wiley & Sons, Inc., Hoboken, New Jersey
Published simultaneously in Canada

For general information about our other products and services, please contact our Customer Care Department within the United States at (800) 762–2974, outside the United States at (317) 572–3993 or fax (317) 572–4002.

Wiley also publishes its books in a variety of electronic formats. Some content that appears in print may not be available in electronic books. For more information about Wiley products, visit our web site at www.wiley.com.

Library of Congress Cataloging-in-Publication Data:

Grim, Ryan, date.
    This is your country on drugs : the secret history of getting high in America / Ryan Grim.
        p.   cm.
    Includes index.
    ISBN 978-0-470-16739-7 (cloth)
    1. Drug addiction—United States.   2. Sociology—United States.   I. Title.
HV5825.G735   2009
306'.1—dc22

                                                                                    2008045527

Printed in the United States of America

10 9 8 7 6 5 4 3 2 1

for elizan

CONTENTS

CHAPTER 1

The Acid Casualty

One day in the fall of 2001, I realized that I hadn't seen any LSD in an awfully long time. I was living on the Eastern Shore of Maryland at the time, where the drug had been a fixture of my social scene since the early nineties. Most of my peers had continued dosing through college or whatever they chose to do instead. Even some watermen and farmers I knew had tripped on occasion.

Because most acid users don't take the drug with any regularity—a trip here or there is the norm—its absence didn't immediately register. It's the kind of drug that appears in waves, so the inability to find it at any given time could be chalked up to the vagaries of the illicit drug market.

I began asking friends who were going to hippie happenings to look for the drug. Eventually, I had a network of people poking around for it at concerts and festivals across the country, as well as in towns where you'd expect to find it, such as Boulder and San Francisco. They found nothing—and no one who'd even seen a hit of LSD since sometime in 2001—even at Burning Man, a gathering of thousands in the desert of Nevada. Strolling around Burning Man and being unable to find acid is something like walking into a bar and finding the taps dry.

● ● ●

In the fall of 2002, I enrolled at the University of Maryland's public-policy school in College Park, in the suburbs of Washington, D.C. Here, too, I continued my search for acid—and found the campus dry. Undergraduate hippies had only high school memories of the once culture-defining drug.

At some point, I decided that the disappearance of acid was nearly, if not totally, complete. I went to see a professor in my department, Peter Reuter, one of the most well-respected drug-policy researchers in the nation.

"Acid is gone," I told him.

"How'd you come to this theory?" he asked.

"I can't find it," I said, "and none of my friends can, either." I knew I sounded like a fool, but that was all I had.

"That's not how we do things in this field," he said. "Drug availability goes in cycles. That's not really a series of trends—that's just how it is." He pointed to a book behind me. "Here, hand me that."

He opened the 2002 *Monitoring the Future* report, which is produced by the University of Michigan and tracks drug use among American teens. "As you'll see," he said, running his finger across the LSD table, "use has been fairly steady over the last . . ." He paused and looked up. "That's interesting," he said, looking at the data for high school seniors. "LSD use is at an historic low: 3.5 percent." He then regrouped and continued with his lecture, telling me about supply and demand and peaks and valleys—and that he was certain the numbers for acid would rise in the 2003 survey.

Drug cycles are widely presumed to be the result of a combination of cultural shifts and the effectiveness of drug interdiction, but they're generally not well understood. Supply and demand, however, inarguably play a large role. When a drug becomes scarce, its price increases, enticing producers and distributors to invest more heavily in it, which increases supply, Reuter explained.

I told him that I wasn't so sure. His theories might not apply this time. There simply was no acid out there, and there hadn't been for several years. I rambled on about the end of the Grateful Dead and the collapse of giant raves. He was unmoved.

"Check the 2003 numbers," he said. "They may be online by now. If levels remain the same, then you've got something."

The 2003 numbers had just come out. I checked annual LSD use: it was at 1.9 percent, nearly a 50 percent drop. I checked a few other sources. Evidence of acid's decline could be found practically everywhere—in the falling statistics in an ongoing federal survey of drug use, in the number of emergency-room cases involving the drug, in a huge drop in federal arrests for LSD. I took the numbers back to Reuter.

"This isn't a trend," he said. "This is an event."

Like all drugs, acid is a bellwether of American society. Its effect on our culture in the sixties and seventies was immeasurable, and its disappearance in the early years of the twenty-first century was limited to the United States. Cultural commentators who look for trends in unemployment numbers, presidential-approval ratings, or car and housing purchases are missing something fundamental if they don't also consider statistics on drug use. Little tells us more about the state of America than what Americans are doing to get high.

Life in the United States, of course, is similar in many ways to life anywhere in the developed world. But our nation diverges sharply from the rest of the world in a few crucial ways. Americans work hard: 135 hours a year more than the average Briton, 240 hours more than the typical French worker, and 370 hours—that's nine weeks—more than the average German. We also play hard. A global survey released in 2008 found that Americans are more than twice as likely to smoke pot as Europeans. Forty-two percent of Americans had puffed at one point; percentages for citizens of various European nations were all under 20. We're also four times as likely as Spaniards to have done coke and roughly ten times more likely than the rest of Europe.

"We're just a different kind of country," said the U.S. drug czar's spokesman, Tom Riley, when asked about the survey. "We have higher drug-use rates, a higher crime rate, many things that go with a highly free and mobile society."

Different, indeed. There may be no people on earth with a more twisted and complex relationship to drugs. Much of our preconceived self-image turns out to be wrong: libertine continentals have nothing on us in terms of drug use, and American piety hasn't prevented us from indulging—in fact, it has sometimes encouraged it. Much of our conventional wisdom about American drug use—that the Puritans and the members of our founding generation were teetotalers or mild drinkers, that the drug trade is dominated by huge criminal organizations such as the Mafia and the Bloods, that crack use has declined significantly since the eighties—turns out to be wrong, too.

If there's one certainty about American drug use, it's this: we're always looking for a better way to feed our voracious appetite for getting high—for something cheaper, faster, less addictive, or more powerful. Drug trends feed themselves as word spreads about the amazing new high that's safe and nonaddictive. Then we discover otherwise—and go searching for the next great high. We often circle back to the original drug, forgetting why we quit it in the first place.

The morning of November 6, 2000, a day before the Bush-Gore election, William Leonard Pickard and his assistant, Clyde Apperson, were busy loading a massive LSD lab they'd secreted in a converted Atlas-E missile silo in Wamego, Kansas, into the back of a Ryder truck. Tubing, buckets, glassware—together with the right industrial chemicals and a lot of expertise, their equipment was capable of rapidly producing millions of doses of acid. When the men were finished, Pickard, a Harvard graduate and a legend in the LSD world for being one of the drug's top producers since the sixties, climbed into a rented Buick LeSabre. Apperson piloted the truck.

Cruising west on Highway 24, the convoy was followed by two police cars, which pulled behind the vehicles and turned on their lights and sirens. Neither Pickard nor Apperson pulled over.

After several miles, a state trooper was able to speed in front of the truck and bring it to a halt. Pickard tried to drive around the stopped vehicles but was blocked. With the Buick still moving, the fifty-five-year-old opened the door and rolled out of the car, then got up and took off on foot toward a nearby housing development. Special Agent Carl Nichols of the Drug Enforcement Administration (DEA), who was following behind the patrol cars, ran after him with trooper Brian K. Smith. Pickard had about a twenty-foot head start.

"Stop! Police!" Smith shouted over and over as he lumbered after a man nearly twice his age. The race went around the corner of a house and up an embankment, then through a yard and a cul-de-sac, then down a street. As if on a Hollywood director's cue, a car zipped down the street in front of Nichols and Smith, who were forced to wait to let it pass. Pickard, meanwhile, showed no signs of slowing. The lawmen legged it up another hill along a driveway. Again as if on cue, Smith, leading Nichols, slipped in the mud and fell. He got up and crested the hill, but Pickard was gone.

"We didn't know beforehand that Pickard was a marathon runner," Nichols told me later. "That would have been useful."

Pickard darted through the woods and down a stream to throw off the dogs that were sent after him. He made it to a farmhouse outside Wamego and spent the night in the cab of a pickup truck parked in a barn as helicopters swarmed overhead. An alert went out for citizens to be on the lookout for one of the world's most notorious drug dealers. He's armed and very dangerous, it said, though neither warning was true. A farmer spotted him in the barn the next morning and called the police.

In Palm Beach County, Florida, 1,300 miles away, thousands of elderly men and women were struggling to decipher the state's butterfly ballots. After weeks of legal battles, the Supreme Court sent George W. Bush to the White House, marking the end of an era that saw the comeback of LSD, the spread of Ecstasy, and the rise to political power of the sixties generation. In reaction to that rise, the ascent of Bush would be accompanied by an aggressive battle against all things liberal, as well as by the virtual eradication of a primary symbol of the American countercultural rebellion—the first of three sins Republicans had long sought to hang on their Democratic opposition by calling it the party of "acid, abortion, and amnesty."

For Pickard, it was the worst two days of his life—"the long night of the soul," as he called it in a letter from Lompoc Federal Prison. He was "shot through with tears, fear, searchlights, the thunder of choppers, fishtailing squad cars and drawn revolvers, Nazi shepherds, breathless running down creekbeds to throw off the bloodhounds, visions of worlds devastated forever, [my wife] two weeks from delivery and alone, and all the other feelings that arise while being hunted and captured by the armed clergy."

Pickard would receive two concurrent life sentences without the possibility of parole for conspiracy to manufacture LSD. DEA officials asserted that Pickard's Kansas lab produced 2.2 pounds of LSD—about 10 million doses, with a street value of $10 million— every five weeks. They had confiscated, they claimed, 90.86 pounds of LSD, by leaps the largest seizure in history.

They also boasted that this single bust had cut off 95 percent of all available LSD in the nation.

In an article published in *Slate* shortly after the new drug numbers had come out, I wrote about the disappearance of LSD. All of the available yardsticks, including data from the federal Drug Abuse Warning Network (DAWN), which charts emergency room data in twenty-one major cities, measured a steep drop-off in LSD use. DAWN, run by the Department of Health and Human Services, isn't a scientific survey; it merely records the "mentions" of drugs by emergency-room patients. (For instance, if you visited the ER with a broken finger and hospital personnel asked if you were on drugs and you said, "Yes, LSD," that would go down in DAWN as an LSD mention, even if you were fibbing. If you answered, "Yes, LSD and pot," both drug mentions would appear.) But DAWN numbers are still a good rough measure of drug use. Between 1995 and 2000, LSD mentions remained relatively stable, hovering at around 2,500 per six-month period. But in the second half of 2001, DAWN LSD mentions dropped below 1,000 for the first time. In the next six-month period, mentions fell below 500.

DAWN project director Dr. Judy Ball told me that what is notable about this decline is that it occurred in every metropolitan area surveyed. The drop in acid mentions was not local or even regional—it was national.

Nobody collects nationwide arrest data for LSD trafficking and possession, but federal arrests for these crimes had also tumbled in recent years. The DEA recorded 203 arrests in fiscal year 2000, 95 in FY 2001, 41 in FY 2002, and 19 in FY 2003. In the first quarter of 2004, the feds arrested only three people on LSD charges. In the

LSD haven of San Francisco, the DEA recorded no arrests in 2000 and just 20 in 2002, according to Special Agent Richard Meyer of the agency's San Francisco office.

One possible explanation for the decline could be that youthful attitudes about LSD had changed for the worse, dragging use down with them. But the high-school surveys for the period show that both perceived-risk and disapproval rates for the drug declined. So why hadn't consumption kept up with perception?

I suggested that Pickard's arrest came at a time when LSD was vulnerable, employing the well-worn "perfect storm" analogy. There's no doubt that Pickard was at some point one of the biggest—if not the biggest—producers in the nation. His incarceration, combined with the two other major cultural events I mentioned to Reuter—the demise of both the Grateful Dead and of giant raves—might have been enough to do acid in.

The LSD market took an early blow in 1995, when Jerry Garcia died and the Grateful Dead stopped touring. For thirty years, Dead tours had been essential to keeping LSD users and dealers connected. The DEA was aware of the connection and wrote about it in a 1994 divisional field assessment. After Garcia's death, Phish picked up part of the Dead's fan base—and the vestiges of its LSD-distribution network. In 1996, LSD use among twelfth graders peaked at 8.8 percent. By the end of 2000, Phish had stopped touring as well, and the survey numbers for LSD began to tumble.

Around the same time, the thousand-plus-person raves that were popular in the nineties—and always swimming with Ecstasy and LSD, a good chunk of which was probably dropped off by the roving delivery system of the Dead or Phish—began to fade out as police began targeting them with more intensity. They were finished off by the RAVE (Reducing Americans' Vulnerability to Ecstasy) Act of 2003, which threatened rave organizers with decades in prison if anyone at one of their events was arrested on drug charges—a virtual life sentence waiting to happen, given the crowd. The death of the massive rave brought on a flowering of a million intimate underground parties. Yet the closed nature of these smaller affairs often put them beyond the reach of not only the police, but also the LSD network.

With the collapse of the Dead, Phish, and the rave, a drug subculture that was maintained by touring musicians and DJs playing for thousands at a time found itself adrift. At the same time, it lost a major producer.

Due to the spiritual qualities of the experience it induces, acid is produced and distributed unlike any other drug—with cultish secrecy and evangelical zeal. LSD is a highly difficult substance to make, and recipes for it, unlike those for Ecstasy or meth, are fiercely guarded. (Recipes on the Internet are generally bogus or not detailed enough to be of any use.) In the early seventies, the government took down several dozen members of the drug's influential distribution network, known as the Brotherhood of Eternal Love. Despite facing long prison terms, the leaders of the group refused to testify against one another, which allowed the network to survive the jailing of Grateful Dead sound engineer Owsley Stanley—who financed the band with proceeds from his acid empire—and other top producers.

"The prosecutors had never seen anything like the Brotherhood," Michael Kennedy, the group's attorney, told author Robert Greenfield for his biography of Timothy Leary. "They brought in some informants from outside and did some infiltration, but nobody ever rolled on anybody else in that organization."

Pickard has hinted to me that he was a member of the Brotherhood. Although it's uncertain whether he was, he was certainly active in the LSD scene at the same time. By 2000, he had attained such status in the acid world that his bust sent shock waves through the system.

My *Slate* piece exploded on the Internet, as one ex-hippie after another forwarded it around the globe. After the story ran, my inbox was flooded with messages—some from people asking if I knew where they could find some acid, others telling stories from the sixties. Not a single person wrote to say that I was wrong, that acid could still be found somewhere in the United States.

A letter mailed to me at the university, though, caught my attention. The return address included a prisoner number and the town of Lompoc, California. It was from William Leonard Pickard. DEA agents never seized 90.86 pounds of LSD, he wrote. They're lying. Check the court transcripts.

• • •

LSD is one of the most powerful drugs ever created. A mere 20 micrograms—that's 20 millionths of a gram—can radically alter one's perception of reality for up to half a day. There is no known lethal dose, although people have gone into comas when exposed to too much. One example: an FBI agent who accidentally drenched himself while searching an LSD lab run by Pickard in the eighties, despite Pickard's attempt to warn him to wear protective gear. The agent had to be induced into a coma with Thorazine. He came to several days later and went home, but the Thorazine—which suppresses LSD's psychedelic effects—wore off while he was in the shower. He started tripping again and slipped back into a coma. He did survive, however.

Albert Hofmann, the Swiss chemist who invented the drug in 1938, called LSD "medicine for the soul." Most subsequent users have followed his lead, describing their trips in spiritual terms. Countless artists, writers, filmmakers, and musicians have sought to document this ineffable experience. Even Tony Soprano has gotten in on the psychedelic act: In the third-to-last episode of *The Sopranos*, he takes peyote, pukes, and strolls through a casino. There he spies a roulette wheel and tells his companion that it operates on the same principle as the solar system—one of the many insights that seem profound while tripping but are more likely nonsense. Religion scholar Huston Smith participated in Leary's infamous LSD experiments at Harvard and noted that his trips seemed similar to transcendental experiences described by the world's great mystics.

Acid inspires an endless stream of questioning that wouldn't be out of place in a Philosophy 101 class. Who am I? Why am I here? What is life? What is reality? The act of questioning everything, regardless of whether it actually leads to any answers, can mark a new level of independence in a person. To the acid initiate, a tripping sixteen-year-old is truly thinking on his own for the very first time. If existence is contingent upon thought, as Descartes suggested, then the LSD experience can mark the beginning of one's existence.

Because the psychedelic experience is so mentally subversive, it's less appealing to people who are relatively content in their worldview. Acid is perfect as a rite-of-passage drug, something to help a person transition from one stage of life to another, which explains why so many traditional cultures have used psychedelics in initiation ceremonies. Researchers in Europe are studying whether psychedelics can ease the fear of death in the terminally ill. Just as it can help kick-start one's life, so the thinking goes, it can help ease a person's departure from it.

The disappearance of LSD didn't mean an absence of melting walls in America. Head-trippers in the first decade of the twenty-first century turned to a variety of other psychedelics, from plant-based drugs such as ayahuasca and salvia to a host of lab-synthesized "research chemicals." Indeed, Americans' desire for inebriation is remarkably resilient. Aside from the occasional spike or dip in use, for the better part of the past four hundred years, the American desire to get blotto has been fairly steady. Dramatic movements toward or away from specific drugs don't happen in isolation. They're often related to changing patterns in the use of another drug.

On the Eastern Shore, my roommate had a healthy magic-mushroom-growing operation going in one of our bathrooms, and we readily consumed his fungal harvest in place of LSD. It wouldn't be too much of a stretch to say that 'shrooms became part of our daily diet, though they became less and less powerful unless we took a few days off. By the third straight day of doing them, they would effectively stop working, no matter how many we ate. Rather than creating a dependence, this diminishing psychedelic return makes them impossible to become addicted to.

Perhaps because our lives were both still in transition—he had just left the U.S. Army—the experience was almost always pleasant and profound. Later, when I was out of school and working toward a career, I found 'shrooming extremely uncomfortable. Federal drug-use statistics indicate that I have a lot of company in "growing out" of psychedelics—the bulk of users are in their mid-to-late teens or early twenties. After that, reported use of psychedelics ebbs toward zero. Of course, drug use itself doesn't disappear as Americans age—just hallucinogenic drug use—which says something about the level of our interest, as adults, in having our minds blown.

By the time acid was criminalized, in 1966, it had gone from the domain of academia to the realm of revolution. LSD fueled an upheaval that was ready for something mind-blowing. Indeed, though the civil rights and antiwar movements had their geneses before acid became prevalent in the hippie underground, it's likely that without LSD, the sixties would have more closely resembled previous waves of American leftism. With it, there emerged a full-grown countercul- ture, a church of opposition to mainstream American values.

Those values, suggested Alexis de Tocqueville, are what you get when you mix democracy with America's fervent Christianity. The idea of the American republic as a self-perfecting phenomenon has blended with our religious idealism to shape the way that we've viewed drugs and insobriety throughout U.S. history. "Religion in America takes no direct part in the government of society, but it must be regarded as the first of their political institutions," wrote the French social scientist in his landmark nineteenth-century travelogue *Democracy in America*. "However irksome an enactment may be, the citizen of the United States complies with it, not only because it is the work of the major- ity, but because it is his own, and he regards it as a contract to which he is himself a party. . . . While in Europe the same classes some- times resist even the supreme power, the American submits without murmur to the authority of the pettiest magistrate."

Of course, Tocqueville also identifies another key component of American society: individualism. But the combination of religious faith and respect for the law has undoubtedly led to the prohibition movements that have coursed through American culture since shortly after the Revolution. "Societies are formed which regard drunk- enness as the principal cause of the evils of the state, and solemnly bind themselves to give an example to temperance," Tocqueville observed, adding in a footnote, "At the time of my stay in the United States"—the 1830s—"the temperance societies already consisted of more than 270,000 members; and their effect had been to diminish the consumption of strong liquors by 500,000 gallons per annum in Pennsylvania alone."

The decision to get high is always a personal one. Ask a fan of psychedelics about drugs and he'll generally tell you that done responsibly, a regimen of recreational mind alteration aids one in liv- ing an examined life. But drug use has consequences for others, too, be they the children of the neglectful user or the doctor who handles highs gone wrong. The battle between common good and individual liberty has long defined the American story, and it has always been fought especially hard over inebriation of any kind.

When it comes to drugs, Americans have put precious little stock in the concept of pleasure, at least officially. Speed is acceptable as long as it boosts a kid's attention span and isn't just a good time. "Euphoria" is listed as a negative side effect of pharmaceutical drugs. Ours is a nation in which medical professionals who prescribe narcotics face the real prospect of prison time even when staying within accepted medical boundaries. Ronald McIver, a doctor from North Carolina, is now doing thirty years in a federal prison for reducing more pain than the government thought appropriate, although his prescribing habits were well within accepted medical practices. When pleasure is suspected, American drug use gets tricky, particularly when that high might do some real good, as in the case of medical marijuana.

Thus it was in drugs that sixties radicalism found its most visible form of cultural disobedience. While mainstream America took prescription uppers and downers and drank eminently legal martinis, the counterculture dropped a new drug that gave it a perception of reality that matched its revolutionary hopes. "There are the makings here of a complete social division: revolution is in the head, along the highways of perception and understanding. The psychedelic experience, being entirely subjective, is self-authenticating," argues Colin Greenland in his book *The Entropy Exhibition: Michael Moorcock and the British New Wave in Science Fiction*, which posits sixties youth culture as an "alien" society. "It gave its first advocates an inexorable sense of rightness in opposing their holistic, libertarian ethos to the discriminatory and repressive outlook of their elders. In legislating against cannabis and LSD, the governments of America and Europe were not only outlawing drugs that encouraged disaffection among the young but . . . were reaffirming faith in Western materialism and a single objective reality."

Psychedelic drugs give one a very real feeling that there's some type of intangible divide between those who have turned on and those who haven't. The psychedelic experience—with LSD's being perhaps the most powerful—defies credible characterization, largely because accounts of it strike the uninitiated as highly unbelievable and seem to the initiated incomplete. "Non-acid takers regard the LSD trip as a remarkable flight from reality, whereas cautious devotees feel they've flown into reality," writes Richard Neville in his 1970 "guide to revolution," *Playpower*. "After an acid trip, you can reject everything you have ever been taught."

LSD didn't disappear after it was criminalized. The American government wasn't toppled, either. Rather, the nation was able to absorb acid and the counterculture into mainstream consciousness— probably because there was something fundamentally American about both from the beginning. LSD is for questers, and Americans have always been on a quest, whether it's to go west, to go to the moon, or to spread democracy around the globe. Timothy Leary, who spent years in prison and was once called "the most dangerous man in America" by President Richard Nixon, went to his end a respected cultural figure in the employ of Madison Avenue. Jerry Garcia's death was commemorated by congressional tributes and fawning cover stories in big-time glossies.

When Barack Obama solicited questions from the public on his presidential-transition Web site and allowed users to vote on the most popular, sixteen of the top fifty questions had to do with liberalizing drug policy. In the midst of war and financial collapse, the question voted most pressing asked whether Obama would legalize marijuana. The media ridiculed the result, but in doing so, they showed how much they misunderstand the importance we currently place on getting high in America. Today, huge majorities support legalizing marijuana for medical purposes, and almost half of Americans support legalizing it for everybody twenty-one and older.

Such widespread acceptance of exploratory drug use helped lead to the comeback of LSD, pot, and other hippie drugs in the nineties. The comeback stalled out just after Nichols and Smith chased Pickard through the Kansas countryside.

America, we like to boast, is an amalgamation of many different cultural strains. One class or community—say, impoverished southern manual laborers—might be doing something completely different to get high from what another group—say, well-heeled northeastern hipsters—would do. Or it might not be: meth has been popular at the same time with both the trailer-park set and the urban gay community. Such odd similarities and stark differences reveal both something particular about a given socioeconomic milieu and something of the essential character of the American people.

In the late sixties Andy Warhol's New York scene was openly driven by meth; the drug only later infiltrated LSD-centered San Francisco. In the spring of 1966, Warhol's performance-art extravaganza/troupe of speed freaks, the Exploding Plastic Inevitable, accepted an invitation to play the Fillmore Auditorium in San Francisco, a legendary hippie venue. The result was a collision of drug cultures, reports Martin Torgoff in his book *Can't Find My Way Home: America in the Great Stoned Age, 1945–2000.*

"We spoke two completely different languages because we were on amphetamine and they were on acid," Warhol follower Mary Woronov told Torgoff. "They were so slow to speak, with these wide eyes—'Oh, wow!'—so into their vibrations; we spoke in rapid-machine-gun fire about books and paintings and movies. They were into . . . the American Indian and going back to the land and trying to be some kind of true, authentic person; we could not have cared less about that. They were homophobic; we were homosexual. Their women—they were these big, round-titted girls; you would say hello to them, and they would just flop on the bed and fuck you; we liked sexual tension, S&M, not fucking. They were barefoot; we had platform boots. They were eating bread they had baked themselves—we never ate at all!"

That disparity had more to do with cultural differences than with drug availability. Warhol and his band had ready access to all the LSD they could have digested, but it didn't fit as well with their lifestyle and values as meth did. The same type of choice was evident among the hippies: bennies and other forms of meth were there for those who wanted them, but the egoism and aggression that those drugs provoke didn't fit the counterculture ethos. Although drugs are often given credit for creating or driving a culture, sometimes it can be the other way around. When a culture can freely choose one drug over another, it will pick the one that fits best with its worldview.

So much has been written on drug use and American culture that it would take weeks to roll all of that paper up and smoke it. In much of that writing, the story of American drug use goes something like this: The party started in the sixties, got crazy in the seventies, and got out of control in the eighties, as greed and addiction took over. That was followed by a period of recovery and maturity. Yet America is not a rock band, and its real history wouldn't fit neatly on VH1. Very few popular authors bother to look at what drugs Americans themselves say they're on—which is a shame, because that information isn't hard to get. In addition to the University of Michigan's federally funded survey of teenagers, which has been going on since 1975, there's the feds' own survey of adult use, now called the National Household Survey on Drug Use and Health. There are also smaller surveys to which these can be compared, as well as data on arrests, seizures, and emergency-room admissions.

What the numbers reveal is that although things were indeed crazy in the seventies, things stayed crazy even after Americans supposedly sobered up. And while the standard drug narrative begins in the oh-so-wild late sixties, let's not kid ourselves. Future Americans were getting obliterated on their way to the continent, and perhaps no decade has witnessed as much better living through chemistry as the 1890s, a time when the movement against alcohol ushered in a buffet of modern highs.

The survey approach has a natural hindrance: not everybody wants to give the federal government detailed answers on illegal drug use. But there are ways to attempt to account for the "lie error" in surveys, and if a certain percentage of people were lying in 1975, it's safe to assume that a roughly similar percentage of people were lying in 2005. A recent study that drug-tested folks immediately after they took a drug-use survey found that the survey results were pretty accurate. Some people who had done drugs fibbed and said they hadn't, but some who hadn't done drugs lied and said they had. Both groups were very small, and they effectively canceled each other out.

However respondents might lie, though, surveys are always useful for reflecting drug trends. And because drug use is at once a private and a social affair, drug trends can tell us a lot about where we've been, where we are, and where we're going. A lot of smart people have spent careers poring over these numbers, and the insights they've come to have often been overlooked. But the data have frequently been presented as if they had no cultural or social implications—as if, for example, cocaine just appeared out of nowhere or LSD simply vanished. A lack of cultural or historical context allows partisans on both sides of the drug-policy debate to fill the void with their own stories: the CIA introduced crack to the ghetto; take acid and you'll jump out a window.

In reality, there's no such thing as drug policy. As currently understood and implemented, drug policy attempts to isolate a phenomenon that can't be taken in isolation. Economic policy is drug policy. Healthcare policy is drug policy. Foreign policy, too, is drug policy. When approached in isolation, drug policy almost always backfires, because it doesn't take into account the powerful economic, social, and cultural forces that also determine how and why Americans get high.

Cultural movements change our drug habits; our drug habits alter our culture. In both cases, the results might not be apparent for years. Yet a sober look at them makes it clear that America's twisted relationship with chemically induced euphoria has left a trail of consequences that have been as far-reaching as they've been unintended.

CHAPTER 2

A Pharmacopoeia Utopia

O n a Sunday in December 1873, around seventy women marched out of a Presbyterian church in Hillsboro, Ohio, led by the daughter of a former governor. "Walking two by two, the smaller ones in the front and the taller coming after, they sang more or less confidently, 'Give to the Winds Thy Fears,' that heartening reassurance of Divine protection now known . . . as the Crusade Hymn. Every day they visited the saloons and the drug stores where liquor was sold. They prayed on sawdust floors or, being denied entrance, knelt on snowy pavements before the doorways, until almost all the sellers capitulated," wrote Helen E. Tyler in *Where Prayer and Purpose Meet: The WCTU Story, 1874–1949*. Born out of these marches, the Woman's Christian Temperance Union became one of the most successful lobbying organizations in American history.

Over the next four decades, the group became a media sensation, grew its ranks to more than 345,000, and spearheaded the effort to transform the personal pledge of its members "to abstain from all distilled, fermented and malt liquors" into a constitutional mandate. By 1920, per capita consumption in the United States was only about an eighth of what it was a century before, and only about a quarter of what it is today.

The WCTU's slogan—"For God and Home and Native Land"—perfectly encapsulates the forces that propelled it: religion, family values, and nationalism. In the nineteenth-century United States, all three were ascendant. The Second Great Awakening fostered the growth of missionary societies, preaching tours, and days-long revival meetings. New periodicals such as *Godey's Lady's Book, Ladies' Home Journal*, and *Good Housekeeping* described women's duties to their nuclear families as near-religious imperatives. The War of 1812—especially Andrew Jackson's drubbing of the British at the Battle of New Orleans—gave Americans a sense of themselves as players equal to any on the world stage and unleashed a wave of patriotic fervor. If the latter ebbed a little during the Civil War, it rose again mightily with the 1876 centennial, marked in Philadelphia with an exposition of homegrown wonders that included Charles E. Hires's root beer, H. J. Heinz's ketchup, and Alexander Graham Bell's telephone.

In other words, if you had a taste for Bible-thumping, homemaking, flag-waving, and teetotaling, it was an exciting time for America. Ditto if you had a taste for cocaine or opiates.

What we think of as today's major drugs almost all entered American culture in the mid-nineteenth century, and all became hugely popular by the end of it. Key to their success was the demonization of beer, wine, and liquor by the WCTU, the Anti-Saloon League, and their various fellow travelers and predecessors, none of which understood something fundamental about America: that it relates to alcohol and drugs much like an addict does—with spasms of morality and sobriety followed by relapse.

Again and again in American history, the use of one substance diminishes while the use of another rises, due to a combination of social, political, and economic factors. A movement against a drug might spring up organically, but it's nurtured by whatever interests it serves. The drug goes from socially acceptable to socially condemned. It often becomes illegal. Then something else takes its place. This process was on full display in the nineteenth century, as the first significant surge of the temperance movement inadvertently created a drug lover's utopia.

The first European settlers of America drank much more alcohol—strong apple cider was soaked up by the gallon—than we do now, despite the reputations of our Puritan ancestors. (Colonists also smoked an enormous amount of tobacco, often a variety that contained around 15 percent nicotine—enough to cause hallucinations and a high far superior to the buzz that now comes from a Marlboro.) Unlike the WCTU, early American temperance advocates opposed drunkenness, rather than drinking per se. In 1619, the colony of Virginia banned "playing dice, cards, drunkenness, idleness, and excess in apparel." The Massachusetts Bay Colony began requiring a governor's permit in order to sell liquor in 1633, observing that many of its people were "distempering themselves with drinke." One unfortunate lush, a fellow named Robert Cole, was made to wear a red "D" around his neck for a year.

But the American temperance movement didn't really get going until 1785, when Dr. Benjamin Rush, a social reformer and signer of the Declaration of Independence, wrote the first major antiliquor treatise in U.S. history. In his *Inquiry into the Effects of Ardent Spirits upon the Human Body and Mind, with an Account on the Means of Preventing, and of the Remedies for Curing Them*, Rush pioneered the conception of alcoholism as a disease, while still advocating Christianity, guilt, and shame as great inducements to sobriety. But he also wrote of the effectiveness of cures including vegetarianism, ankle blisters, a "violent attack of an acute disease," "an oath, taken before a magistrate, to drink no more spirits," and "suddenly, and entirely" abstaining from liquor—perhaps with the aid of a touch of laudanum.

Unlike the teetotalers he inspired, Rush restricted his finger-wagging to the consumption of liquor. Drinks such as beer and wine, he wrote, were "generally innocent, and often have a friendly influence upon health and life." Indeed, when America's most prominent physician was recommended by Thomas Jefferson to help prepare Meriwether Lewis and William Clark for their journey west, Rush suggested outfitting them with, in addition to such things as eight ounces of Turkish opium and six hundred mercury-laden laxatives of his own concoction, thirty gallons of "medicinal wine"—although the doctor did admonish, "The less spirit you use the better."

Rush suggested that the overuse of spirits could lead to everything from "a puking of bile," "a husky cough," and "frequent and disgusting

belchings" to "falsehood . . . fraud, theft, uncleanliness, and murder."
Liquor tears apart families, ruins fortunes, and corrupts children.
"The social and imitative nature of man," he warned, "often disposes
him to adopt the most odious and destructive practices from his companions," meaning that a drunkard begets other drunkards, until so
many are about that the very nation is at risk. "Should the customs
of civilized life preserve our nation from extinction . . . they cannot
prevent our country being governed by men, chosen by intemperate
and corrupted voters. From such legislators, the republic would soon
be in danger."

Like-minded men such as Jefferson and John Adams similarly wanted the nation to be built on "virtue"—a democratic society, they reasoned, requires the selfless and civilized participation of
upright citizens. Shortly after the Constitution was ratified, Treasury
Secretary Alexander Hamilton pushed through Congress a tax on liquor that he said was meant "more as a measure of social discipline
than as a source of revenue." (Though Hamilton also conceded that
he "wanted the tax imposed to advance and secure the power of the
new federal government.") Americans, it turned out, had as much
love for taxes on whiskey as they had for taxes on tea, and the levy
was met on the frontier with fierce resistance. Protesters launched
the Whiskey Rebellion of 1794, which had to be beaten back by
George Washington.

The movement against insobriety has risen and fallen at different points in the history of this nation founded on high idealism. But
whenever the American campaign against drunkenness has gathered
strength, whether in the 1830s, the 1870s, or the 1980s, the call for
temperance has evolved into a demand for full abstinence—zero
tolerance, in today's terms. Abraham Lincoln told a temperance
organization in 1842 that Americans used to assume that problems
with alcohol come from "abuse of a very good thing," but then came
to realize that the culprit is "use of a bad thing." The WCTU still
proudly displays a line from the ancient Greek philosopher Xenophon
on its Web site: "Temperance may be defined as: moderation in all
things healthful; total abstinence from all things harmful."

Members of various waves of the American temperance movement
have distributed copies of Rush's *Inquiry*, but once total abstinence

became the goal, they left his kudos to beer and wine on the editing-room floor. Other positive portrayals of drinking were edited out of American history, too. An 1848 engraving of George Washington making a toast to his officers shows him holding a glass and a bottle of liquor or wine on the table. When the image was reprinted for the centennial, as the temperance movement rose, the glass was removed and the bottle was replaced with a hat.

The temperance movement's drift toward extremism is understand-able. In the nineteenth century, temperance advocacy rose in tandem with organized efforts in support of both the abolition of slavery and equal rights for women, movements that tended to favor uncompro-mising positions. Lincoln supported a moderate stance on slavery and still went to war over it. And women either deserved equal rights or they didn't—although the suffrage and temperance movements were so closely connected that opponents of the latter often opposed the former so that women wouldn't have a chance to vote on alcohol in the way that they'd promised.

Future president Warren G. Harding, an early opponent of pro-hibition, summed up that political positioning in 1916 when he was a senator from Ohio. "I am not sure how I will vote, but think I will vote against suffrage," he said, according to an article from the time in *The Nation* magazine. "I don't see how I can vote for suffrage and against prohibition."

By 1812, when Rush published his extremely popular *Medical Inquiries and Observations upon the Diseases of the Mind*, he'd con-cluded that drinkers, not just drinks, could be generally innocent. Their will, he writes, was the "involuntary vehicle of vicious actions." But that didn't stop him from suggesting, after a little hand-wringing over issues of personal liberty, that alcoholics be confined to "sober houses" in order to initiate a "complete and radical cure of their disease."

The transition from moderation to the radical cure of abstention was further assisted by the Reverend Lyman Beecher, a brilliant orator and evangelist who had no fewer than six children who would make a mark on literary and political history. (Harriet Beecher Stowe of *Uncle*

Tom's Cabin fame is the best known today.) Beecher and his children, several of whom were prominent abolitionists, were what we would now call liberals or progressives. Although Democrats are the ones usually tagged as being "soft on drugs" today, throughout American history, movements against drugs and alcohol have generally come from the left, as they cited concerns about the common good, public health, and religion. Republican president Harding and his attorney general famously played poker and drank bootlegged whiskey during Prohibition, while *The Nation* magazine, then and now a leader of liberal thought, was a supporter of the Eighteenth Amendment. The Prohibition Party, founded in 1880, was emphatically leftist—it had as a primary goal the implementation of the income tax. Only the relatively recent rise of a more secular left has altered the dynamic.

In 1814, Beecher delivered a series of six sermons on insobriety designed to appeal to the growing sense of American identity. "Intemperance is the sin of our land, and, with our boundless prosperity, is coming in upon us like a flood," he preached. "[I]f anything shall defeat the hopes of the world, which hang upon our experiment of civil liberty, it is that river of fire, which is rolling through the land, destroying the vital air, and extending around an atmosphere of death."

As the words of Beecher and other Second Great Awakening preachers were printed and distributed around the country, the shift to absolutism came rapidly: within ten years of its 1836 founding, the American Temperance Society had officially redefined "temperance" to mean "abstinence." The position cost the movement the early support it had enjoyed from the beer lobby, which then joined forces with the liquor industry against the society.

Beecher's river-of-fire rhetoric wasn't necessarily disproportionate to the problem. Despite the hopes of the nation's founders, drinking had risen steadily in the United States after the Revolution, according to drug and alcohol historian David F. Musto. Anti-British sentiment led to a decline in the importation of British beer and an increase in domestic whiskey consumption, which in turn strengthened the temperance movement—the effects of the more potent beverage, it was assumed, being that much more deleterious to society. By the 1800s, the movement had gained enough momentum to force schools to teach fearmongering in the style of the more recent D.A.R.E. (Drug Abuse Resistance Education) program. It demanded that antialcohol messages be a part of every child's education. "The majority of beer drinkers die of dropsy," children were taught. "When alcohol passes down the throat it burns off the skin leaving it bare and burning. Alcohol clogs the brain and turns the liver quickly from yellow to green to black. Alcohol is a colorless liquid poison."

Referring to "alcohol" as a "poison" was the culmination of the shift in attitude. Once beer and whiskey and gin had become "alcohol," they became easier to vilify. Once alcohol had become "poison," the fight was just about over. These days, poisonous alcohol is mostly confined to chemistry labs and cleaning agents; the respectable label for the drinkable stuff in educational settings is "drug," which associates it with something already prohibited. "There were days when we called it Bourbon whiskey and Tom gin, and when the very name of it breathed romance," wrote Stephen Leacock in 1918. "That time is past. The poor stuff is now called alcohol. I wish somehow we could prohibit the use of alcohol and merely drink beer and whiskey and gin as we used to."

In a 2007 *New Yorker* article, Jill Lepore summed up the conventional understanding of why American drinking collapsed beginning in the 1830s.

> If you were to look at a map, and chart these changes, you'd see that they follow the course of the nation's growing network of canals and railroads. The canal or railroad arrives, and the people join churches; the people join churches, and they drink less. How do historians account for these correlations? The answer, at first, seems obvious: preachers spread the Gospel; the same boats and trains that carried cash crops from farms to towns brought revivalist ministers from towns to farms. But, once they got there, why did anyone listen to them?

> The most widely accepted answer to that question was proposed by Charles Sellers, author of *The Market Revolution: Jacksonian*

America, 1815–1846, who argued that capitalism drove people from the taverns because the industrializing marketplace needed sober workers. It's one thing for a field hand to be wasted, the thinking went. It's another for a brakeman to be hammered.

An insurgent historical camp, led by UCLA professor and Pulitzer Prize–winning historian Daniel Walker Howe, insists that there was no market revolution in the 1830s. The nation's development, he holds, began earlier and gradually expanded—much more an evolution than a revolution. It certainly didn't take place within a decade. Howe suggests that people listened to the preachers simply because they were authority figures who represented an even greater authority figure, God. A problem with using his theory to explain the decline of boozing is that drinking didn't plummet in the early 1700s, during the First Great Awakening.

Clearly, there was more to the downturn than just the Almighty or the almighty dollar. Human behavior is very difficult to change. So if Americans all of a sudden stopped getting drunk, what did they do instead? They tended to their families. They prayed. And yes, they labored. But they also got high.

Although whiskey has long been used to self-medicate depression, nothing takes the edge off quite like a good narcotic. And in the 1830s, when the temperance movement began its first great push, which helped reduce per capita U.S. alcohol consumption from four gallons per year to just one gallon in the span of a decade, Americans had quite the edge on. The Panic of 1837 was set off when banks in New York City essentially shut down. Across the country, paper notes became worthless. For five years, the United States was ravaged by its most severe economic downturn to date. Economist Milton Friedman called it "the only depression on record comparable in severity and scope to the Great Depression of the 1930s." America had hit bottom. The religious revival was one response—the Second Great Awakening culminated in the 1830s—but Americans also turned to opium to ease the pain.

By the 1870s, when the temperance movement began another great push, the one that eventually led to Prohibition, America's long-standing affection for opium products such as laudanum combined with other cultural forces such as war, economic development, and immigration patterns to move opium from the medicine cabinet to those infamous urban dens. And surveys from the time show that the drug was even more popular in rural areas.

Twenty-four-year-old Warren Delano made his first overseas journey in pursuit of opium in 1823 on behalf of the Boston-based importer Russell & Co. Within seven years, he was a senior partner in the company and heavily involved in the lucrative opium trade. His grandson Franklin Delano Roosevelt would later sign a constitutional amendment undoing Prohibition. In the intervening century, America went through a relationship with drugs that makes our current one appear almost functional.

In 1827, the first year the federal government began tabulating opium imports, almost none was brought into the United States. Five years later, the number had climbed to around fifty thousand pounds. In several years during the 1830s and early 1840s, importation peaked at more than seventy thousand pounds. If a dose is less than half a gram—and it can often be much less—then seventy thousand pounds would be enough for more than thirty million opium highs in a nation with an 1840 population of roughly seventeen million. Importation statistics suggest that use continued to rise throughout the 1840s and 1850s.

Opiate use rose just as drinking declined, increasing in the very midst of the temperance surge. As America's first real introduction to a drug other than alcohol, the opium boom enjoyed a long honeymoon. For decades, the benefits of the drug were cherished as its downsides remained unknown or ignored. Although Chinese immigrants, who came to work on the rapidly expanding railroad network, are often credited for bringing opium and addiction to it with them to the United States, immigration statistics suggest that the American taste for opiates might be inborn. By 1880, there were more than a hundred thousand Asian-born immigrants living in the United States, and their entry into American culture certainly aided the growth of the opium trade. But the U.S. Census Bureau says that there were just over one thousand people born in Asia living in the United States in 1850, by which time the rise of opium was already well underway.

It has long been assumed that Civil War doctors gave out mor-phine injections to wounded troops like candy, and that the men then brought their opiate addictions home after hostilities ceased. But the government's own *Medical and Surgical History of the Civil War*, published just after the conflict, debunks that theory: "The hypoder-mic syringe had not yet found its way into the hands of our officers," it states.

The report's conclusion jibes with the history of medical technol-ogy. It was in the 1850s that the first syringe injected morphine into a patient, in Britain, and the practice didn't spread to Civil War bat-tlefields until late in the war. Morphine was more commonly dusted into wounds, and as in civilian life, opiates were also administered as tinctures, pills, or salts. Historians have long debated how many addicts that might have produced, but there's strong evidence that so-called soldier's disease is to some extent either an invention or a supposition.

That doesn't settle the question, of course, of what role the war played in the spread of drug use that came after it. No doubt the many horrors that troops witnessed were traumatic enough to lead some to self-medicate, but men weren't the primary users of opium. Most studies from the time reveal a roughly 60-to-40 percent female-to-male division among opium users. In the nineteenth century, opium was also a distinctly midlife drug: the average user was about thirty-five years old, and she most likely got her first taste from her doctor. Nineteenth-century opium users were predominantly middle- and upper-class, too, hardly the proletarians who fought in the war.

As use and addiction rose, the temperance movement finally caught up with opium. The Chinese became scapegoats. The first American narcotics law was passed in San Francisco in 1878, and it targeted not opium but opium dens, which were run by Chinese immigrants and attracted a multicultural crowd. By 1885, opium was less socially acceptable than alcohol, which it had begun to replace only a half-century earlier. A *New York Times* article about a courtroom scene displays the prevailing attitudes of the decade:

James Bradford was nobbily attired in a tight-fitting Prince Albert coat, carried a new-market on his arm, and he held a silver-headed cane and a high hat in his hand. He was an ideal of the creature known as "dude." He denied having smoked the drug.

"Well, Officer Reynolds caught you in the place," said the court. "How do you account for that?"

"Well, Judge, to tell the truth," he replied faintly, "I was a little bit—a little bit—well, I must admit that I was full, and I don't know how I came to go into such a disreputable house."

"The officer further claims that you had an opium pipe in your mouth," said the magistrate. "What is your explanation of this charge?"

"That I can't tell," he answered meditatively, "unless some fellow put it in my mouth for a joke. I was full, you know, and they could have done anything they pleased without my knowing it."

Assistant District Attorney Purdy said that the case was a very clear one, and from the evidence he thought the prisoner guilty of the charge of selling opium to be smoked on the premises. He said he thought it was bad enough for a Chinaman to be charged with this offense, but it was a crime of more importance when one of our own race is caught in the act of selling this cursed drug, and he implored the court to show no leniency to the accused.

The opium den's owner was sent away for three months and fined five hundred dollars, which the *Times* reported was the highest penalty given to date in New York. Bradford got a twenty-five-dollar fine and ten days in the city jail. "He was unable to pay his fine and he stepped down stairs a very crestfallen 'dude,'" notes the story's kicker.

As amusing as the story seems, its author was working with some seriously held assumptions: that opium use should be confined to the Chinese, that drinking—or being "full"—is more acceptable than getting high, and that opium is a "cursed drug."

• • •

Opium and alcohol are rather different experiences that don't mix—either physically or psychically—which might account for the dude's memory lapse. Thomas De Quincey, the popular author of the 1822 *Confessions of an English Opium-Eater*, describes it well:

> The pleasure given by wine is always rapidly mounting . . . after which as rapidly it declines; that from opium, when once generated, is stationary for eight to ten hours: the first, to borrow a technical distinction from medicine, is a case of acute, the second of chronic, pleasure; the one is a flickering flame, the other a steady and equable glow. But the main distinction lies in this—that whereas wine disorders the mental faculties, opium, on the contrary (if taken in a proper manner), introduces amongst them the most exquisite order, legislation, and harmony.

At the time, there was little research done exploring the relationship between opium use and drinking. But there was at least one noteworthy study: an 1872 look at the opium boom by the Massachusetts State Board of Health. The reason for the dramatic upswing in opiate use, it concluded, wasn't the Chinese or the Civil War—it was the temperance movement.

This unintended consequence of the call for sobriety wasn't unique to the United States, the board found. "It is a significant fact . . . that both in England and in this country, the total abstinence movement was almost immediately followed by an increased consumption of opium," it noted. The study suggested that easy accessibility to the drug through pharmacies was part of the reason for the increase, but that many other sources existed as well. One official, referred to as a state assayer, reported to the board:

> Opium has been recently made from white poppies, cultivated for the purpose, in Vermont, New Hampshire and Connecticut, the annual production being estimated by hundreds of pounds, and this has generally been absorbed in the communities where it is made. It has also been brought here from Florida and Louisiana, while comparatively large quantities are regularly sent east from California and Arizona,

where its cultivation is becoming an important branch of industry, 10 acres of poppies being said to yield, in Arizona, twelve hundred pounds of opium.

Although this description of a thriving domestic opium crop might sound surprising today, the board's characterization of that crop's consumers certainly doesn't: "[T]he opium habit is especially common among the manufacturing classes," it asserts, "who are too apt to live regardless of all hygienic laws." It puts some of the blame for such lower-class use on doctors, who are "in no small measure responsible for the moral, as well as physical, welfare of their patients," and shouldn't be allowed to get away with the "injudicious and often unnecessary prescription of opium." America's better half made up "so large a proportion of opium takers," the study suggests, because women were "doomed, often, to a life of disappointment . . . of physical and mental inaction, and in the smaller and more remote towns, not unfrequently, to utter seclusion."

The "most important cause" of opium taking, however, was "the simple desire for stimulation," an urge hitherto satisfied by alcohol consumption. Opium, the report noted, was both more available and more socially acceptable than alcohol. The narcotic "can be procured and taken without endangering the reputation for sobriety. In one town mentioned, it was thought 'more genteel' than alcohol." The report went on to say that it was "between 1840 and 1850, soon after teetotalism had become a fixed fact, that our own importations of opium swelled"—citing a rise of 350 percent. In England, one doctor noted, "opium chewing has become very prevalent, especially since the use of alcoholic drinks has been to so great an extent abandoned, under the influence of the fashion introduced by total abstinence societies." The board also found it "curious and interesting" that as wine drinking advanced in Turkey, opium eating retreated.

As always in America, the limits of what exactly is moral behavior depend on what the meaning of "is" is. By following their version of God's code to the letter, teetotaling Americans of the nineteenth century freely violated its spirit.

●   ●   ●

Opium's boost was not only due to its acceptability as a booze replacement, but also because it was a good fit for the times in other ways. As the Massachusetts Board of Health and De Quincey both noted, opium made for a good remedy for the negative side effects of the century's rapid industrialization and urbanization—boredom, back pain, anxiety, and, because of poor sanitation, all sorts of stomach problems.

In the United States, the negative consequences of using a particular drug are typically dealt with not only by condemnation, but also by searching for a better, less harmful drug—as optimistic, potentially profitable, and quintessentially American a project as any that can be conceived.

Morphine was isolated from opium around 1805. The nineteenth-century version of Big Pharma got into the business of manufacturing and distributing the drug, usually dissolved in alcohol. In the 1830s, just as folks were starting to put down the bottle, pharmaceutical companies in Philadelphia became major morphine producers. Medicinal opiate imports doubled per capita between 1870 and 1890. By the 1890s, there were a quarter of a million morphine addicts living in the United States.

Significantly, these new drugs came with no baggage. Opium wasn't perceived as an evil poison like alcohol, at least initially. Morphine taken through a needle, it was first assumed, had no chance of causing addiction. When that myth was dispelled, the search was on for a nonaddictive substitute. Bayer, the world's first pharmaceutical giant and the maker of aspirin, claimed to have found it and trademarked the wonder drug Heroin because it made people feel heroic, or, in German, *heroisch*. "It possesses many advantages over morphine," claimed the *Boston Medical and Surgical Journal* in 1900. "It's not hypnotic, and there's no danger of acquiring a habit."

Heroin had been synthesized from morphine in 1874, but its commercial value wasn't recognized until Bayer began selling it in 1898. It took off in the United States, where manufacturers were soon lacing products ranging from lozenges to pills to salts that dissolved in water with Bayer Heroin.

An ambitious drug connoisseur might have been able to find meth back then, too. German scientists synthesized amphetamine in 1877, and Japanese researchers developed methamphetamine in

1893 (but didn't come up with crystal meth until 1919). In 1933, the first amphetamine derivative met the mass market, in the form of the Benzedrine inhaler sold by Smith Kline & French. It quickly integrated itself into bohemian culture to such a degree that it was regularly referenced by the earliest members of the Beat Generation, but speed wasn't much a part of the Progressive Era pharmacopeia.

That doesn't mean there was no way to get a rush. Cocaine, isolated from the coca plant, added to the libertarian utopia. Merck was the first pharmaceutical company to manufacture it, and the drug was commercially available in the United States by 1884. Coca-Cola, introduced in 1886, was a mixture of coca, sugar, and another mild stimulant, the West African kola nut. It was marketed as a temperance beverage, a substitute for alcohol—an intoxicant without the poison. Even Coca-Cola, though, hasn't always been safe from temperance activists: a movement leader took the drink to court in 1911, charging that its caffeine was dangerously addictive. After drawn-out litigation, Coke cut the caffeine by half.

With the power of industry marketing behind it, cocaine swept across the nation. The new drug could "supply the place of food, make the coward brave, the silent eloquent," promised the Parke-Davis Company, which sold cocaine kits complete with a syringe.

So there we were, at the turn of the last century, with full legalization. Coke, heroin, and morphine were all readily available. It wasn't just a druggie's paradise; it was the natural experiment that present-day drug-policy experts dream of.

What would happen if drugs were legalized? Well, it happened. And history suggests that if we ever legalize them again, it won't be long before we ban them all over again.

Yet legalized drugs weren't an accidental by-product of the nineteenth century's economic and technological advances. They were its foundation. By the late 1800s, levies on alcohol, tobacco, and tea made up almost half of all British government revenue. They financed the country's imperialist aspirations and, along the way, cost it the American colonies—which financed their own war for independence with tobacco proceeds.

The role of opium in furthering British colonial ambitions is well known. Rum propped up the transatlantic slave trade. "With these psychoactive products [colonial powers] paid their bills, bribed and corrupted their native opponents, pacified their workers and soldiers, and stocked their plantations with field hands," writes David Courtwright in *Forces of Habit: Drugs and the Making of the Modern World*.

By 1906, tens of thousands of opium-containing medical preparations had been patented. In America, producing and selling these nostrums was a massive and far-reaching undertaking, one that helped create the modern advertising industry and the mass media—not to mention the monolithic, multibillion-dollar business that is Big Pharma. With the advent of the twentieth century, however, the world's elite began to embrace a much different stance toward drugs, a reversal that Courtwright calls "one of history's great about-faces, however slowly and imperfectly executed."

This about-face was driven by the United States. As the country emerged from World War I a preeminent power, it sought to enact its own tightening drug policies on a global scale, creating a regime of worldwide narcotics control that persists today even as other forms of American dominance falter.

CHAPTER 3

Prohibition, Inc.

I n the early 1800s, the state of medical technology offered the suffering few options for pain relief. Essentially all a doctor could
do was use drugs to help a patient get high. Even the most
temperate-minded were reluctant to decry an evil of such obvious necessity. But when pain relief unaccompanied by inebriation
became available, attitudes began to change—or, more accurately,
attitudes and interests that had been kept in check by the undevel-
oped state of medicine were finally unleashed.

Aspirin, X-ray machines, and other commonplace elements of
today's medical arsenal wouldn't be around until the very end of the
nineteenth century. The lack of an effective product, however, never
stopped a good American businessman from trying to make a buck.
Indeed, a person of that time with a headache, an infection, or any
other malady had a bewildering array of supposed remedies to choose
from. The commercialization of pain relief had allowed drug control
to slip from the hands of the medical profession.

The once flourishing patent-medicine industry, which produced
herbal and medicinal concoctions that often didn't work, lives on in
familiar descendants such as Vicks VapoRub and Geritol. The industry left a profound mark on American culture. The modern advertising industry was essentially launched by patent-medicine companies,
which sold their wares without a prescription at a huge markup and
had to compete with scores of similar producers. Thus the dawn of

brand building: Accept no substitutes! Medicinal advertising in turn fueled journalism and the rise of mass media and mass marketing. The hyperpartisan media that had previously been driven by political parties was nothing next to the commercialized journalism funded by patent-medicine firms. Major American newspapers were founded for the sole purpose of promoting certain patent medicines. This relationship, of course, would eventually become rather complicated, as some of the journalists supported by the patent-medicine industry turned on their fraudulent benefactors. But in the meantime, there were enormous profits to be made.

When one product generally isn't much better than another, it's difficult for any particular company to dominate the marketplace, which accounts for the multitude of now-defunct patent firms. But there's no mystery behind those patent meds that were actually effective: they were made with alcohol, cannabis, cocaine, or opium. In the unregulated capitalist jungle that grew wild then, ingredients were almost never listed, but people knew which products worked. Naturally, addictions developed—brand loyalty at its most loyal.

As the more potent patent medicines helped spread drug addiction across the country, it moved to poor and working-class communities. It also began to be associated with a criminal element. In 1909, New York City Police Commissioner Theodore Bingham sounded a warning that was becoming more common at the time: "The classes of the community most addicted to the habitual use of cocaine are the parasites who live on the earnings of prostitutes, prostitutes of the lowest order, and young degenerates who acquire the habit at an early age through their connection with prostitutes and parasites." Five years later, New Haven police chief Phillip Smith told a meeting of the International Association of Chiefs of Police that "nowadays drugs have become a regular diet with harlots and their pimps, and criminally inclined persons of all kinds."

Heroin had been assumed to be nonaddictive when introduced commercially in 1898. But it didn't help improve the image of the drug user after it had been around long enough for people to learn otherwise. "In many instances [heroin addicts] are members of gangs who congregate on street corners particularly at night, and make insulting remarks to people who passed," reads a 1915 New York

State Hospital psychiatric bulletin. Around the same time, New York addiction specialist Alexander Lambert called heroin a "vice of the underworld." Taking the drug, he noted, differs from morphine use, the point of which is "to forget bodily pain and mental suffering." Morphine users of the era typically got their drugs from a doctor and tended to be both better off and over thirty years old. Heroin users scored on the street, hung out on the corner, and tended to be in their teens or early twenties.

The rhetoric of American drug use was taking on an adversarial edge, one that still exists today.

Both morphine and heroin, of course, ease bodily pain and mental suffering—but the question as to whose body and mind were being eased was becoming crucial. As more people left rural areas for the exploding cities, members of the general public in these new urban environments didn't appreciate the mental suffering they had to endure as the target of, as the psychiatrist put it, "insulting remarks" from "gangs who congregate on street corners." In turn, addicts lined up outside of a New York City clinic were harassed and gawked at by sightseers. Inevitably, there was also a racial component to early-twentieth-century addiction: a turn-of-the-century study in Jacksonville, Florida, found that blacks, only a few decades removed from slavery, were twice as likely as whites to be snorting cocaine—a phenomenon perhaps more significant as it relates to perception than to reality.

When users were predominantly middle- to upper-class whites and getting high was associated with medicine, there was little incentive for the government to criminalize drugs. After all, the ruling class tends to rule itself least. But as the twentieth century progressed, addiction that originated with medicinal use—the most common way for rich people to get hooked—declined substantially, while street use rose. Two Chicago doctors who examined more than five thousand cases they had treated between 1904 and 1924 noticed the shift. "Fifteen or twenty years ago," they wrote, "most addicts acquired the habit through the physical disease or discomfort. Today the number of new addictions through physicians' prescriptions is small. The great majority of cases now result from association with other addicts, following their advice in taking a 'shot' or a 'sniff' for 'what ails you' and searching for new sensations. These are the pleasure users."

The patent-medicine market made it difficult enough for Big Pharma to compete. The growing black market made it even harder. The further drug use got from the medical community, the less interest pharmaceutical companies had in defending it. For decades, the industry had been one of the biggest obstacles to outlawing the drugs that it had been making a fortune selling. But advances in medicine—as well as Big Pharma's declining share of the pleasure-user market—gave it reason to rethink. Aspirin, patented in 1900 by heroin inventor Bayer, gave patients a nonaddictive analgesic and the company a new product to sell. Cocaine became less medically necessary with the invention of its synthetic versions, tropacocaine (1891), stovaine (1903), and novocaine (1904). Novocaine was perfect for the dentist's chair, and it had no potential to cause the dreaded side effect of euphoria.

Big Pharma needed the help of the state to push the multitude of patent firms out of business. It also needed public opinion, which was turning against drug use and the people who enabled it, thanks not only to the visible consequences of the pharmacopeia utopia, but also in large part to a more unlikely source: the women's suffrage movement.

Opium had entered the American bloodstream through laudanum and other opium-laced products available at pharmacies and recommended by doctors. When the backlash against drugs began, the opposition went straight for the pharmacist—and, to a lesser extent, the physician, who wasn't always seen as a trustworthy professional. In 1911, Hamilton Wright, the government's top drug official, went after both occupations in the pages of the *New York Times*. "A proportion of our doctors and a much larger ratio of our druggists regard their liberty to prescribe and sell as a license to advise and furnish to its victims the narcotic curse on demand," he lamented. "The contrast between European and American professional ethics in this matter is deplorable, and the dark side of the picture is America's."

Such mistrust was a by-product of the growing movement for women's rights, which was closely allied with the temperance movement. To the members of the era's many women's temperance leagues, druggists were little better than tavern owners—people, in essence, invested in intoxication. But the movement's actions against pharmacies and saloons were more than an effort to clean up a few drunks. As the Woman's Christian Temperance Union's version of its history makes clear, it was "a protest by women, in part, of their lack of civil rights. Women could not vote. In most states, women could not have control of their property or custody of their children in case of divorce. There were no legal protections for women and children, prosecutions for rape were rare, and the state-regulated 'age of consent' was as low as seven."

The tavern, long a symbol of unruly male behavior, was also the place where rules were made. Most political meetings were held in saloons, which women were generally barred from. They didn't much care for that arrangement, or for the public priorities that resulted. "At the end of the 19th century, Americans spent over a billion dollars on alcoholic beverages each year, compared with $900 million on meat, and less than $200 million on public education," noted Helen E. Tyler in *Where Prayer and Purpose Meet: The WCTU Story, 1874–1949*. By the 1890s, the WCTU was endorsing women's suffrage, more than half of its departments worked on nontemperance issues, and it had one of the first full-time lobbyists in Washington.

Similarly, pharmacies became a target of the movement because regulating their wares was a way to secure some of that elusive legal protection for women and children. In 1892, *Ladies' Home Journal* editor Edward Bok barred patent-medicine advertising from the publication. Over the next several years, he published numerous pieces revealing the true ingredients of many patent medicines and explicitly called the WCTU to action. In 1904, Bok declared that Doctor Pierce's Favorite Prescription, a favorite patent preparation of pregnant women, contained not only alcohol and opium, but also the potentially deadly plant extract digitalis—too late, it turned out: Pierce had changed his formula since the magazine secured its sample. After losing a $200,000 lawsuit, the *Journal* hired lawyer-cum-journalist Mark Sullivan to help continue Bok's crusade in a more law-savvy, and financially prudent, manner.

Sullivan delivered, contributing to exposés on unethical patent-medicine business practices. One Washington journalist made a career of securing testimonials from senators and representatives, charging companies seventy-five dollars for the former and the relatively cut-rate forty dollars for the latter. Sullivan also helped Bok uncover the brisk business in supposedly confidential letters from female nostrum users, which, along with the writers' addresses, traded hands by the thousands among patent-medicine companies—and anyone else who was willing to pay for them. When companies wrote these women back—after employees had giggled over their missives' "spicy" parts—they frequently answered with a form letter, and sometimes with the wrong medication. "The medicines are put up by young girls who are constantly making mistakes and sending men's remedies to women, and vice versa," Sullivan wrote in a 1906 story. "They can't do otherwise because they have to send out a certain number of treatments in a given time."

As such pieces galvanized women against the industry, Jane Addams, the legendary Chicago suffrage and antiwar activist, campaigned for a ban on the common patent-medicine ingredient cocaine, which passed in her hometown in 1904. In 1905, muckraking journalist Samuel Hopkins Adams published an eleven-part investigative series in *Collier's Weekly* exposing much of the patent-medicine industry as fraudulent. Upton Sinclair's *The Jungle* followed soon after, helping convince President Theodore Roosevelt and the American public that a law regulating both drugs and food was needed. Historian James Harvey Young describes the coalition that got the Pure Food and Drug Act of 1906 through Congress as made up of "agricultural chemists, State food and drug officials, women's club members, the medical profession, sympathetic journalists, [and] the reform wing of business." The Equal Suffrage League, the General Federation of Women's Clubs, and the WCTU were all involved.

Women's groups that supported the Pure Food and Drug Act were concerned with protecting consumers from adulterated products. The American Pharmaceutical Association, however, didn't have such untainted motivations.

Public opposition to patent medicines came at a time when American drug use was declining, after a peak in the 1890s. It was the corruption of the industry, as exposed in the *Collier's* investigation, that was the most troubling drug issue for most Americans. Big Pharma was happy to play along. It was in its clear interest to have its intoxicants marketed through doctors rather than through unregulated pharmacies: It would disassociate its products from patent medicines and help crush competition from smaller firms. In 1903, the American Pharmaceutical Association had already proposed legislation that would make the sale of cocaine, opiates, and chloral hydrate illegal without a prescription. Congress implemented the law in the District of Columbia, and a few state legislatures followed suit.

In 1905, Congress banned opium imports and prohibited the drug's use in the Philippines. Opium smokers quickly switched to morphine, heroin, and cocaine, which were still legal. In opium, politicos had found an issue that they could use to win favor with China in opposition to Europe, which had violently forced opium into Chinese lungs as a method of commercial subjugation. Allying with China against opium was a useful foreign-policy tool, though it wasn't of particular concern to Americans back home.

Although temperance advocates included drugs in their condemnation of insobriety, booze remained a much bigger public-health issue among most progressives. Reliable estimates put the number of drug addicts at only around half a million nationwide, out of a total population of under one hundred million. In 1910, President William Howard Taft told Congress that cocaine was "the most dangerous drug in America," but attempts to push through comprehensive drug prohibition legislation went nowhere. So drug opponents took a more modest approach. Hamilton Wright, the U.S. Opium Commissioner, led the effort, with the press as Taft's able assistant. A five-thousand-word profile of Wright published in the *New York Times* in March 1911 began, "Read this paragraph and gasp."

> "Of all the nations of the world," Dr. Hamilton Wright, who knows more of the subject than any other living man, told me the other day, "the United States consumes most habit-forming drugs per capita. Opium, the most pernicious drug known to humanity, is surrounded, in this country, with far fewer safeguards than any other nation in Europe fences it with. China now guards it with much greater care than we do;

Japan preserves her people from it far more intelligently than we do ours, who can buy it, in almost any form, in every tenth one of our drug stores. Our physicians use it recklessly in remedies and thus become responsible for making numberless 'dope fiends,' and in uncounted nostrums offered everywhere for sale it figures, in habit-forming quantities without restriction."

Elsewhere in the piece, the *Times*, perhaps the first to militarize the discourse of the drug-policy debate, called Wright's effort a "battle with the evil" and suggested that "it is to be devoutly hoped" that he prevails. As with many of today's drug epidemics, it took the media to alert the citizenry that there was one. "Few people realize how serious the opium habit has become in the United States," the story maintained. "Ask most men where most opium is used and they will answer, 'China,' without the slightest hesitation; but the fact is definitely otherwise. Our per capita consumption equals and probably exceeds that of the dragon empire, and there the habit is being intelligently killed, while here it is increasing with so great a speed that we may well stand startled at the contemplation of its spread."

Wright proposed going after the pharmaceutical industry. "As a result of the illicit traffic in these drugs the pharmaceutical profession in this country has lost much of its dignity," he told the reporter, "and this is fully justified by facts; the medical profession must include within its ranks a multitude of arrant knaves, the greater number of them, possibly, themselves victims of the drug and robbed by it of all sense of their responsibility to their patients and society." But Big Pharma would make that strategy problematic.

Wright's plan was to limit narcotic sales to licensed, monitored pharmacies, which could deal only with patients with prescriptions. He refused to compromise with the pharmaceutical industry, which sought to use his legislation only to put smaller vendors of patent medicines out of business. His bill died in House committees in 1911, 1912, and 1913, blocked by Big Pharma.

Wright, a State Department official, had better luck internationally. In 1906, at Wright's urging, Roosevelt called for an international convention on drugs. Underscoring China's interest in the issue, the convention was held in Shanghai in 1909, with a follow-up conference—this one with treaty-making authority—taking place two years later. The Hague Opium Convention, the beginning of the international antidrug effort, was contentious, because many of the thirteen participating countries benefited from the opium trade. Nonetheless, Wright succeeded in getting participants to pledge to pass laws regulating opium, morphine, heroin, and cocaine—thus obligating Congress to enact his own legislation.

Despite the international mandate, Wright was still stymied at home. Secretary of State William Jennings Bryan, a fervent prohibitionist, convinced Wright to sit down with the drug lobby. A few compromises later, the legislation was finally moving. Marijuana, then still known as cannabis, was excluded from the plan. So was chloral, a sedative popular at the time but almost unheard of today. (Mary Todd Lincoln took it for insomnia, though it was supplanted in the twentieth century by Quaaludes, Benzedrine, and other depressants. Anna Nicole Smith's death, however, was reportedly the result of a chloral-and-Benzedrine cocktail.) Pharmaceutical bookkeeping requirements were standardized and simplified so that the reform wouldn't be costly to major firms. The large companies didn't want an overly complicated system of paperwork, but they weren't opposed to regulation per se—after all, it affected smaller, undiversified companies the most.

The labeling regulations of the Pure Food and Drug Act had already dented the business of the once-secretive patent-medicine vendors. Now their profits from soon-to-be-regulated drugs would be vulnerable to investigation.

Big Pharma was winning.

Probably the biggest concession Wright agreed to, however, was exempting from his proposed legislation products containing a small amount of narcotic—at the time, such products were big earners for both Big Pharma and the patent-medicine companies. This leniency was attacked by members of Congress who wanted tighter legislation, but one of the bill's backers explained on the floor that this was as good a situation as they could hope for, given the power of the pharmaceutical lobby. "Unfortunately I am forced to believe that if we should attempt in this way to attack all the proprietary medicines which contain opium, the bill would have a rocky road to travel, and would be consigned to oblivion," said Representative James Mann of Illinois. "That may not be a very good excuse, but, after all, it is practical."

Bryan and Wright pushed hard for passage. After the narcotic exemption was loosened further in the Senate to allow higher concentrations of heroin and morphine, the bill finally passed in December 1914. The event merited barely a mention in the *New York Times*, even though the Harrison Narcotics Tax Act, as Wright's legislation was known, was the first major federal law to regulate drugs, defined as "opium or coca leaves, their salts, derivatives, or preparations." It banned the distribution of narcotics—including cocaine, which isn't a narcotic—for anything but medical purposes.

"Tax" is in the name instead of "Ban" because most early-twentieth-century legislators, regardless of party affiliation, tended to view federal power as limited by the Constitution. Then, a pharmaceutical company could argue successfully that cocaine refined in New York could be sold in New York without any federal interference. By using the power to tax, however, Congress could, to some extent, legally interfere with activity that didn't cross state lines. It was a foot in the door that the states would repeatedly try to push back.

Congress, exercising its constitutional authority to levy taxes, required all narcotics distributors to register with the forerunner of the Internal Revenue Service and pay a one-dollar-per-year tax. Only doctors and legitimate medical companies were allowed to register, which meant that nonmedical distributors would be committing a tax crime. This legislative maneuver effectively banned the nonmedical use of narcotics—although there was a major industry-friendly loophole:

> The provisions of this Act shall not be construed to apply to the sale, distribution, or giving away, dispensing, or possession of preparations and remedies which do not contain more than two grains of opium, or more than one-fourth of a grain of morphine, or more than one-eighth of a grain of heroin, or more than one grain of codeine, or any salt or derivative of them in one fluid ounce, or, if a solid or semi-solid

preparation, in one avoirdupois ounce, or to liniments, ointments, and other preparations which contain cocaine or any of its salts or alpha or beta eucaine or any of their salts or any synthetic substitute for them. . . . Provided, that such remedies and preparations are sold, distributed, given away, dispensed, or possessed as medicines and not for the purpose of evading the intentions and provisions of this Act.

The Harrison Act was far from a reactionary, authoritarian crackdown. Rather, like Prohibition, it was the essence of progressive reform. Its purpose was to regulate a chaotic market in the name of public health and the common good. It was passed by a Democratic Congress and signed by a Democratic president. But the act did come at a time when Americans readily gave up their civil liberties in the name of the war effort. The infamous Espionage Act was passed in 1917, banning "disloyal" speech and leading to the imprisonment of Socialist presidential candidate Eugene V. Debs.

World War I affected the American drug market in other ways. First, the global conflagration disrupted drug trade routes and diminished supply. Second, prohibitionist sentiment merged with nationalist fervor to promote the idea that sobriety was a way to strengthen the nation. Xenophobia played a major role. Anything German was despised: sauerkraut was renamed Victory Cabbage, and beer fell out of favor. A 1918 *New York Times* editorial exemplified the nexus of the period's antidrug and anti-German attitudes:

Into well-known German brands of toothpaste and patent medicines—naturally for export only—habit-forming drugs were to be introduced; at first a little, then more, as the habit grew on the nonGerman victim and his system craved ever-greater quantities. Already the test had been made on natives in Africa, who responded readily; if the German Staff had not been in such a hurry German scientists would have made their task an easy one, for in a few years Germany would have fallen upon a world which cried for its German toothpaste and soothing syrup—a world of "cokeys" and "hop fiends" which would have been absolutely helpless when a German embargo shut off the supply of its pet poison.

The 1916 congressional elections brought a wave of temperance candidates to Washington. The Eighteenth Amendment, the first addition to the U.S. Constitution to restrict rights rather than expand them, was passed the next year and ratified in 1919. Just a few years after its passage, the Harrison Act was being used to prosecute doctors and pharmacists who supplied narcotics to addicts. Several medical professionals were locked up in high-profile cases that sent the message that the feds were serious.

Pharmaceutical companies cooperated by opening their books to investigators, though a 1918 committee appointed by the secretary of the treasury determined that an extensive, well-organized illicit drug trade had arisen in response to tightening restrictions. The Federal Bureau of Narcotics' first major crackdown came in the early twenties, when opiate use had started to rise. They invested more in policing efforts, and federal arrests jumped from fewer than three thousand in 1921 to more than seven thousand in 1925.

The feds claimed success: the bureau did several nationwide surveys purporting to show a significant drop in narcotic use, with the number of American addicts down to as few as twenty thousand by the end of the twenties. Drug historian David Courtwright, however, filed a Freedom of Information Act request and got his hands on the surveys and related memos. The statistics turned out to be made up.

Given the controversial nature of the expansion of federal powers needed to regulate drugs, the government had strong incentive to show that its new drug laws were working. Not coincidentally, the fabricated numbers show a big drop. Courtwright also found a private memo in which Bureau of Narcotics Commissioner Harry Anslinger himself confessed that the figures were all bogus. A top Treasury Department official, Stephen B. Gibbons, called them "absolutely worthless." Courtwright and others have taken a look at arrest data, hospitalizations, treatment-center records, and other sources and concluded that opiate use was generally steady in the United States until around 1940.

While federal authorities were focusing on opiates, the next "most dangerous drug in America" was slowly making its way north. When the West Indies banned slavery in the 1800s, plantations there began hiring workers from India. They brought cannabis with them, and smoking it recreationally soon became a part of everyday life in Jamaica and on other nearby islands. In the early nineteenth century, thousands of Jamaicans traveled to Panama, Cuba, and Costa Rica looking for work and bringing pot with them. As early as 1916, American workers building the Panama Canal were smoking it.

A military commission looked into the situation in 1932—which suggests that the trend must have started a good decade or more earlier—and found that Panamanian farmers were growing marijuana and selling the excess to American soldiers. During that same period, around a million Mexicans migrated to the United States following the 1910 revolution in their homeland. They, too, smoked marijuana, and they, too, brought the practice with them.

In the United Sates in 1885, about 5 prescriptions out of every 10,000 involved cannabis as a fluid extract; in 1895, 11.6; in 1907, 8. By 1926, however, the number was down to 2.3 prescriptions in 10,000, and by 1933, 0.4. But as the use of ingested cannabis faded along with the patent-medicine industry, the use of smoked cannabis increased. In 1936, the New York City Police Department destroyed forty thousand pounds of marijuana found growing in town. The next year, a bill was introduced in Congress to ban the plant.

The American Medical Association, which had two decades earlier opposed the Harrison Act, strongly opposed this federal incursion into the doctor's office, as well. This time, though, the AMA was up against the pharmaceutical industry, which had little ability to profit from a freely growing plant with the potential to cut into revenue from laboratory-made products. DuPont and other synthetic fabric makers lobbied hard, too, hoping to take down hemp, which they saw as competition. Temperance advocates, licking their wounds from the overthrow of prohibition in 1933, were happy to take on pot. The federal government, undergoing a massive expansion under the New Deal, was eager to gobble up any extra power it could. The AMA at the time was a fierce opponent of President Franklin D. Roosevelt, so the administration and the Democratic Congress didn't hesitate to kick some dust on it.

It started by rolling over Dr. William Woodward, the AMA's top lobbyist, when he came to testify before the House Ways and Means

Committee about marijuana taxation in May 1937. He told the lawmakers:

> That there is a certain amount of narcotic addiction of an objectionable character no one will deny. The newspapers have called attention to it so prominently that there must be some grounds for their statements. It has surprised me, however, that the facts on which these statements have been based have not been brought before this committee by competent primary evidence. We are referred to newspaper publications concerning the prevalence of marihuana addiction. We are told that the use of marihuana causes crime. But yet no one has been produced from the Bureau of Prisons to show the number of prisoners who have been found addicted to the marihuana habit. An informed inquiry shows that the Bureau of Prisons has no evidence on that point. You have been told that school children are great users of marihuana cigarettes. No one has been summoned from the Children's Bureau to show the nature and extent of the habit, among children. Inquiry of the Children's Bureau shows that they have had no occasion to investigate it and know nothing particularly of it. . . .
>
> The trouble is that we are looking on narcotic addiction solely as a vice. It is a vice, but like all vices, it is based on human nature. The use of narcotics, as is trite at the present time in the medical profession, represents an effort on the part of the individual to adjust himself to some difficult situation in his life. He will take one thing to stimulate him and another to quiet him. His will is weakened in proportion as he relies on drugs of that sort. And until we develop young men and young women who are able to suffer a little and exercise a certain amount of control, even though it may be inconvenient and unpleasant to do so, we are going to have a considerable amount of addiction to narcotics and addiction to other drugs.

Importantly, from the AMA's perspective, Woodward opposed congressional action because of marijuana's medical potential:

> I say the medicinal use of Cannabis has nothing to do with Cannabis or marihuana addiction. In all that you have heard here thus far, no mention has been made of any excessive use of the drug by any doctor or its excessive distribution by any pharmacist. And yet the burden of this bill is placed heavily on the doctors and pharmacists of the country; and I may say very heavily, most heavily, possibly of all, on the farmers of the country. To say, however, as has been proposed here, that the use of the drug should be prevented by a prohibitive tax, loses sight of the fact that future investigation may show that there are substantial medical uses for Cannabis.

Asked specifically about its medical benefits, Woodward mentioned two that are often referred to by today's medical-marijuana advocates. "Indian hemp is employed in various preparations for internal use as a sedative and antispasmodic," he said, using a term that was common at the time because of marijuana's origins in India. (Today, marijuana is used to treat spasms associated with multiple sclerosis and other diseases.) Asked whether the AMA "favored the passage of the Harrison Narcotic Act," Woodward replied, "I will not say we favored it. We felt it was an experiment."

When the bill came to the floor for a vote, someone asked if Congress had consulted the AMA. Democrat Carl Vinson, who served more than fifty years in the House and would be awarded the Medal of Freedom by President Lyndon Johnson, had questioned Woodward at length as chairman of the Ways and Means Committee. He rose to answer. "Yes, we have. A Dr. Wharton"—presumably Woodward; he was the only AMA representative to testify—"and [the AMA] are in complete agreement," he said.

The Marijuana Tax Act quickly became law.

CHAPTER 4

America's Little Helper

The week before I went on leave from my day job to write this book, I visited my doctor. "I want some type of amphetamine, like Ritalin or something," I told him.

"Have you ever been diagnosed with ADHD?" he asked.

"No."

"Do you want to see a psychiatrist?"

"No."

"Do you have trouble concentrating?"

"No," I said, "but I've taken it before when friends have had it, and it makes it easier to work." He looked at the results of my blood work and said there was nothing to indicate that the drug would hurt me.

"How much do you want?"

The next day, a woman was in front of me at the local Rite Aid as I waited to pick up my prescription for Metadate, time-released speed that, according to my doctor, is better than Adderall. She asked for a packet of generic pseudoephedrine—which, of course, is stored behind the pharmacy counter, safe from the Washington area's meth manufacturers.

The clerk asked for ID, and the woman pulled out her wallet. "I have a couple credit cards with my name on them, but no ID with me," she pleaded fruitlessly.

Danielle Black, a Johns Hopkins University student, was smoking with a friend outside the pharmacy after her request was denied. She explained that she was visiting from Baltimore. She'd recently moved from New York City and doesn't drive, so she has no driver's license. "I usually carry my passport, but I didn't bring it this weekend, so no Sudafed for me," she said. "I swear I'm not a meth dealer or anything."

Such is the result of a one-hundred-year effort to regulate a product that is at once medically useful, recreationally enjoyable, and potentially harmful. It's also the result of Big Pharma's role in the drug trade, especially its efforts to ban some drugs while keeping others freely available. In the case of speed, the industry managed to do both to the same drug. When amphetamine is made and sold by major corporations, it's no big deal. When methamphetamine is made by bikers or imported from Mexican manufacturers, we have a cri-sis—never mind that levels of use were higher when Big Pharma was the sole pusher. Reaction to speed's underground resurgence in the sixties opened the door to the modern war on drugs, becoming the impetus for a series of federal initiatives that refocused American drug policy from public health to law enforcement.

Speed is ubiquitous in the United States, whether shoved into a child's mouth before school in the form of Ritalin or injected as crys-tal meth by that scary guy in the trailer park. A DEA-sponsored audit at the turn of the millennium showed that the United States was con-suming 85 percent of the world's prescription speed, with 80 percent of that going to children. More than 15 million prescriptions were written annually in the late nineties, amounting to more than 350 million daily doses. And that was just the legal speed. Today, around one in four Americans has used some illegal form of the drug, and no surprise: as abusable substances go, speed is most American in its effect. It makes you want to work, and work hard.

The Protestant quality of the amphetamine high was documented more than seventy years ago. A 1938 study in Denmark administered a local brand of Benzedrine to one hundred men and women and found that the amphetamine derivative "increased their desire for work in general." Speed makes it easier to begin a task and get it done, and the latter requires that the drug be long-lasting—or at least availa-ble to the user in ample supply. Where I grew up, we could often spot evidence of meth trips that had petered out before the workload did: the contents of a fully dissected pickup truck strewn about someone's front yard. It would take another dose to get the truck together again. Unlike the buzzes from crack and powder cocaine, which begin to diminish after just a few minutes or half an hour, respectively, a meth spree can keep a user going anywhere from eight hours to several days—and for only about twenty-five dollars a dose.

Speed's current status in America is a relic of the libertine days when Big Pharma consolidated its control of an unregulated drug trade. It's a reminder, too, of the fact that no drug can be viewed in isolation. Policies enacted to counter other drugs—marijuana and cocaine, for example—have ended up encouraging the meth trade, as have laws against meth itself. Indeed, American drug policy can safely claim credit for the superstrength meth that we have today, as well as for the bodily devastation that has come with it. Every well-meaning law intent on cutting down the drug has been met with adaptation by its producers and dealers and an upturn in the underground market.

Among the first popular amphetamine products was a Benzedrine inhaler that could be purchased at pharmacies in the 1930s, no prescription needed. The small white tube came stuffed with a saturated cotton wick and was marketed as a decongestant for cold and allergy sufferers. Benzedrine dilates the nasal passages, but patients soon focused their attention on the drug's remarkable side effects, which also included weight loss. Word quickly spread that the drug-soaked wicks could be removed and then dissolved in coffee or alcohol or simply chewed and swallowed, allowing the user to stay focused on a cross-country drive or to resist that second helping of meat loaf. Or just to get high.

Amphetamines are generalized brain stimulants; they trigger a massive release of the neurotransmitter dopamine, which in turn amps up body temperature, heart rate, and blood pressure. Users experience increased movement—rats, for example, start running around in circles, while humans might talk too much. Extended use can contribute to depression, paranoia, and even some of the jittery symptoms associated with Parkinson's disease. But the heightened attention to detail and decreased sense of fatigue users experience in the short term is why the military still gives pills to pilots and others who need to be awake and alert. In drugging its soldiers, the

United States places itself in the company of Nazi Germany, which doled out meth liberally during the Blitzkrieg and throughout the European occupation. Pervitin, the German brand, was first sold in 1938 by the Berlin-based Temmler pharmaceutical company.

Otto Ranke, a military doctor and director of the Institute for General and Defense Physiology at Berlin's Academy of Military Medicine, tested Pervitin on ninety university students in September 1939 and concluded that the drug could help win the war. The German military ordered more than thirty-five million tablets of it and a modified version called Isophan between April and July 1940. The drug was banned in 1941 under the Opium Law, yet that same year, ten million pills were sent to the frontlines. Adolf Hitler, a vegetarian teetotaler, was injected daily with speed from 1942 on, making him the first meth-head to have the power of a major industrial economy at his command.

Early on, as is often the case with a new drug, many doctors believed that amphetamine and its derivatives had nearly unlimited potential. Meth was considered a possible treatment for all manner of disorders, including epilepsy, Parkinson's, schizophrenia, and alcoholism—in addition to, of course, depression, obesity, and fatigue. The harmful side effects were as yet unnoted—or at least considered manageable.

Average Americans glommed on to amphetamines as a way to work harder, stay up longer, or lose weight. Amphetamine pills became available by the late thirties, marketed as a way to get a little lift or curb the appetite. By 1943, half of the prescriptions for Benzedrine written in the United States were for patients seeking an energy boost or weight loss. A 1950 trade ad for Dexedrine urged doctors to prescribe the drug to women: "Many of your patients—particularly housewives—are crushed under a load of dull, routine duties that leave them in a state of mental and emotional fatigue. Dexedrine will give them a feeling of energy and well-being, renewing their interest in life and living." Norodin, its makers promised, "is useful in reducing the desire for food and counteracting the low spirits associated with the rigors of an enforced diet." According to the FDA, by the late sixties, 80 percent of amphetamine prescriptions were written for women.

With the imprimatur of corporate America, the pills escaped banishment to prohibition's underground marketplace. Although a prescription was needed, "pep pills" weren't hard to obtain legally, and a healthy chunk of them was surely diverted to unsanctioned users. (It still is: within an hour of picking up my prescription, I had split a pill with a friend, who promptly took it to study for the bar exam.) In 1958, Americans took 3.5 billion amphetamine tablets. In 1967, they took 8 billion.

Early concerns about the potential for the drug to be habit-forming resulted in halfhearted efforts to control its availability. The FDA banned using certain amphetamines in inhalers in 1959 but, in a significant concession to Big Pharma, continued to allow drug companies to use merthamphetamine, which closely resembles methamphetamine. By the early sixties, however, the ride was coming to an end. President John F. Kennedy, himself an amphetamine user, told Congress in 1962 that "[o]ne problem meriting special attention deals with the growing abuse of non-narcotic drugs, including barbiturates and amphetamines. Society's gains will be illusory if we reduce the incidence of one kind of drug dependence, only to have new kinds of drugs substituted. The use of these drugs is increasing problems of abnormal and anti-social behavior, highway accidents, juvenile delinquency, and broken homes."

A new progressive wave was cresting. America was bound not westward but upward, dedicated to reaching the moon and winning a moral struggle against Communism. The civil rights movement was gaining national acceptance and broadening minds. Such times of national pride can breed abstinence and antidrug legislation, and sure enough, the Senate pushed a radical overhaul of earlier tax acts, intent on replacing them with stricter controls.

But if the national mood was progressive, expansive, and idealistic, how could there have been such an explosion of drug use among young people? The answer lies in the significant difference between their drugs and their parents'. Alcohol and amphetamines create experiences that are essentially escapist. An acid trip is certainly a departure from everyday reality, but it's no drunken stupor or exhilarating high. The term "high" isn't used by acid aficionados, who associate the drug with expanding consciousness, and dub themselves "psychonauts," or psychic explorers. Though it's true that marijuana use can often result in little more than lethargy, it can also induce a more introspective experience, with some psychedelic flavor to it. Both drugs, acid and marijuana, allowed an emerging youth culture to define itself against its elders and their preferences—which in turn led to a conservative backlash and even stricter drug controls.

The 1963 assassination of President Kennedy might have sharpened youthful opposition to an American culture that seemed out of control, but it also aided the development of the counterculture by delaying a federal drug crackdown. Presidential successor Lyndon B. Johnson had little initial interest in waging a drug war, partly because the man who would be prosecuting it, Attorney General Robert F. Kennedy, was a political enemy. Kennedy had opposed Johnson's vice presidency, and the two men were to become divided over issues as diverse as urban development, American travel to Cuba, and the Vietnam War. To halt congressional action on amphetamines, Johnson promised renewed vigor and coordinated federal action—a time-tested method of doing nothing. With the lobbying assistance of the American Medical Association and the Pharmaceutical Manufacturers Association, Johnson was able to stop in the House a 1964 attempt to control drugs that had already passed the Senate.

The next year, in a bit of undercover journalism, CBS News managed to buy more than a million barbiturate and amphetamine pills by setting up a fake company with little more than a post-office box. The drugs supposedly had a retail value of $500,000 on the black market and had cost CBS only $628. The Senate reintroduced its bill amid a public outcry. Freshman senator Robert Kennedy was a cosponsor, and with him out of the Justice Department, the White House dropped its opposition.

Big Pharma was closely watching the deliberations between Congress and the White House. It sensed that continuing opposition might be futile, thanks to the combined impact of Robert Kennedy's leaving the White House and joining the Senate, the CBS News investigation, and the rise in amphetamine use in the counterculture. The lobbying prowess of the pharmaceutical industry had long protected its lucrative amphetamine market from government intervention, but no good lobby wants to be on the losing side of a national issue, so Big Pharma decided to get behind the new legislation—for a price.

Pharmaceutical companies produce pills for a few pennies and sell them for well upward of a few dollars. The only thing preventing a competitor from underselling them is copyrights and patents. For a long time, Big Pharma had wanted better protection. It figured that if this new drug-control law had momentum, it ought to use the law as a vehicle to combat generic and counterfeit producers.

Lobbyists for Big Pharma saw to it that the counterfeit production of, say, aspirin was no longer an issue for Bayer to investigate and resolve in the courts on its own. Now it was the responsibility of the FDA, which was given the authority to arrest and jail violators. It was a significant but unsurprising concession to the pharmaceutical industry. After all, the FDA and Big Pharma had a history of mutual assistance: in 1962, one top FDA official with oversight of the drug-approval process, Henry Welch, was found to have taken more than $300,000 in "honoraria" from Big Pharma for various promotional speeches and articles. But the new law took that cooperation to another level.

The sophisticated PR campaign on behalf of the Drug Abuse Control Amendments of 1965 mostly involved hysterical accounts of speed-freak truckers causing highway pileups. A representative of the American Trucking Association testified before Congress that despite this heated rhetoric, only about a dozen of the twenty-five thousand truck accidents in the previous seven years had been tied to speed—and that, in fact, the drug generally improved driver performance. Much like the AMA's testimony on pot three decades earlier, the Trucking Association testimony was dismissed and then distorted. ("We had testimony last week from . . . a representative of the American Trucking Association that such occurrences were rather rampant all over the country," said Democratic Chairman Oren Harris of the House Committee on Interstate and Foreign Commerce. Lyndon Johnson would make him a district judge later that year.) The bill passed 402–0 in the House and cruised through the Senate.

In an attempt to curb diversion to the black market, the law required closer record keeping by producers and pharmacists. First, though, the FDA had to deal with the fallout from the Welch scandal.

George Larrick, a protégé of drug warrior Harry Anslinger and a proponent of the Drug Abuse Control Amendments, was forced out of his top position at the agency. To its chagrin, the drug industry was unable to anoint one of its own to the commissioner's position. Instead, the job went to James Goddard, a doctor with a background in consumer-protection and public-health advocacy. In his first year, drug recalls increased 75 percent, according to the FDA—not quite what Big Pharma had bargained for.

Goddard came to the agency with a moderate view of illegal drug users, if not of illegal drugs. He told Congress:

> Let me explain that the Food and Drug Administration is not engaged in tracking down the users of these dangerous drugs. But we are actively engaged in closing down the man- ufacturers, counterfeiters, wholesalers, and peddlers of these drugs. To the user, we hold out a compassionate hand: we are ready to aid the drug abuser to find his way back to reality with the help of proper medical expertise. I believe that the job we have is far greater in scope than the one which the Government has waged thus far against the hard narcot- ics: cocaine, morphine, heroin, and the opiates. The FDA's efforts take in thousands of drug manufacturers, jobbers, dis- tributors, repackers, and dispensaries where illegal diversion of the controlled drugs may take place.

That scope soon became even greater. Using the Drug Abuse Control Amendments, the government quickly added LSD to the list of drugs that Goddard was to suppress. No bill needed to be debated or signed by the president this time, because the act had given the executive the power to expand the law to include any "stimulant, depressant, or hallucinogenic" drug that it thought was danger- ous. Legislation that had been written for the purpose of contain- ing speed now began to apply to drugs associated with the rising counterculture.

The man pushing hardest against acid was Robert F. Kennedy. He wasn't the chair of the Senate subcommittee that looked at LSD in 1966, but he was nevertheless allowed by his seniors to lead much- covered hearings on the dangers of the drug. Goddard was reluctant to play along, even though the actual chairman of the subcommittee, Senator Abraham Ribicoff, had made clear the panel's intention. "Only when you sensationalize a subject matter do you get reform," advised Ribicoff, a longtime friend of the Kennedys. "Without sensationalizing it, you don't. That is one of the great problems. You scientists may know something, a senator may know something, but only when the press and television come in and give it a real play because it hits home as something that affects all of the country, do you get action."

Kennedy, trying to get Goddard to sensationalize acid's dangers, mentioned the potential of suicide while tripping. "Those suicidal tendencies I would suppose probably existed prior to taking the drug, in latent form," Goddard suggested. Acid was banned anyway.

In 1968, President Johnson officially made drug use a law-enforcement issue rather than a public health one. By executive order, he created the Bureau of Narcotics and Dangerous Drugs, transferring enforcement of all drug laws from the Department of the Treasury and the Department of Health, Education, and Welfare to the Department of Justice. That same year, Americans installed in the presidency the man who, on June 17, 1971, would officially declare the nation's war on drugs: Richard M. Nixon. "We have the moral resources to do the job," he said in a press conference outlining his national and international drug policy. "We now need the authority and the funds to match our moral resources. I am confident that we will prevail in this struggle as we have in many others."

Johnson's attorney general, Ramsey Clark, had taken a far more humanitarian approach. In 1966, he had urged presidential approval of the Narcotic Addict Rehabilitation Act, which allowed users to serve civil-commitment sentences in the custody of the surgeon general rather than prison time and provided $15 million in funding for research and local treatment centers. Keith Stroup, founder of the National Organization for the Reform of Marijuana Laws, told me that before he launched his marijuana-legalization group, in 1970, he'd been personally encouraged by Clark to make the effort.

Nixon's Justice Department had no such liberal leanings. Will Wilson, Nixon's second in command in the Department of Justice, typified the new administration's attitude when he described the problems he had with Clark's approach. "Clark's trouble was that he was philosophically concerned with the rights of the individual," Wilson said. "Our concern is more an orderly society through law enforcement. Clark put too many restraints on the law-enforcement agencies. He was like a football coach warning his players not to violate the rules, when he should have been telling them to go in there and win. I'm not opposed to civil liberties, but I think they come from good law enforcement."

That mind-set was common among people who'd been shocked by the protests and riots and far-out movements of the sixties. One thing that could be associated with participants in each of those movements, from the antiwar effort to black nationalism, was drugs. It wasn't much of a stretch to extend that association to liberal humanitarianism as a whole, which is what Nixon's camp did when it called the Democrats the party of "acid, amnesty, and abortion." Going after drugs was the easiest way for the establishment to defend itself against the counterculture, and it had decided to so with the full force of the law.

More than thirty-five years later—and more than two decades after President Ronald Reagan's call for a "nationwide crusade against drugs, a sustained, relentless effort to rid America of this scourge"— roughly five times as many drug offenders are sent to prison as are treated for addiction. Speed was the original impetus for the legislative charge that resulted in this situation. As the drug drifted from Mom's medicine cabinet to hippie stash, it fueled hysteria about both drug use in general and the imminent collapse of America at the hands of the counterculture. Each successive federal drug initiative from 1965 on pushed U.S. drug policy closer to an enforcement-based approach. In 1973, the DEA was created, and the battle fully joined.

Once a year, the Department of Health and Human Services releases its drug-use data. In theory, these numbers should mean a lot to the DEA, whose mission includes "reducing the availability of illicit controlled substances on the domestic and international markets." In practice, however, the stats hardly matter at all, at least in terms of funding: If they're up, the DEA will ask for more money to combat the growing threat. If they're down, it will ask for more money to finish drugs off once and for all.

In the fall of 2005, the numbers were down—and by 2006, the DEA had managed to secure its largest ever budget: $2.4 billion, enough to pay for a record 5,320 special agents. In the meantime, though, some self-congratulation was in order. Then drug czar John Walters and Charles G. Curie, head of the Substance Abuse and Mental Health Services Administration, which runs the annual survey, were happy to provide it, speaking for more than an hour to a Capitol Hill auditorium speckled with a cross section of local, national, and international media. "Our partnerships and the work of prevention professionals, schools, parents, teachers, law enforcement, religious leaders, and local community anti-drug coalitions are paying off," said Curie.

Then the show's dogs gave the stage to its ponies: Diedre Forbes and her daughter, Carrick Forbes, and Vicki Sickels, all recovering from addictions to meth, heroin, or coke or some combination of them. Their stories were harrowing: lives of privilege squandered (the Forbeses were from affluent Hastings-on-Hudson, New York, Sickels from a middle-class home in Iowa), homelessness, recovery, relapse, and finally the treatment that made the difference. Their stories were proof that, yes, a personal victory over drugs is possible.

Scarlett Swerdlow, then head of Students for Sensible Drug Policy, had a question about Sickels's particular about-face, which included not only triumphing over addiction, but also becoming a substance-abuse counselor and social worker. Sickels had spoken of a raid on her house after which she had avoided prison because her brother was one of the cops—and because meth "wasn't that big of a deal at the time." Under current law, Swerdlow explained, you would have been denied federal aid for school after your arrest. What effect would that have had on your recovery?

"It would have been disastrous," Sickels told her, adding, "I've heard of that. It's not a good rule." I followed up: "Do you think you would have benefited from being sent to prison? In general, do you think it's worthwhile to imprison recreational and addicted drug users?" Carrick Forbes stood and walked to the podium. A former heroin addict, she was attending Hunter College in New York.

The speech that followed touched on the many reasons she thought that drug addicts ought not to be imprisoned. "There is very little treatment in prison," she said. "Prisons are just a place to warehouse addicts. . . . I've heard a lot of times that people are actually introduced to new drugs while they're in prison. I never went to prison, but a good friend of mine went for four years. It definitely changed his life, but it didn't help his addiction." She concluded by saying, "We need to focus on treatment, not punishment."

Her assertion prompted Walters to retake the podium to note that there is a "movement toward interest in treatment" over incarceration for addicts like Sickels and the Forbeses, and that most cases are diverted from the prison system to treatment through "drug courts." As Walters sat down, I asked him if he could back up his claim with data. "I'll get that for you," he said.

What his office sent me instead was a report on the number of arrestees that the government sent to treatment for marijuana use, not for addiction to coke, heroin, or meth. I told Walters's office that this couldn't be what he meant to give me. Nothing else was provided.

I found Sickels outside the event as she was being whisked away by federal officials. She called out her e-mail address and asked me to write. Later that day, I did, and she wrote back: "If I'd had a chance to respond to your question about prison versus treatment . . . I probably would have said something inflammatory about the criminalization of addiction. . . . In my neck of the woods, the courts and jails are clogged with people who have committed crimes related to their addiction to meth and crack cocaine. The drug courts are a great thing and I have seen them work for many, but Far Too Few have access to them."

Estimates of the U.S. population in prison for drug offenses vary, but Eric Sterling, head of the Criminal Justice Policy Foundation, has been able to cobble together a number from government data, and he puts the figure at around 500,000. In the government survey released at the press conference, the feds noted that in 2004, 1.4 million people were treated for illicit drug use in a specialty facility. The number of those who were diverted from prison wasn't available, but the 2002 numbers indicate that of the 655,000 who were referred to treatment through the criminal justice system, 25 percent came from a state or federal court, a prison, or a diversionary program. That would be 164,000 people. The same report says that another 6.6 million needed treatment but didn't receive it.

While Nixon was pushing law enforcement to tackle drug use, a significant effort was under way to find a different solution. It was similar to the one advocated by Ramsey Clark and the Johnson administration — and it was embraced by none other than Richard M. Nixon.

In Chicago in the late sixties, psychopharmacologist Jerome Jaffe established an experimental methadone clinic to help heroin addicts. At the time, psychiatrist Robert DuPont had just moved to Washington, D.C., to work for the National Institutes of Health on drug-policy issues. In 1969, he was able to persuade District mayor Walter Washington to establish a small methadone program modeled after Jaffe's.

DuPont's interests paralleled those of Nixon, who had not only promised a moral victory over drugs but had also vowed to reduce crime in the District. Presidential aide Egil "Bud" Krogh Jr. called DuPont—who would later work for President Jimmy Carter and even later set up a lucrative drug-testing business—into his office and asked if he believed he could expand his methadone program across the city. He did. With increased funding secured by Krogh, the Narcotics Treatment Administration became a startling success. Washington's crime rate, which had been climbing throughout the sixties, fell by 5.2 percent as the national rate continued to rise.

Nixon was impressed. By the middle of 1971, he had tapped Jaffe to run a national version of the NTA, which proceeded to spend hundreds of millions of dollars in federal funding. A year later, treatment was available to any heroin addict who wanted it. The national crime rate, after rising every year since 1955, dropped by 3 percent in 1972. In the District, it fell by 27 percent. Each month in 1972 saw fewer people die from heroin overdoses than the month before. Just as Nixon was able to travel to China because of his unimpeachable anti-Communist credentials, he was able to advocate a treatment-based approach to drug addiction because of his solid law-and-order reputation. It was in Nixon's best interest to bring the crime rate down leading into the 1972 election, and weaning addicts off drugs seemed like one way to do it.

Soon, however, Nixon had other problems to deal with, thanks partly to Krogh, who authorized a proto-Watergate break-in relating to Pentagon Papers leaker Daniel Ellsberg. The drug-treatment effort foundered. Under Nixon, two-thirds of that budget had been directed toward curbing addiction. During Reagan's presidency, the NTA was allowed to collapse entirely as his administration spent four-fifths of its drug-war money on enforcement.

By the time DuPont established his methadone program in Washington, the counterculture heavily overlapped with an underground of a different type. The strongest link between the two was the Hell's Angels, a gang of speed-dealing bikers who mingled freely with drug-using hippies. The trade was dominated by the gang so much so that the drug was known as "biker speed" or "biker meth." As the Angels' product crossed from the criminal underworld to the hippie counterculture, the New York Times wrote of speed freaks hanging out at Tracy's doughnut shop in Haight-Ashbury and strung-out "meth monsters" haunting the East Village. Some turned-on kids, much to the alarm of speed-eschewing psychonauts, were doing their parents' drug. During the Summer of Love, "Speed Kills" buttons were distributed by a Haight-Ashbury free clinic as the counterculture tried to correct itself with a self-devised antimeth campaign.

By the fall, the buttons had made an ironic cameo in a lurid Time magazine rape-and-murder story informing readers that "[d]rug-induced violence is nothing new to the neighborhoods where hippies live." From its opening scene of "a tawdry tenement at 169 Avenue B on Manhattan's Lower East Side" with "cockroach-scampered walls" to its description of the killings of twenty-one-year-old sometime speed dealer James "Groovy" Hutchinson and his eighteen-year-old girlfriend, Linda Fitzpatrick, carried out with boiler-room bricks by "turned on" speed freaks who presumably "demanded to 'make it' with Linda," the piece vividly embodies mainstream America's worst prejudices and fears about the counterculture:

Police later arrested three Negroes. Donald Ramsey, 26, who wears the fez of the Yoruba sect, a Black Nationalist cult, and whose apartment on the fifth floor of the murder building is decorated with Black Power posters; Thomas Dennis, also 26, a pot-smoking wino who hung out on the hippie fringe and proclaimed a code of racial violence; and Fred Wright, 31, assistant janitor in the building who lived in a small room just off the cellar, and who was held on "related" charges of raping and robbing another hippie girl just hours before the slayings.

For the most part, the new crop of speed freaks eschewed inhalers and pills; they injected liquid amphetamines obtained through the black market or cooked up in secret labs. A 1970 feature in the *Times* described the new image of meth in now-familiar terms: "The speed epidemic blossomed about three years ago in San Francisco's Haight-Ashbury district and quickly popped up in the nation's other hippie drug haven, New York's East Village. Quiet flower children became ravaged scarecrows. The cannibalism of speed was easy to spot: emaciated bodies cocked in twisted postures; caved-in jaws, grinding and grinding; pockmarked skin, torn and scratched and white, and a constant talking, talking, talking." The story states that, according to the FDA, methamphetamine was the "most popular drug of clandestine chemists." The *Times* had the course of the epidemic backward, however: New York's underground arts scene had embraced meth in the sixties. The drug only later—though not much later—infiltrated San Francisco, drifting up the West Coast from San Diego, by 1970 dubbed the Meth Capital of the United States.

In terms of chemistry and pharmacology, there isn't much of a practical difference between methamphetamine cooked in home labs and amphetamine derivatives sold by pharmaceutical companies. The main difference for users is in the way the drugs are administered. Home cooks don't put their product in pills. The chemicals get bagged up in raw form, designed for injecting, snorting, and, with pure crystal meth, smoking. These methods send the drug almost straight into the bloodstream and on its way to the brain—delivering a bigger, faster rush than orally ingested pills, which must first pass through the stomach, the intestines, and the liver, journeys that take time and dilute the power of the high.

The first Americans to inject speed were likely soldiers stationed in Japan and Korea in the early fifties, where the practice was widespread. Back home, injectable meth was easily available at pharmacies with a prescription, rarely a deterrent for a determined customer. Injection caught on, and in 1963, following increased reports of intravenous abuse, the state of California finally asked manufacturers of injectable amphetamines to stop selling their products in the state. When drug makers complied, home-based speed kitchens started booming. The Drug Abuse Control Amendments of 1965 law gave black-market manufacturers a second boon, helping to take high-powered pills off the street and leaving the home labs with a near monopoly.

In 1970, over the objections of the pharmaceutical industry, which was seeing its pill sales plummet, President Nixon unified American drug legislation under the Controlled Substances Act. The regulatory centerpiece of today's drug laws, it utterly rejected the notion that Congress could regulate drugs only through its power to tax, claiming authority over the drug trade through the Constitution's long-debated Commerce Clause. The law divides drugs into five categories, called schedules, based on their perceived harmfulness, addictive potential, and medical value. Marijuana, which is relatively safe, is not addictive, and has medical value, was placed into Schedule I, where it remains, along with heroin and LSD. Cocaine is in Schedule II. Liquid meth was originally put into Schedule II but was bumped up to I; regular amphetamines started in III but were moved up to II. Schedule V includes low-potency preparations of codeine and opium.

The laws also kicked speed down the social scale, at least for a while. The Controlled Substances Act managed to reduce production of amphetamines by American pharmaceutical companies, from 165,000 kilograms in 1958 to just 1,000 kilograms in 1973. Rather than turn to the biker-associated drug, wealthier users began to shun speed for another upper that was becoming available again: cocaine, which ticked up in use in the mid- to late seventies. Quaaludes and other downers, including heroin, also quietly rose in popularity as meth use consolidated on the fringes. The more the feds cracked down on speed, the more it traveled in the underground—and the more powerful it got.

A 1970 ban on phenyl-2-propanone, known as P2P, had sent home cooks scrambling for a new meth precursor. By the early eighties, they found it in the readily available pseudoephedrine, which Big Pharma had fought to keep legal in bulk sales. The ephedrine-reduction method of speed production turned out to produce a much more powerful drug, especially once Mexican cartels began obtaining pure ephedrine powder in large quantities from pharmaceutical suppliers overseas. In the 2007 book *No Speed Limit: The Highs and Lows of Meth*, journalist Frank Owen writes of the profoundly changed meth experience:

> Taking what I presumed was a modest amount, half a gram, which barely covered the bottom of a small plastic baggie, I ground up the chunks into a fine powder and separated them into eight lines, which were to be taken twice a day over four days, to be accompanied by the occasional nap and lots of fluids. At least, that was the plan. I had a pile of boring fact-checking work to do and I figured meth would make the task easier.
>
> Right from the first line, I could tell this was different from the old biker meth I used to do. Some new plateau of intensity had been reached here. This was powerful, maybe too powerful. Still, for the first twelve hours, I managed to stay on an even keel, working at the computer, dropping off dry cleaning, going to the Korean deli to pick up some beer and cigarettes. Then, as night fell on Sunday evening just before Thanksgiving 2006, I was sitting at my desk in my twenty-second-floor midtown Manhattan apartment when I was startled by a fierce blast of music that filled up the whole room: "O Tannenbaum, O Tannenbaum."

The music was merely coming from a department store across the street, but Owen didn't realize that until five days later, when he eased out of the fantasyland meth had created. In those five days, he had hallucinated being arrested by FBI agents for communicating with an underground organization and believed that he was having sex with "half-human, half-animal creatures." Owen realized when he came down that the new meth "was so powerful that it had given me this extraordinary ability to surrealize reality, animate my surroundings like a cosmic cartoonist. I had experienced meth hallucinations before, but never with such intensity or duration. If a half a gram of Mexican ice spread out over four days could do this to me, imagine what an eight ball could do."

Today, the DEA tacitly acknowledges the P2P ban's role in the creation of the new supermeth. "The ephedrine/pseudoephedrine reduction method is preferred over the P2P method for several reasons," reads one agency report. "First, it is a simpler route of synthesis. Second, ephedrine/pseudoephedrine is less strictly controlled than P2P, and, therefore, is more readily available to clandestine laboratory operators."

But the newly empowered drug warriors had more important intoxicants to attack than meth. The early eighties were dedicated to uprooting as much marijuana as possible. The focus then shifted to cocaine. By the mid-nineties, when the feds turned back to marijuana—this time branded as medicinal—meth had managed to spread eastward across the country in its new, more potent, Mexican form.

The first step in meth's nationwide march was the legislation that pushed its production below the border. The second was the treaty that opened that border: thanks to NAFTA, the North American Free Trade Agreement, meth would be back—and in force.

CHAPTER 5

New Coke

Perfect, thought Keith Stroup as he put down the phone after a call from Griffin Smith, a speechwriter for President Jimmy Carter. Smith had invited Stroup to his apartment at the Watergate, where he needed some help composing a presidential statement on drug policy. Stroup was a pro-pot lobbyist running the National Organization for the Reform of Marijuana Laws (NORML). Drug culture, it seemed, was about to go mainstream.

"He and I were about the same age and had smoked together," Stroup recalled from his K Street office, where he still heads the organization. "I said, 'Whoa,' and I grabbed my best stuff and headed over there." Indeed, it was Stroup who came up with Carter's most memorable formulation of his liberal drug policy: "Penalties against possession of a drug should not be more damaging to an individual than the use of the drug itself."

"We ended up with a statement that I thought was awfully good," he said. "Even though they toned the statement down, it is still to this day the best statement any president has had on marijuana."

The 1977 meeting wasn't public knowledge, but even if it had been, America's relationship with drugs was such that the idea of pro-marijuana advocates consulting with the White House would have drawn little protest. Marijuana use had risen steadily through the sixties, in tandem with the countercultural revolution. "By the time we started going to the antiwar demonstrations, between sixty-five and sixty-eight," said Stroup, "one of the things we noticed was there was a lot of marijuana smoking. It was a way to let the news people covering the protest know that, yes, we were there primarily to protest the war in Vietnam, but there were a lot of other things about the government [we opposed], as well, and one of them was its marijuana laws."

Drugs were the counterculture's consolation prize, instead of a quick end to the Vietnam War, a new egalitarian society, or even a Democratic president. President Richard M. Nixon's war on drugs had been aborted when he resigned in 1974. Though Nixon had explicitly sought to divide the country along cultural lines in order to rule, his successor made healing the national psyche his highest priority. President Gerald Ford both pardoned Nixon and granted conditional amnesty to draft dodgers, actions that were together the essence of seventies détente.

Across America, mainstream acceptance—or at least tolerance— of drug use and drug culture was evident. Head shops publicly selling drug paraphernalia, sometimes thinly labeled as "For tobacco use only," were as common as Auntie Anne's Pretzels and other mall-based chains are today. News reports gradually became more favorable toward marijuana, and the attitude of the general public and legislators alike tended toward a pro-pot stance. In 1973, Oregon became the first state to decriminalize pot, making possession of under an ounce a civil offense akin to speeding. Two years later, California followed. In 1978, Nebraska brought to eleven the number of states that had decriminalized possession of small quantities of the drug.

Tens of millions of people were living in places where smoking pot was effectively legal. Half of the high-school seniors polled by the University of Michigan in 1974 said that they had smoked marijuana in the last year, but there was little public outcry about any kind of "epidemic." As early as 1972, a commission had recommended to Richard Nixon that pot be decriminalized nationwide. He rejected the advice, but three years later, Carter campaigned under a promise to do just that.

"At that time, virtually everyone in the California pot movement thought we'd already won," recalls Jack Herer in the dedication of the cult classic *The Emperor Wears No Clothes: The Authoritative Historical Record of Cannabis and the Conspiracy against Marijuana* . . .

and How Hemp Can Save the World! "They'd begun to drift away from the movement and had gone back to their lives, thinking the battle was over and that the politicians would clean up the loose ends."

In the midterm elections following Nixon's resignation, the American people elected forty-nine new Democrats to the House of Representatives, creating a huge majority. Democrats also picked up four Senate seats, meaning that they had gained virtually dictatorial power in Congress. When Carter moved into the White House, Democrats had fully consolidated power. The GOP hollered here and there about rising pot use and the perennial scourge of heroin, but without control of either branch of the government, it was essentially powerless.

It was in this context that Stroup and Smith sat down to craft Carter's drug policy—and in which, a year later, Peter Bourne, Carter's top drug official, sat down to blow lines at a 1977 NORML Christmas party with Stroup, Hunter S. Thompson, and an assistant to newspaper columnist Jack Anderson.

It's no surprise that coke was their drug of choice. Rapidly gaining in popularity among the educated elite, cocaine was in its honeymoon phase—again. And just as in the previous century, its rise was facilitated by circumstances aligning against another drug. This time around, the drug wasn't demon rum but rather a substance that American culture was on the very verge of declaring respectable: marijuana.

"I clearly fucked up," Stroup told me. The coke session with the drug czar, which had gone down at a Georgetown home, had been strictly private. But to get to it, Bourne and his companions had had to walk up a spiral staircase in full view of the entire party. Stroup, Hunter Thompson, and the government's drug man all ascending together made an interesting threesome. Word inevitably leaked out—in fact, Anderson broke the story, with Stroup agreeing to be quoted in the *Washington Post*. He was subsequently forced out of NORML and not allowed to return until many years later. Carter, deeply embarrassed, never again entertained decriminalizing marijuana or any other liberal drug policies.

Stroup narc'd because he was pissed. While speaking softly about drugs at home, Carter had been vigorously prosecuting the drug war abroad. Well before the scandal broke, Stroup and Bourne had been feuding over a carcinogenic chemical being sprayed on Mexican pot by the Drug Enforcement Administration (DEA). It was supposed to kill the plants, but growers learned that if they harvested their crops immediately after they were sprayed, their pot would still at least appear normal. Pot smokers across the country were getting sick, and NORML, as their largest consumer-protection group, lobbied to have the spraying stopped. Bourne refused, and the rejection played some part in Stroup's outing of him to the *Post*.

The spraying was part of Operation Condor, a joint Mexican–American venture aimed at eradicating Mexican pot that had been going on since 1975. General José Hernández Toledo, fresh from the 1968 student massacres in Mexico City, led ten thousand soldiers into the hills of Sinaloa, Durango, and Chihuahua. "Tons of drugs were destroyed, production was reduced, prices rose, but drugs continued to flow into the American market, although in lesser quantity of Mexican origin," writes sociologist Luís Astorga in the paper "Drug Trafficking in Mexico: A First General Assessment."

The action had several consequences. One, a rise in the price of pot in the United States, was intended. Others were not. The growth of domestic marijuana farming might have eased pot shortages slightly during the seventies, but the industry was hardly the high-tech, high-efficiency bud-producing machine it is today. The encouragement of a shift from pot to cocaine importation among drug smugglers was a much more significant development in the short term. Coke, more valuable by weight and with a less detectable odor, was more profitable and much easier to move. A minor player in the coke trade in the seventies, Mexico would a decade later come to rival the Caribbean. By the late nineties, it would dominate the industry.

As domestic pot production began to take off in northern California, the quality of homegrown marijuana available to Americans was steadily improving. Ken Kesey's former girlfriend and the future wife of Jerry Garcia, Carolyn "Mountain Girl" Adams, was among the first to grow gourmet bud in northern California, in the early seventies. Some Vietnam vets who had picked up a taste for drugs while fighting Communists were happy to employ camouflage and booby-trapping skills learned in the Asian jungle in the forests of northern California, and as they followed Adams's lead, U.S. pot farming was allowed to expand with near impunity.

Neither California governor Jerry Brown nor the Carter administration was particularly concerned with going after West Coast growers. Brown smoked pot himself, and he was almost brought down by it when, at the behest of federal agents, Timothy Leary's wife, hoping to free her husband from prison in the seventies, shared a joint with Brown in an entrapment scheme. (She ultimately decided not to cooperate, saving Brown's political career, which continues to this day.)

The DEA, for its part, had no clue as to how much marijuana was being grown in the United States. In 1984, the agency estimated that domestic annual production was 2,100 metric tons and represented only 12 percent of total consumption. Government officials "were still screaming about all these dynamite, superstrength strains of Mexican marijuana, when we had moved on to Canadian or Thai sticks or stuff people grew domestically," said Stroup. "Their continued preoccupation with imported marijuana gave the domestic industry a chance to get on its feet."

The American marijuana market, however, remained dependent on imported and outdoor herb, both of which are susceptible to shortfalls. Pot grown outdoors is harvested in the fall—meaning that, by summer, supply would be depleted nationwide. Combined with foreign eradication efforts, these seasonal shortages helped open the door for cocaine, as users substituted an available drug for an unavailable one.

"Without question, in the mid- to late-seventies, there were frequently months where even working at NORML we would have a drought," said Stroup. "But there was never a shortage of cocaine, because it didn't have anything to do with a growing season. Sometimes I'd go [to my dealer], and he didn't have any marijuana, but he always had cocaine."

Federal survey data show that coke use among eighteen- to twenty-five-year-olds doubled from 1977 to 1979. By the end of the decade, 40 percent of Americans in that age bracket admitted to trying the drug. "If present trends go unchecked," prophesied a 1979 DEA report, "a vast new youth market for the substance could be opened. High cost, rather than restricted availability, will remain the principal deterrent to regular use among less affluent persons."

Historian Christopher Lasch's 1979 book *The Culture of Narcissism: American Life in an Age of Diminishing Expectations* captures the mood of those who made up this vast new market. "To live for the moment is the prevailing passion—to live for yourself, not for your predecessors or posterity," he writes. "We are fast losing the sense of historical continuity, the sense of belonging to a succession of generations originating in the past and stretching into the future. It is the waning of the sense of historical time—in particular the erosion of any strong concern for posterity—that distinguishes the spiritual crisis of the '70s."

Nothing creates a more narcissistic high than cocaine, and post-Watergate, mistrustful Americans were more inclined to listen to themselves than to the government when it came to drug use. They lied to us about pot, the thinking went. Why should we believe them about coke?

Timothy Leary, whose bizarre career trajectory placed him at the heart of the American counterculture for decades on end, popped up again as a defender of the powder. "Obviously, cocaine is the drug of the day," he told an interviewer in the early eighties. "It is well-adapted to our times. Of course the narcs who are cracking down on its use rant and rave about the dangers of the miserable substance, which is, in reality, a harmless substance. It's a drug that causes euphoria, quite pleasant and sparkling like champagne. You feel powerful, as if you controlled the world—and intelligent, much more than you actually are."

"I've never turned down cocaine," he added, "except after midnight if I want a good night's sleep."

The nation's new enthusiasm for the drug was positively nineteenth century. Harvard University drug expert Dr. Lester Grinspoon testified at a 1979 congressional hearing that "people, generally speaking, don't use cocaine quite as recklessly as they did at the turn of the century and are more sophisticated about their use of it. At present, chronic cocaine abuse does not commonly appear as a medical problem." Users, he said, were not "very much at risk." That same year, *High Times*, which had been solely dedicated to pot, was running ads for "cocaine kits." The magazine showed readers how to heat coke and smoke the vapors. In Colombia, said the ad, "the natives call their Snow Vapor Base. For over 100 years, in every village, it's been the Toke of the Town!"

Carter's own top drug-policy official, Bourne, saw little danger in cocaine, writing in a 1976 article that coke "is probably the most benign of illicit drugs currently in widespread use. At least as strong a case could be made for legalizing it as for legalizing marijuana. Short acting—about 15 minutes—not physically addicting, and acutely pleasurable, cocaine has found increasing favor at all socioeconomic levels in the last year."

In July 1981, *Time* magazine illustrated its cover story "High on Cocaine" with a shot of a martini glass filled with coke. In it, the piece suggests,

> Whatever the price, by whatever name, cocaine is becoming the all-American drug. No longer is it a sinful secret of the moneyed elite, nor merely an elusive glitter of decadence in raffish society circles, as it seemed in decades past. No longer is it primarily an exotic and ballyhooed indulgence of high-gloss entrepreneurs, Hollywood types and high rollers, as it was only three or four years ago—the most conspicuous of consumptions, to be sniffed from the most chic of coffee tables through crisp, rolled-up hundred-dollar bills. Today, in part precisely because it is such an emblem of wealth and status, coke is the drug of choice for perhaps millions of solid, conventional and often upwardly mobile citizens—lawyers, businessmen, students, government bureaucrats, politicians, policemen, secretaries, bankers, mechanics, real estate brokers, waitresses.

Time's Michael Demarest was nearly as good a pitchman for cocaine as Leary:

> Superficially, coke is a supremely beguiling and relatively risk-free drug—at least so its devotees innocently claim. A snort in each nostril and you're up and away for 30 minutes or so. Alert, witty and with it. No hangover. No physical addiction. No lung cancer. No holes in the arms or burned-out cells in the brain.

Instead, drive, sparkle, energy. If it were not classified (incorrectly) by the Federal Government as a narcotic, and if it were legally distributed throughout the U.S. (as it was until 1906), cocaine might be the biggest advertiser on television.

As the DEA had noted, though, coke's high price tag kept its use somewhat in check—at least until President Ronald Reagan revived the war on drugs in earnest. As the seventies closed out, the nation reacted against what came to be known as the "excesses" of that decade and the sixties. Drug use was certainly among them. As gas lines, stagflation, and a hostage crisis brought, as Carter famously put it, a "malaise" to the nation, news reports on pot turned negative.

Pot smoking, according to survey data, began to trail off. Nebraska would be the last state to decriminalize marijuana possession.

"We're making no excuses for drugs, hard, soft, or otherwise," pronounced Reagan on June 24, 1982. A veteran of many pitched pissing contests with the counterculture while governor of California in the late sixties, he was eager to take it on again when he became president. "Drugs are bad, and we're going after them. As I've said before, we're taking down the surrender flag and running up the battle flag. We're going to win the war on drugs."

Reagan redoubled efforts at curbing imports, further militarized drug policy, and brought about mandatory minimum sentences for minor drug offenses. In 1980, the FBI's Uniform Crime Report listed fewer than a hundred thousand arrests for heroin and cocaine, which were tabulated together. By 1989, that figure had jumped to more than seven hundred thousand.

But the first battle Reagan would fight in his war was against marijuana, which required laying siege to the once-ignored base of liberal resistance, northern California. His Campaign against Marijuana Production began in the harvest season of 1983. U-2 spy planes and military helicopters flew over the Golden State looking for green crops. (By the fall, corn, wheat, soybeans, and the like have turned brown, making cannabis easy to spot from the sky.) The DEA reported seizing 64,579 plants with an estimated value of $130 million.

Federal law-enforcement figures marched in the streets chanting, "War on Drugs! War on Drugs!" The opposition printed bumper stickers demanding, "U.S. Out of Humboldt County."

The 1984 haul was three times larger. Nationally, pot plant seizures rose from about 2.5 million in 1982 to more than 7 million in 1987, an amount that rivals the government's previous estimate of the *entire* domestic crop. Reagan even began to go after "ditchweed," a wild variety of hemp that has no potential to get a user high. The first year that the White House kept data for ditchweed eradication, it claimed to have uprooted about 9 million plants. That number was up to more than 120 million by 1989 and reached half a billion in 2001.

Unsurprisingly, such sustained effort drove up the price of marijuana. The DEA closely tracks drug prices and purity, although it doesn't often make the data available publicly. It did so most recently in 2004, and the numbers include a startling, if misunderstood, observation. "The marijuana price trends . . . are not highly correlated with trends in prices of other drugs over time," the report reads. "While the price of powder, heroin, and, to a lesser extent, crack were falling during the 1980s, the average price of marijuana generally rose." An eighth of an ounce of pot in 1981 was going for twenty-five dollars. It stayed roughly the same in 1982. By 1986, it was up to fifty-three dollars, and it hit a high of sixty-two dollars in 1991, a 150 percent rise over ten years. Coke, meanwhile, become much more affordable. It cost nearly six hundred dollars a gram in 1982. As Reagan directed resources toward the pot battle, coke's price began to tumble. By 1989, it was down to two hundred dollars a gram, cheaper in real terms than it had been during the last national coke binge a century earlier. At the same time, average purity levels nearly doubled.

Clearly, the price trends are highly correlated, but the correlation is a negative one: in the eighties, price increases in marijuana drove demand toward other drugs. The war on drugs hard, soft, or otherwise helped persuade pot smokers to put down the bong and pick up the pipe, the mirror, or the needle.

Pot smoking plummeted under Reagan. About half of twelfth graders in 1979 told the University of Michigan researchers they had smoked pot that year, the same as five years before. The numbers fell through the eighties and dwindled to one-fifth of twelfth graders in 1992. The use of other drugs either stayed the same or increased as people started looking for a different cheap high. Reported use of inhalants nearly doubled, from 4 to 7 percent between 1981 and 1987. Cocaine, heroin, and meth use all rose in the eighties.

Heroin dropped in price by a third between 1981 and 1988. By 1996, it had dropped by two-thirds. The price of crack was falling as well. The DEA started tracking it only in 1986, around the time the drug's use became widespread. Its price fell by about half over the next five years. In rural areas, the price of meth fell by a quarter from the early eighties to the middle of the decade. The stated goal of U.S. drug policy is to lower demand by increasing price. Reagan's drug war did precisely the opposite, with pot as the lone exception.

While the president focused on pot in California, cocaine was exploding in Florida.

Miami was the perfect base for large-scale drug smuggling. As the countercultural wars petered out, hippies who didn't drop back in or go back to the land went south to Miami. Coconut Grove was bursting with hippies by the mid-seventies, the type of smart, antiauthoritarian troublemakers that embody the perfect smugglers. Business makes strange bedfellows. The Carter administration had pulled back on the effort to overthrow or assassinate Cuban leader Fidel Castro. The move left south Florida with an idle army of well-trained, mostly Cuban American adepts of dark arts that would become valuable in the coke business: how to acquire and use weapons, how to hide money, how to surreptitiously pilot planes and boats. A speedboat could zip through any one of the Everglades' hundreds of little waterways to find a hidden place to unload or dock elsewhere along Florida's more than three thousand miles of coastline. That was mostly unnecessary throughout the seventies, however, because smugglers could dock at almost any marina, back up a truck, and drive off. Interdiction was not a major concern.

The infrastructure for this multibillion-dollar import business wasn't created solely for cocaine or even for marijuana before it. South Florida had a long history of smuggling coffee, tobacco, and any other product subject to tariffs. A "mother ship," either from the

Caribbean or directly from Colombia, would anchor near the shore, though not close enough to be seen from land. Yachts or cigarette boats—named for the vessels that smuggled bootleg tobacco—zipped out to the offshore vessel to load up with coke. The drug also came in by air. In the late seventies and early eighties, customs officials estimated that more than eighty cocaine-laden planes landed in the United States every night, mostly in Florida. In 1980, the Customs Service seized two hundred cigarette boats and fifty airplanes, one of which was a World War II–era bomber. It had previously been used by customs agents investigating drug operations.

"The best thing about Miami is how close it is to the United States," goes one favorite local saying, and for a while, the rest of the country really did behave as if the Florida coke trade were happening overseas. Criminologist Paul Goldstein, who focuses on cocaine, told me that the nation essentially ignored Miami's gradual takeover by cocaine because it wasn't happening up north, even though the city was America's murder capital throughout the seventies. "Then when crack came [to Washington and New York] in the eighties, you couldn't pick up your paper without seeing a story about it. It led people to say, 'Crack is so much worse. We've never had this problem before.' Well, they had that problem in Miami," he said.

Miami residents today talk of the seventies and eighties in almost wistful terms. There's a certain pride in having lived through the insanity that was the uncontrolled drug trade. In a 2005 memoir for the alternative newsweekly the *Miami New Times*, Carlos Suarez De Jesus, a former waiter at the Mutiny Hotel, a notorious dealer hangout, writes of how cocaine took over:

> Around town the lure of easy cash was leading friends to dabble in the drug trade's quick-strike opportunities. Guys I knew who were perennially broke and literally stealing food from the backs of parked Holsum bread trucks weeks earlier would drop by my job in brand-new BMWs, waving their Rolexes in the air. Some had been driving coke shipments to New York or Chicago for their employers, others had been unloading boats by moonlight. It was remarkable how they shrugged off the risks and bragged only of the money.

Almost everybody at work was using drugs in some form or another, and if brass was aware, they didn't act on it. It was a price they paid to keep the wagons rolling. I recall being astonished how coke seemed to permeate everything. It was the rare hospital where I didn't party with orderlies, nurses, or interns on duty. It was everywhere.

Weapons were everywhere, too. More than two hundred thousand guns were sold in Miami in the late seventies. In 1980, nearly a quarter of the city's murders were committed by machine gun. That year, Fidel Castro opened up his prisons and asylums, flooding south Florida with refugees known as Marielitos, immortalized in the movie *Scarface*. The Cubans went to war with the locals and the Colombians for control of the state's drug trade, quickly relegating most of their homegrown competition to marijuana dealing. That was no small consolation, but the marijuana market paled in comparison to the coke trade. In 1980, police seized 3.2 million pounds of pot worth more than $1 billion in south Florida. They also seized 2,353 pounds of coke worth nearly $6 billion.

John Spiegel, now an attorney, was a homicide detective during coke's heyday, and he remembers the corruption and the depravity of the criminality. "I saw several of my colleagues get into major trouble after they elected to dabble in the business themselves," he recalled. One victim was blown to pieces to prevent identification—but the killers, men working for trafficker Ricky Cravero, Spiegel said, forgot to remove the guy's driver's license, which landed nearby. That case was solved, but by 1980, three of the FBI's top-ten crime-ridden cities were in south Florida: first-place Miami, then West Palm Beach, and Fort Lauderdale. In response, Dade County added 1,000 new cops to its then-1,700-person force. Many were immediately corrupted. Starting salaries were just shy of $18,000. One night running a cigarette boat could net $50,000.

Miami was flooded with dollar bills. Around a fifth of all real-estate transactions in Miami were paid in cash, the *New York Times* reported in the late eighties. In a study by a Florida International University professor, the underground economy was estimated to be $11 billion, a third of Miami's economic output. The Federal Reserve branch in the city built up a currency surplus of $5 billion, mostly in fifties and hundreds, as crooked banks deposited dirty money. The surplus was greater than at all other Federal Reserve banks combined. Miami's U.S. attorney, Dexter Lehtinen, told a reporter that $220 million in cash was spent on cars in Miami between 1986 and 1989, many times more than in other cities.

This new local industry couldn't have come along at a better time. It has become commonplace to say that cocaine fit the mood of a decade whose affluence was bracketed by recessions. Even Leary indulged in this cliché: "It's the drug of the eighties because this decade is facing the fact," he said at the time. "We're in an age of realism and toughness." Robert Sabbag, in his 1976 book *Snowblind: A Brief Career in the Cocaine Trade*, suggests that cocaine was a way to restore a fading American spirit. "[C]ocaine's presence in the blood, like no other drug, accounts for a feeling of confidence that is rare in the behavioral sink of post-industrial America," he wrote.

The collapse of American manufacturing left more than a psychic need, however. It also left a vacuum in the economy, which the non-goods-producing service industry rushed to fill. According to a 1992 *New York Times* story, "There were more jobs created within New York City in the 1980s—overwhelmingly high-skilled, high-paying managerial, professional and technical jobs—than there are people in Buffalo, the state's second largest city." We became a nation of middle managers, of bankers and bureaucrats, of adjusters, accountants, and waitpersons. And drug dealers—from the importer to the distributor to the guy on the corner.

Peter Reuter, the University of Maryland professor who helped me with my original LSD article, has made a career out of examining the economics of illegal businesses. One of his most startling observations is that the coke trade—indeed, the entire drug trade—is essentially a service industry, because the street price of a dose of cocaine is many, many times higher than the cost of merely manufacturing it. As with any other retail good, some of the excess covers the seller's profit. Some covers what accountants call transportation-in costs. But much more goes toward reducing the risk of product seizure and employee arrest, the principal perils of providing an illegal service.

Those perils became less significant the more the south Florida coke industry became entrenched. As cocaine's price fell throughout the decade, it became available to consumers of more moderate means. It trickled down, so to speak, spreading across the country in both powder and crack form.

During its high-priced heyday, however, coke was known as a professional's drug—as Suarez De Jesus observed. Employees of the legal service industry benefited from this product of the illegal service industry as they worked long hours in their burgeoning sector of the economy. Its exclusivity evoked a cloistered world that both the upwardly mobile and the severely impoverished dreamed of being a part of.

Unemployment had climbed in the late seventies as plants shut down and American cities crumbled. Stagflation meant that wages and job growth were falling while prices were rising—a phenomenon that some economists had thought impossible. By the close of the decade, inflation was approaching 15 percent and interest rates had risen above 20 percent. To lasso the beast, Reagan severely tightened monetary policy, cutting the money supply and intentionally driving the country into a recession. The Reagan Recession, as it became known, hit hard in the summer of 1981 and persisted for the next year and a half. The president's approval rating bottomed out in the mid-30, and in the 1982 midterm elections, Democrats picked up more than two dozen congressional seats.

America was no longer a place where things were made; it was a place where things were shuffled around. Cocaine slotted nicely into the new economy. The Reagan Recession had disproportionately affected urban blacks and Latinos, and American cities were teeming with unemployed men eager to earn a living distributing the drug, cutting it, or defending territory where it was sold. De Jesus describes one of the coke trade's typical recruits:

A childhood friend named Celia was dating one of the city's rising dealers. His name was Manolito and he was a ruthless thug who'd been the leader of a local street gang, the Utes, and had a reputation for being trigger-happy. He once fired a shotgun into a crowd of Hialeah rivals during a quince party in Miami Beach.

Manolito, who was in his early twenties, was working for an uncle in the "shrimping business" and apparently had been involved in major trafficking. Suddenly the guy was driving a new Corvette and picking up tabs all over town. Celia showed off a shiny new Volvo and diamond tennis bracelet he'd given her for her birthday.

Both people like Manolito and the economy needed the pick-me-up that selling coke provided. The banking industry had been banged up by the recession, and it was glad to have the influx of capital brought by the cocaine biz. The *Economist* reported that forty-four Miami banks were given international charters in 1982, compared to ten in 1978. Another thirty-six foreign banks opened branches in Miami during that period. At least forty city banks refused to report cash deposits of more than $10,000, as required by law, throughout the seventies and into the eighties. And at least four banks, authorities estimated, were bought and controlled by drug dealers. As their trade spread across the country, dealers found still other banks eager to deal in cocaine cash. Much of the money that went to foreign producers ended up back in the American economy, too, laundered through the Panamanian branches of U.S. banks.

By the late eighties, a few banks had begun to come under suspicion as their money laundering became too blatant. But the penalties were so laughably small that even when the banks did get caught, they often still benefited from the transaction. A Beverly Hills branch of the American Express Bank was caught laundering $100 million belonging to Juan Garcia Abrego, operator of a notorious cartel with close connections to the then Mexican government. In a 1994 congressional hearing, Chairman Henry Gonzalez, a Texas Democrat, noted that the $950,000 fine—less than 1 percent of the laundered cash—meant that the bank still profited from the exchange. Citibank, which since the 1950s had been the most active U.S. financial institution in Mexico, was in a perfect position when cocaine trafficking moved from the Caribbean westward. Mexican playboy Raul Salinas was discovered to have laundered hundreds of millions through Citibank. His brother, President Carlos Salinas, a prominent ally in the U.S. drug war, was estimated to have made off with some $5 billion himself.

In two and a half years of investigation beginning in 1986, Senator John Kerry's committee looking into links between the Central Intelligence Agency and the Contras also turned up ties between drug cartels and the banking industry. One hearing involved the Medellín cartel's top accountant, Ramon Milian Rodriguez, who had been busted laundering billions through the New York–based bank First Boston. A committee member suggested that he "must be very clever" to have cleaned up so much cash. "Well, First Boston paid a fine of $25,000 and I'm doing 42 years," Rodriguez responded. "Who do you think is cleverer?"

Carter and Reagan, for different reasons, had both ignored cocaine as it grew in popularity in the late seventies and early eighties. The market had become so flooded that the price of a gram of coke plummeted from $600 in 1982 to $400 in 1984. The coke industry pulled itself out of this apparent death spiral through an innovation that helped it reach thousands of new consumers: crack. Cheap and packing a quick punch, crack was the perfect $5, five-minute escape. It began to spread throughout the nation, especially in poor African American communities.

Since the eighties, skeptics have cast doubt on the severity of the crack epidemic. In 1984, when coke use peaked in the United States, around 18 percent of people between the ages of eighteen and twenty-five had used cocaine, but the numbers for crack were much more modest. *Monitoring the Future* first began to break out crack as a category in 1986, when it found that 4.1 percent of high-school seniors had used it in the previous year. In 1987, the number was down to 3.9 percent. That year, the survey broke use down by race and found that white kids were twice as likely as black students to have used crack—with Latinos leading everyone at 5.5 percent. Use was concentrated, according to the survey, in the Northeast and in the West and in big cities. A survey of nineteen- to twenty-eight-year-olds found that only 6.3 percent admitted to ever having used crack; 1 percent had used it in the past thirty days.

For obvious reasons, surveys have some difficulty reaching hardcore drug addicts, which is why they're better at measuring trends than at establishing absolute figures. But they do show that during the peak of the eighties cocaine panic, the number of people using the drug recreationally remained relatively small. Critics of the Reagan-era response to drugs see these data as proof that the cocaine hysteria was cooked up by politicians and the media. It's easier to blame poverty and urban decay on drugs and lock up the people than it is to treat the problem, goes the argument. And while there was certainly no shortage of scapegoating, the rise of cocaine in those years was a very real phenomenon. Although occasional use was declining—as it was for all drugs at the time—the number of people using an awful lot of the drug was increasing.

Two studies, both done by the National Institute on Drug Abuse's Division of Epidemiology and Prevention Research, reflect this. The first looked at nonlethal and lethal cocaine overdoses in hospitals between 1976 and 1985 and then between 1984 and 1988. In the first study, nonlethal overdoses increased five times over the decade in question, while lethal ones went up six times. From 1984 to 1988, at the height of the panic, nonlethal overdoses jumped another five times and lethal ones by only two and a half times, presumably because the community of users had become experienced enough to know exactly how much coke will kill you. Though the crack boom was exaggerated, it can't be said that it didn't exist.

The introduction of the new drug came, predictably, with violence, as rival organizations struggled to control territory and competition. Miami in the late seventies and early eighties was mirrored by Los Angeles, Washington, D.C., and New York in the mid-eighties. Murders committed by African Americans surged beginning in 1984, rising from just over 30 per 100,000 people to more than 50 in the early nineties, according to Justice Department statistics. Meanwhile, just under 30 black people per 100,000 were killed in 1984; by the early nineties, that number had risen to 40. Black males aged fourteen to twenty-four were particularly hard hit, with their murder rate doubling after 1984 before falling in the early nineties. Indexes that measure social misery—infant mortality, children in foster care, arrests for violent crimes or gun possession, incarceration rates—all worsened significantly during the same period.

In September 1989, a record 64 percent of respondents to a *New York Times*–CBS News poll said that drug abuse was the United States' most pressing problem. By August 1990, that number had dropped to just 10 percent, where it more or less remained for the rest of the decade.

Coke use fell steadily throughout the late eighties and leveled off toward the end of the decade—just as the hysteria was at its peak. It has remained fairly flat since, though the DEA sporadically claims big victories in disrupting supply. The most recent chest pounding began in August 2007. Drug czar John Walters began making the press rounds, which included riding up New York Avenue NE to the compound of the *Washington Times*, tucked away in a postindustrial wasteland on the outskirts of Washington, D.C. The paper often provides the most receptive audience for a GOP administration's messengers. Walters came with a small staff and a stack of glossy pages making the case that the war on drugs was being won, said a source who was at the meeting. Prices for cocaine, he said, were rising fast. That can only mean a decline in supply, he explained.

Congress was in the midst of a debate over a controversial $1.4 billion aid package intended to help Mexico wage its own drug war. With Plan Mexico, as it was called, on the table, the news couldn't have come at a better time for the White House. The drug czar, however, had a credibility problem: in the past, he'd pointed to several other price increases and supply drops that quickly reversed themselves and left him and the media looking silly. A *Times* editorial staffer said that the reception to Walters's presentation was fairly cool. It took more than a month for anyone to bite (although the *Times* did tout the benefits of Plan Mexico). *USA Today* finally took the bait, making the price increase its lead story in a September edition. From there, word spread that there was a shortage of coke out there.

The administration gave itself the credit, citing increased Mexican cooperation, Colombian eradication efforts, and a number of high-profile seizures for the alleged supply downturn. "Drug kingpins are having a harder time moving illegal drugs and chemicals and pocketing the illicit proceeds because they are up against the full-court press of sustained, joint initiatives by a historic three-way partnership among Colombia, Mexico, and the United States," said DEA administrator Karen P. Tandy at a press conference staged in Colombia when the numbers were officially released. "This rock-solid, international lineup has disrupted the world's highest level narco-traffickers, made illegal drugs costlier and less pure, forced traffickers into an uncertain reactive mode, and formed the linchpin to greater stability throughout the Western Hemisphere."

The DEA released its price data for 2007 to make its case. I asked the agency for the numbers for years 2005 and 2006 so that I could put the current price in historical context, but the agency declined to provide them. I filed a Freedom of Information Act request and was told in a letter that there was no "public benefit" to releasing the data.

So did the DEA really have the cocaine cartels in retreat? Quite the opposite, actually: coke exporters were simply finding more lucrative markets than the economically stricken United States. Producers are "not going to see a significant impact [from a decline in American consumption] because they've seen huge increases in demand, and therefore profit, from Europe," André Hollis, who was the senior counternarcotics adviser to Pentagon chief Donald Rumsfeld from 2001 to 2003, told me. Just a few years prior, he explained, Americans were doing about five times more blow than their Old World fellows. Today, coke-consumption levels in the United States and Europe are roughly equal. It's hard to confirm his claim statistically. But United Nations surveys have shown rapid rises in cocaine use in Western European countries during the early years of the twenty-first century. And press accounts from across Western Europe have talked about a continental coke binge similar to America's in the eighties.

True, the U.S. government can point to a number of high-profile seizures, including one that landed more than 20 metric tons of coke in Mexico. Tighter border enforcement as a result of efforts to curb terrorism and immigration has likely played a small role in shrinking the American coke trade, too. But the biggest factor is probably the rise of the euro and the concomitant decline of the dollar, which has made it less profitable to sell cocaine to Americans. "The euro has replaced the dollar in the Western Hemisphere as the currency of choice among these traffickers, which is an extraordinary shift," said Karen Tandy, head of the DEA, at an antinarcotics conference in April 2007 in Spain. "As cocaine use has declined in the U.S. dramatically, in the European market it has risen." Officials at the conference said that a kilogram of coke that would fetch $30,000 in the United States was worth $50,000 in Europe—and the dollar has fallen further against the euro since then. On April 1, 2007, a dollar was worth about 0.74 euros; a year later, it was worth only 0.63 euros. Because of this price differential, it's now a theoretically profitable enterprise to smuggle cocaine out of the United States. Buried in its 2009 National Drug Threat Assessment, the Department of Justice cited the currency exhange rate as one possibility for decreased imports coming into the U.S. "The declining value of the U.S. dollar provides a financial incentive for drug traffickers to sell cocaine in foreign markets where the wholesale price of cocaine is already much higher than in the United States," the report said.

Donald Semesky, the DEA's chief of financial operations, has noted that 90 percent of the 1.7 billion euros that were registered as having entered the United States in 2005 came through Latin America, "where drug cartels launder their European proceeds." As the cocaine market has shifted, use along its new trade routes has grown. A UN report notes increases in use not only in South and Central America but also in Africa, where seizures jumped tenfold from 2003 to 2006 and then doubled again between 2006 and 2007. West African nations, which make Colombia and Mexico look like models of transparent governance, have become important stopping-off points for coke traffickers on the way to Europe. Out-of-work African youth make cheap foot soldiers, and drug runners with expensive equipment and weaponry have little to fear from airport security when the places have little access to electricity and cop cars with empty gas tanks. "Africa is under attack," warned the UN's Office on Drugs and Crime executive director Antonio Maria Costa in a *Washington Post* op-ed in 2008. "States that we seldom hear about, such as Guinea-Bissau and neighboring Guinea, are at risk of being captured by drug cartels in collusion with corrupt forces in government and the military." From West Africa, the coke heads to Spain and Portugal. Spain, according to the UN, had levels of coke use equivalent to those in the United States for the first time ever in 2006.

From the drug cartels' perspective, the beauty of shifting exports to Europe is that the resulting decline in shipments to the United States does indeed lead to an increased price here. While expanding their business elsewhere, the cartels are getting more money per unit of American product. That increase in wholesale cost has led

U.S. coke retailers to take action—by diluting their wares, the easiest way for drug dealers to pass on increases in cost. The DEA found a 15 percent decrease in U.S. cocaine purity in the first six months of 2007.

What's the real-world impact, then, for your average American coke user? As with sentencing, it depends on who you are. "There are no crackheads going without crack," Dale Sutherland, a narcotics investigator with the Washington, D.C., police department, told me. "But the white guy from the suburbs may be paying a little more." Here's why: a typical crackhead knows more dealers than a casual user. If one dealer raises prices or too heavily cuts his product, an addict can find another seller across the street—meaning that in order to keep addicts as customers, a dealer will have to accept less profit while stepping on the product just a little. Casual users, however, tend to have only one dealer and are less willing to go shopping around for the best price. And that dealer isn't very concerned about losing his business by selling them inferior product—they don't buy much, anyway.

There are data that back up this market logic. To support its assertion that supply is down, the DEA has cited a survey that measures the number of people who fail workplace drug testing for cocaine. By the end of 2007, one-third fewer workers were failing coke tests, a rather remarkable decline. Because drug addicts have some difficulty holding steady jobs, it's safe to assume that this sample includes mostly casual users—exactly the sort most likely to decrease their consumption in response to a price increase.

The ultimate goal of the war on drugs, of course, is to reduce addiction, and there are signs that raising the price of coke hasn't done it among hard-core users. Up-to-date data are tough to come by, but some cities have begun drug-testing folks who get arrested. Here, we can presume a much higher number of regular users.

In D.C., where the practice of drug testing arrestees began in 1984, a little more than 40 percent of them tested positive for cocaine in January 2007. That percentage barely budged as the price rose. Eventually, though, the price increase seems to have taken a toll: by the end of the year, the number of arrestees testing positive had indeed dipped—to just below 40 percent.

CHAPTER 6

D.A.R.E. to Be Different

I n the summer of 1999, the sixties generation celebrated itself by throwing a concert for Woodstock's thirtieth anniversary. The do-over event was organized by the same ponytailed businessman who'd put the first one together, and typical of something organized by an aging boomer, it was a corporate shit show. Pizza sold for six dollars a slice, and in the middle of a heat wave, water cost four dollars for a tiny bottle. For those who couldn't make it to the concert in upstate New York—at a Superfund-listed former U.S. Air Force base—the entire festival was available on pay-per-view.

More than 200,000 young people did show up, though. And unlike their gate-crashing parents, they paid $150 each to get in.

The sixties crowd might have lost their idealism somewhere along the way, but their children showed some antiestablishment—or at least antisocial—spirit on the last day of the festival, breaking into a riot, setting fires, looting vendor booths and ATMs, and allegedly raping four female concertgoers.

It's a notorious instance of the way that boomers' children simultaneously embraced and rejected the mythology of the sixties. A less-well-known expression of that attitude involves those kids' drug use: during the mid- to late nineties, American teens got as high as any group of young folks since the seventies, right under the noses of the people who had kicked off the last national indulgence.

For most of American history, drug-use trends among younger and older people have moved roughly in harmony—if not to the same degree, then at least in the same direction. The late sixties were an exception: use rose first among college students and then increased among high schoolers and the rest of the country. Since then, young people have been the leading indicator of drug trends.

The next deviation was in the nineties. In 1991, eighth graders, according to their answers to the University of Michigan survey category concerning "any illicit drug," started getting high more often, but no other segment of the population did. The next year, eighth, tenth, and twelfth graders all showed increases in use, while college-student and adult use remained largely flat. The trend continued over the next few years, as middle- and high-school students continued to show more drug use while older groups' use remained steady.

By 1996, tenth graders were doing more drugs than their adult counterparts. In 1997, their use equaled that of college students; by 1998, it had eclipsed college-age use. The wave broke that year, as eighth graders finally reported a decline in drug use. As those younger kids grew up, they took their temperate ways with them, and at the very end of the decade, use among tenth and twelfth graders took a downturn. By 2004, tenth graders were once again using drugs less often than college students and adults. The party didn't completely die down, however: Twelfth-grade use, even while eighth- and tenth-grade use fell, stayed roughly constant.

The Michigan researchers who first noticed the trend call it a "cohort effect." The pattern is clearly visible moving through the charts over time. Take cocaine use: among eighth graders, it rose from 1991 to 1998; among tenth and twelfth graders, from 1992 until 1999; among college students, beginning in 1994; and among young adults, starting in 1996. Clearly, these are the same people doing coke.

Understanding why begins with recognizing that the survey numbers are only a partial reflection of the reality of drug distribution and consumption.

•   •   •

If the availability and price of a drug are constant yet its use goes up or down, it means that a couple of different things could be happening. Perhaps a new drug has hit the streets and has begun to corner the market on a particular kind of high. Or maybe the change isn't economic but cultural, with changes in use reflecting new levels of approval or disapproval for a certain substance.

The forces that drive these phenomena can be captured only roughly by the Michigan survey, which asked kids about their personal disapproval of using a drug even once, and about the amount of perceived risk associated with taking a drug. If an antidrug campaign actually works, surveys should first show attitudes hardening against the drug, then a decline in its use. In a pro-drug environment, attitudes will soften—users will see less risk in trying a drug once and will disapprove of it less—and then, a few years later, use will predictably rise.

The survey also measures "perceived availability," which can affect drug trends as well. Many younger users, studies have shown, get their drugs from other casual users, rather than from a specific dealer. So when there are more casual users of a drug, there are more sources for other casual users. As use declines, those sources disappear and the trend feeds on itself, further bringing use down. When use of a drug goes down among a group of casual users, perceived availability follows it. However, if perceived availability declines at the same time as, or before, a registered drop in use, then the reduction is probably supply- rather than demand-driven.

In the early nineties, kids reported that the supply of their favorite drugs was steady. It was demand that was up.

In a span of five years in the early nineties, "personal disapproval" of marijuana fell by a fifth. Disapproval dropped first for eighth graders, a year before their use increased, and the same pattern held for the older kids. The number of young people who thought that the drug is dangerous also dropped significantly. Both beliefs are leading indicators in the survey: when kids don't disapprove and aren't afraid of a given drug, a rise in use is on the way.

The high-school class of 1996 was the first one to increase its use of drugs since the across-the-board decline of the eighties. That group of students had entered kindergarten around 1983, the same year that the Drug Abuse Resistance Education program, now D.A.R.E. America, was founded by Los Angeles Police Department chief Daryl Gates.

The idea behind D.A.R.E. is simple. If drug use spreads like a virus, the thinking goes, then inoculating children before they're exposed could slow the spread. Early on, however, D.A.R.E.'s creators made a decision that has been critical to both its success and its failure: they chose cops as the ones to deliver the vaccine. The current course includes some essay writing and test taking, but it's mostly about watching and listening as a uniformed officer conducts an intentionally frightening version of show-and-tell.

Using cops as the public face of the organization—though not surprising, given Gates's background—won it a vocal and politically popular champion. Police forces appreciated the rare opportunity to forge relationships with children outside the cops-and-robbers matrix. The police officer as public servant is a role cops understandably enjoy playing. "D.A.R.E. 'humanizes' the police: that is, young people can begin to relate to officers as people," offers the organization's PR material. "D.A.R.E. permits students to see officers in a helping role, not just an enforcement role."

Officers chosen to be part of the program first go through eighty hours of training in child development, classroom management, and teaching. Those who take on high-school classes get an additional forty hours' worth. Though versions of the program are available for all grades, D.A.R.E. concentrates on fifth and sixth graders. The curriculum is highly standardized, with seventeen sessions focusing on the dangers of drugs and drug addiction, as well as the "Three R's": "Recognize, Resist and Report." The officer shows the kids what drugs look like and tells stories of lives ruined or ended. He or she teaches students how to avoid peer pressure and how to build their own "self-esteem"—which, it's assumed, will give kids the strength to say no.

D.A.R.E. cops often stick around for lunch and recess to talk further with the kids about drugs—and much else. As a 1988 federal Bureau of Justice Assistance study explains, "Students have an opportunity to become acquainted with the officer as a trusted friend who is interested in their happiness and welfare. Students occasionally tell the officer about problems such as abuse, neglect, alcoholic parents, or relatives who use drugs."

The campaign has succeeded on many fronts, as any parent who's been scolded for drinking by a young child knows all too well. And it has inspired more than mere scolding. In 1992, a Maryland girl told her D.A.R.E. officer that her parents were growing pot, and each parent spent thirty days in jail, according to the *Washington Post*. Two kids in Boston reported their parents the same year; the year before, a Colorado child called 911 and said, "I'm a D.A.R.E. kid," then told the operator about a baggie of pot that he'd found. A nine-year-old Georgian called the cops after stumbling on some speed in his parents' bedroom. "At school, they told us that if we ever see drugs, call 911 because people who use drugs need help," said Darrin Davis to a reporter for the *Dallas Morning News*. "I thought the police would come get the drugs and tell them that drugs are wrong. They never said they would arrest them."

The D.A.R.E. program is now in three-quarters of all school districts, reaching more than twenty-five million American kids. It also has branches in more than fifty nations worldwide. Ironically, it was born just as more than a decade of rising drug use was ebbing among all age groups, including baby boomers, who now had the sorts of responsibilities that can preclude taking recreational drugs: careers, mortgages, and, most important, children.

Apprehensive new moms and dads in the eighties and early nineties helped make D.A.R.E. a global phenomenon, but they were surrounded by countless other sources of parenting help. Best sellers such as Melody Beattie's *Codependent No More* and Charles Whitfield's *Healing the Child Within: Discovery and Recovery for Adult Children of Dysfunctional Families*, both published in 1987, helped to build a massive market in recovery and wellness literature during the period. Self-esteem, self-actualization, and self-help, pop-psychological leftovers from the individualistic sixties and narcissistic seventies, became buzzwords to live by as millions of Americans were introduced to their "inner child" and the potentially catastrophic consequences of neglecting it. "With our parents' unknowing help and society's assistance, most of us deny our Inner Child," Whitfield writes of this hidden, wounded aspect of the psyche. "When this Child Within is not nurtured or allowed freedom of expression, a false or co-dependent self emerges."

Motivational speaker John Bradshaw further popularized the notion with his 1990 best seller, *Homecoming: Reclaiming and Championing Your Inner Child*. He went on to host a ten-part TV special by the same title and to author four more self-help best sellers. Together, his books would sell more than ten million copies. He and Whitfield both identified a national psychological crisis that had been caused by neglectful, unloving, and "spiritually abusive" parents.

They urged boomers not to make the same mistakes while rearing their own children—whether the one within or the ones without. "Give your child permission to break destructive family roles and rules," advises Bradshaw. "Adopt new rules allowing pleasure and honest self-expression." He also assures readers that "mistakes are our teachers—they help us to learn." Kids will make more mistakes than adults, he suggests, because "they have lots of courage. They venture out into a world that is immense and dangerous. Children are natural Zen masters; their world is brand new in each and every moment." Children, therefore, shouldn't be held back by rigid rules but allowed the freedom to explore. They shouldn't be scolded but reasoned with. Parents should be friends and confidants, not authority figures. In a 1990 *New York Times* article, Wendy Kaminer summed up the codependency movement's attitude toward parenting: "Shaming children, calling them bad, is a primary form of abuse."

The movement was strong enough—and ostensibly permissive enough—to disturb some of the more conservative elements of American society. A columnist in Georgia's *Fayette Citizen* was perplexed as late as 1998 by the proliferation of "parenting classes," many taught by folks just out of college. He called one of the programs and spoke to its director. She told him that "the most prevalent problem is improper parental discipline," which probably reassured spare-the-rod types. But that wasn't all. "You wouldn't believe how many parents still don't realize that under no circumstances should spanking or hitting be used to discipline children," she added. And "the second most frequent problem," she said, "is not parents endangering children, but rather parents who try to 'control' their children, which stifles self-expression."

She was working from a set of assumptions that was backed by more than just pop psychology. At a 1995 Aspen Institute program called "The Challenge of Parenting in the '90s," those gathered heard from Harvard professor Stuart T. Hauser, then director of the school's Judge Baker Children's Center. Relying on a longitudinal study he published in 1991, he told the conference that the "chances of a teenager experimenting with new ideas and embracing new perceptions are greatly increased when he or she is in a family where curiosity and open-mindedness are valued, and uncertainty is tolerated." The goal of his research, he said, was to "enhance" parenting "so that it will not interfere, obstruct, or aggravate the greatest difficulties during the teenage years." The title of his lecture, "Adolescents and Their Families: Paths of Ego Development," is telling—the family belongs to the child.

Few parents, of course, wanted no structure or discipline at all. Hauser, in his talk, recommended required educational programs dealing with violence, drugs, pregnancy, and school failure. For young potential psychonauts, the rise of the codependency movement and the spread of D.A.R.E. dovetailed fortuitously: kids were encouraged to satisfy their curiosity, which uniformed officers piqued by waving baggies of pot in their faces during school.

Health-care activist Mykey Barbitta says that his first exposure to marijuana came during a D.A.R.E.-like field trip to a police station in fourth grade. "They had that cabinet that had all the drugs in it, and they said, 'These are all dangerous,'" he recalled. "I saw marijuana sitting there at the bottom, right in the middle, and I'm like: this I can see, the needles, the pills. I can understand, in fourth grade, that those can hurt you. But how can that little leaf hurt you? I just had my doubts ever since then."

Today, Barbitta is a drug dealer: he runs a state-sanctioned medical-marijuana shop in San Francisco.

Not surprisingly, the University of Michigan survey shows that just as the inner child was breaking out, LSD use among the children of the most educated parents—the sort who might watch a John Bradshaw special on PBS—began rising. According to most surveys, it's almost always the children of the least educated parents whose drug use is the highest. But not for LSD in the nineties, especially in the Northeast and on the West Coast among white, educated young males.

In 1975, 11.2 percent of all twelfth graders said that they'd used "hallucinogens" at least once that year. Use skewed toward males, with 13.7 percent claiming to have used compared to 9 percent of women. Use of LSD specifically stood at 7.2 percent. The numbers for both hallucinogens and LSD slowly declined over the next fifteen years, dipping to a low of 5.5 percent of all seniors having taken hallucinogens in 1988.

Then the trend started turning around, and by 1994, use of LSD was back to 1975 levels. Mid-nineties acidheads differed demographically from those of twenty years before, however. The Michigan survey breaks the nation into the Northeast, the North Central, the South, and the West. Acid use in the seventies was spread evenly throughout the country, save for the South, which lagged behind. As far back as the surveys go, blacks barely register on the hallucinogen scale. Whites top it, although Latinos aren't far behind. The level of education of a child's parents, however, played little role in whether that kid would try acid or hallucinogens.

Beginning in the late eighties, children of the most highly educated parents took the lead in acid use. In 1975, kids with uneducated parents used hallucinogens at precisely the same rate as kids of highly educated parents—and both groups used it less than children with moderately educated parents. By 1990, the kids of the highly educated were more than twice as likely to trip.

Meanwhile, kids in the Northeast cracked 13 percent for hallucinogen use in 1996 and 1997 and nearly hit 12 percent for acid in those years—the highest of any subgroup for both categories. Numbers for the West for these years are high, too, with a peak of 8.8 percent LSD use in 1996. Whatever their parents' educational background, kids who said they wouldn't be going to college or would be going for fewer than four years dropped acid at a significantly higher rate than others.

Acid's sixties-era distribution network was there to meet the demand. The Grateful Dead, long known to be something of a psychedelics delivery service, had continued to tour throughout the eighties and dropped a top-ten comeback album, *In the Dark*, in 1987. The year before, *Skeletons from the Closet: The Best of Grateful Dead*, which had been released in 1974, earned platinum certification by finally reaching one million copies sold. The nineties, though, saw sales really take off. *In the Dark* went double-platinum in 1995, and the neophyte-friendly *Skeletons* hit double-platinum in 1994 and triple-platinum just six months later, in early 1995. The cultural comeback the Dead made was in evidence following that year's drug-related death of front man Jerry Garcia, which played out on the cover of *Newsweek* and was memorialized with congressional speeches. LSD use among high-school and college students peaked at the same time.

College campuses in the early to mid-nineties were dominated by tie-dyes, some of which came from Dead shows, where hard-core fans set up not only T-shirt booths, but also a drug bazaar known simply as the Lot. There, youngsters all over the country could get a night of mind-blowing psychic exploration for as little as five dollars—and often for free. The Dead had company on the road, too. New England–founded jam band Phish and its southern counterpart, Widespread Panic, grew in popularity during the period. So did gatherings such as the Furthur Festival, which featured projects by various members of the Dead and replicated the Lot scene.

Psychedelia, despite the loss of Jerry, was on the rise.

In 1999, due to clamoring demand from the East Coast, the annual Rainbow Gathering—a meeting of tens of thousands of hippies in a national forest—was held east of the Mississippi River for the second time in its history and the first time in two decades. The rise of acid in the Northeast coincided neatly, in fact, with the growth of the then regional band Phish.

Several musical streams converged to form a river of explicit pro-drug peer pressure never seen before. West Coast hip-hop was one, especially for nonurban youth sufficiently removed from the music's lyrical concerns to find them seductively exotic. *The Chronic*, Los Angeles–area rapper Dr. Dre's 1992 solo debut, announced its drug policy right on the CD: a symmetrical green pot leaf on a simple black background. Tipper Gore and the Parents Music Resource

Center might have lamented the misogyny and violence threaded throughout the work of Dre's old group, N.W.A., but the suburban and rural kids who helped make his solo effort a triple-platinum hit discovered something infinitely more interesting: the chronic itself. With a heavy influence from pothead George Clinton, the album glorified the gangsta lifestyle. But because most suburban and rural kids weren't about to join a gang and start packing a nine, they had to channel their "inna gangsta" in other ways. The easiest options were to dress like Dre and smoke pot.

The Chronic also introduced mainstream America to Snoop Doggy Dogg, whose love of violence seemed eclipsed only by the joy he took in smoking "endo." "Rollin' down the street, smokin' endo, sippin' on gin and juice," raps Snoop in the chorus of one of the more popular songs from his 1993 album, Doggystyle. Eventually, censors figured out that by "endo" he meant marijuana, so the radio version became "Rollin' down the street, smokin' smokin', sippin' on gin and juice." Suburbia also glommed on to ghetto-culture renditions in film, as Boyz n the Hood (1991) and Menace II Society (1993) earned cult followings.

Cypress Hill, Latino rappers from California who loved the sound of bubbling bong water, can take a share of credit, too. Almost every one of the group's songs had something to do with cannabis, and it even quoted the Bible in defense of legalization, referencing Genesis 1:12: "and God gave all seed bearing plants on Earth to use." The group's self-titled 1991 debut spawned three top-twenty rap singles and sold two million copies over nine years. In 1993, the group smoked pot on the stage of Saturday Night Live, earning a lifetime ban.

Hip-hop artists had plenty of help in exposing American youth to the joys and sorrows of drug use. Neopsychedelia flourished in the import bins of hip record stores in the early nineties in the forms of dream pop and space rock, with drone-obsessed British outfit Spacemen 3 proclaiming it was "taking drugs to make music to take drugs to." Between 1990 and 1994, members of grunge bands Mother Love Bone, 7 Year Bitch, and Hole had all died of heroin overdoses, which didn't stop the concept of "heroin chic" from gaining currency in the fashion world. In 1997, President Bill Clinton described the trend as "glorifying death."

By 1992, antipot propaganda from the previous generation was being used for its ironic value on top-40 radio, where kids frequently heard a snippet of dialogue from the 1970 film *Beyond the Valley of the Dolls*. "She was living in a single room with three other individuals. One of them was a male and the other two, well, the other two were females. God only knows what they were up to in there. And furthermore, Susan, I wouldn't be the least bit surprised to learn that all four of them habitually smoked marijuana cigarettes—reefers." The clip, the intro to the ska band Sublime's first hit, "Smoke Two Joints," is followed, Cypress Hill–like, by the sound of somebody pulling bong hits—then gives way to talk of smoking two joints before smoking two joints. The album on which the track appeared, *40 oz. to Freedom*, was certified gold in 1997. It went platinum just a year later. In terms of straightforward messaging, "I smoke two joints in the morning" is hardly "Lucy in the sky with diamonds"—no druggie decoder needed.

Acid house, the music of 1988's so-called Second Summer of Love in Britain, helped rave culture blossom in the United States. Despite the "acid" of the genre's name, its defining substance was Ecstasy, and the thousand-plus-person raves that sprang up in U.S. cities in the late eighties and early nineties were an easy place to score that drug, as well as genuine acid and, with less frequency, ketamine and GHB. The urban rave scene was made possible by the postindustrial collapse of the American city in the seventies and eighties. Abandoned warehouses, office buildings, and, in a famous case in New York City, an Episcopalian church, hosted the weekend hedonism for mostly suburban, mostly teenaged partygoers who streamed over bridges and through tunnels.

Peter Gatien, a rave pioneer in New York, owned the iconic clubs the Tunnel, the Palladium, and the former church he dubbed the Limelight. He also ran a multimillion-dollar drug business, charging dealers license fees to operate in his establishments and creating a semicorporate structure to organize the trade, according to employees who flipped on him after he was arrested in 1996. In his defense, he claimed that he was too high on coke at the time to have run such an elaborate business. He was acquitted and deported to Canada, where he now owns the Toronto nightclub CiRCA. The nightlife scene in Miami's South Beach was run much the same way, largely by Mafia associate Chris Paciello, a close friend of Madonna's who was arrested for murder just before his latest club, Liquid, was to open.

The nineties saw an increase in the supply of psychedelic drugs just in time to meet the growing demand. The Brotherhood of Eternal Love and other acid syndicates met most of their precursor needs by using Eastern European suppliers. Those connections began drying up in the late seventies and early eighties as authorities caught on. But the 1991 collapse of the Soviet Union reopened the taps.

Acid kingpin William Leonard Pickard, in correspondences with me, was always careful about not admitting to any illegal activity, because his appeal was still ongoing. I asked him if it was true that the collapse of Communism allowed ergotamine tartrate (ET), the crucial LSD precursor, to again flow into the West. "An interesting anecdote is that the Aum Shin Rikyyo group of terrorists were found to have some kgs of ET of Russian origin, as an oblique answer to your question," he responded. "From my reading, research, and interviews, I believe ET availability declined rapidly with the installation of the [United Nations International Drug Control Programme] controls in signatory nations."

The controls he's referring to weren't implemented until near the end of the decade, and they appear to have played a significant role in the decline of acid that took place around then. But immediately after the Soviet Union imploded, the precursors flowed freely. According to the Michigan survey, American kids took advantage—and the last thing that could have stopped them was D.A.R.E.

Instead, it did just the opposite. As the organization grew, it set out to prove its worth with statistics. In the early nineties, D.A.R.E. lobbied the Department of Justice to do a nationwide study of the program. The resulting report by the Research Triangle Institute concluded that D.A.R.E. does not prevent drug use.

It did find that shortly after going through the program, kids have a more negative opinion of drugs than students who never took the class. That difference dissipates within one or two years, however, with D.A.R.E. and non-D.A.R.E. kids becoming indistinguishable with regard to attitudes toward drug use. Even worse, among kids in suburban school districts, drug education, the study found, leads to a significant increase in the likelihood that a kid will get high.

Subsequent studies—and there have been many—have also discovered either that there's no connection between D.A.R.E. and drug use or that D.A.R.E. has had a contrary effect. Talking to kids about marijuana, it turns out, makes them less frightened of it, not more. The Michigan survey has consistently found that twelfth graders were drastically less likely to think that occasional pot smoking is harmful—about a quarter said so in 2008—than eighth graders, half of whom that year said that it could cause great harm.

The U.S. Surgeon General's office, the National Academy of Sciences, the U.S. Government Accountability Office, and the National Institute of Justice, among other groups, have all concluded that the program is ineffective. The GAO found it to be counterproductive, as did researchers at Indiana University, who discovered that kids who had completed the program had higher rates of psychedelic drug use than those who had not. Research by Dennis Rosenbaum, a professor at the University of Illinois at Chicago, found that D.A.R.E. grads were more likely to drink alcohol, smoke tobacco, and use drugs. "Across more than 30 studies, the collective evidence from evaluations with reasonably good scientific validity suggests that the core D.A.R.E. program does not prevent drug use in the short term, nor does it prevent drug use when students are ready to enter high school or college," concluded Rosenbaum. "The basic question then becomes: How can we reconcile this state of knowledge with the reality of worldwide support for D.A.R.E.?"

D.A.R.E. has defended itself by pointing to the popularity of the program and its ancillary benefits for cops. D.A.R.E. is indeed extremely popular, according to the same studies—with parents.

And why wouldn't it be? Parents often find the "drug talk" intimidating, and federal surveys show that some of them might find it hypocritical, too: there's a roughly 50 percent chance that the potential talk givers themselves have gotten high. For many parents, it's difficult to oppose the notion of having a trained and presumably unblemished police officer teach their kids about right and wrong. D.A.R.E. is also a ready-at-hand answer to the parental question of what schools are doing in terms of drug education.

But even without the cultural pressures and renewed drug availability of the early nineties, D.A.R.E. was doomed to fail. What better way to get a kid to do something than to dare him not to?

A sign that the program was backfiring at my school was that kids who were known to be getting high were ironically slapping D.A.R.E. bumper stickers on their lockers or skateboards. It didn't help that the administration complemented D.A.R.E. by trotting First Lady Nancy Reagan around the country asking kids to "Just say no," a phrase that became one of the more lampooned attempts at public persuasion ever attempted. (One joke involved Reagan's answer to homelessness: "Just buy a house.")

Reagan's national finger-wagging came along with a multibillion-dollar advertising campaign centered on the unforgettable image of a frying egg. "This is your brain," a stern voice said of an uncooked egg. "This is your brain on drugs," it said as the egg sizzled in a pan. "Any questions?"

The query, of course, was meant to be rhetorical. But it shows how little interest the government had in answering real questions that kids might have had about drugs—even ones raised by the frying egg: Which drug does that to my brain? Why? What's it feel like? Will it kill me instantly?

The curious went elsewhere for answers.

CHAPTER 7

Border Justice

During the first year of his administration, President Bill Clinton made free trade a top priority, pushing for the passage of the controversial North American Free Trade Agreement. It wasn't an easy task. Having helped Democrats take the White House for the first time in twelve years, organized labor was in no mood to see manufacturing jobs shipped to Mexico. The debate was difficult enough without having to talk about the sprawling Mexican drug trade and its attendant corruption and how the agreement would end up benefiting the cartels. So Clinton ordered his people not to mention it.

"We were prohibited from discussing the effects of NAFTA as it related to narcotics trafficking, yes," Phil Jordan, who had been one of the Drug Enforcement Administration's leading authorities on Mexican drug organizations, told ABC News reporter Brian Ross four years after the deal had gone through. "For the godfathers of the drug trade in Columbia and Mexico, this was a deal made in narco heaven."

The agreement squeaked through Congress in late 1993 and went into effect January 1, 1994, the same day that the Zapatistas rose up in southeast Mexico. With its passage, more than two million trucks began flowing northward across the border annually. Only a small fraction of them were inspected for cocaine, heroin, or meth.

In a 1999 report, the White House estimated that commercial vehicles brought roughly 100 tons of cocaine into the country across the Mexican border in 1993. With NAFTA in effect, 1994 saw the biggest jump in commercial-vehicle smuggling on record—an increase of 25 percent, a massive annual upsurge for any type of drug-related statistic. The number of meth-related emergency-room visits in the United States doubled between 1991 and 1994. In San Diego, America's meth capital, meth seizures climbed from 1,409 pounds in 1991 to 13,366 in 1994.

As far as the Clinton administration was concerned, the cost of increased drug smuggling was far less than the benefit of increased trade. In this case, the White House knew very well that economic policy couldn't be separated from drug policy; it simply chose to pretend otherwise. It's a tactic in which the United States frequently engages. The ongoing foreign-policy goal of taking out the Taliban in Afghanistan, for instance, has been pursued in spite of its potential effect on the heroin trade. That Afghan heroin exports have increased in the wake of regime change is a typical result of such a compartmentalized approach. But drug policy per se doesn't exist. Because altering one's consciousness is a fundamental human desire, any public policy is also drug policy.

When broad economic policies collide with narrowly focused drug policies, unintended consequences multiply. The opening of the border by NAFTA came at an opportune time for Mexican drug runners, who had recently expanded their control of the cocaine trade and made major investments in large-scale meth production. Both were unintended consequences of U.S. policies in the seventies and eighties aimed at crushing meth and cocaine with a militarized, enforcement-heavy approach. The return of meth across the Mexican border was one more sign that the get-tough policies of the eighties had backfired.

Meth production had been driven underground and pushed into Mexico in the late sixties and seventies as a result of federal legislation. It fell into the waiting arms of a drug-smuggling establishment that itself had also been created by U.S. drug policy. The 1914 U.S. law that banned opium had created a situation in which the drug was illegal on one side of the border and legal on the other, where it had been grown since the 1800s. The Mexican government was in the midst of a revolution and unable to stop northward smuggling.

Sociologist Luís Astorga, in his study "Drug Trafficking in Mexico: A First General Assessment," cites Los Angeles customs officials claiming that Baja California's then governor, Esteban Cantú, a Mexican army colonel, was suspected of playing a major role in the drug trade by reselling product seized from other traffickers.

Mexican smugglers got another boost when the United States banned alcohol with passage of the Eighteenth Amendment. It took them decades, though, to get into the cocaine business. In the seventies, South American cocaine producers were running almost all of the cocaine imported into the United States through the Caribbean, into Miami, and then out to the rest of the nation. In the eighties, the feds brought the hammer down on the mound of coke that was Miami and the Caribbean smugglers. While the government focused on the powder that then began to waft across the country, Mexican meth smugglers seized a perfect opportunity.

The opening salvo of the U.S. war on coke might well have been a 1981 *Time* magazine cover story on Miami's burgeoning drug trade, which put an intolerable situation before the eyes of the whole American public. The report, titled "Trouble in Paradise," led directly to federal intervention, with Vice President George H. W. Bush repeatedly traveling to Miami to oversee the response personally.

Unsettling and shifting a multibillion-dollar drug trade, however, was no simple affair. With tighter enforcement in Florida and the Caribbean, producers increasingly moved their product by tuna boat or airplane to Mexico or another nearby nation and then overland across the U.S. border. Mexico had the infrastructure ready: by the late seventies, it was the world's largest heroin exporter, with thousands of acres of poppy fields. The late sixties and seventies had also seen a dramatic increase in demand for Mexican marijuana; by the mid-seventies, it was among the world's foremost pot exporters.

The extensive South and Central American smuggling network was built at a time when the United States' primary foreign-policy goals were to oppose communism and to support enemies of communism — regardless of whether they were also drug traffickers. When relations with the Soviet Union began to thaw, in the mid-eighties, the United

States was left with a superpower-sized military that had no obvious enemy. Drugs would have to do.

"Two words sum up my entire approach," President George H. W. Bush's drug czar, William Bennett, announced in 1989: "'consequences' and 'confrontation.'" He and Bush doubled annual drug-war spending to $12 billion and pressed fighter planes, submarines, and other military hardware into service for the cause. In 1989, Secretary of Defense Dick Cheney secured $450 million to go after Caribbean smugglers; billions more were spent in the source countries of South America.

In the early nineties, a White House report notes, more than 250 tons of coke were smuggled into the United States through Florida in a year, while only about 100 tons flowed across the southwestern border. By the end of the decade, just under 200 tons each came across both boundaries. In subsequent years, the amount coming through the Caribbean steadily fell, and by 2004, the Interagency Assessment of Cocaine Movement determined that the route accounted for less than 10 percent of all coke smuggling into the United States.

Spreading the market out didn't have a noticeable effect on supply north of the border. But it had an important impact south of it: it solidified the strength of Mexican drug-running organizations, which quickly realized that they could make a nice extra profit by packing another drug with their shipments of cocaine. U.S. restrictions on pharmaceutical companies, which had lowered domestic meth production, had also created a thriving Mexican meth industry. The Mexican cocaine cartels were flush with capital, having taken over major portions of the business from the Colombians—thanks, in large measure, to successful U.S. efforts to decapitate Colombian drug organizations. These two circumstances led directly to the industrialization of the meth trade.

The Mexican traffickers renegotiated their deals with the Colombians, taking an ownership stake rather than a flat fee for transport, and then reinvested some of this capital in building meth factories. Their product was then shipped northward in unprecedented volumes.

The return of meth—or, more precisely, the evolution of meth—was a throw-your-hands-up moment for drug warriors. Federal surveys show a long and slow decline in the use of amphetamines in the United States from 1981 to the early nineties. But between 1994 and 1995, meth use jumped in the United States. Among nineteen- to twenty-eight-year-olds in the Michigan survey, annual use ticked up by a third. (It remained lower, however, than the American media would have you believe: Even after the jump in meth use, only 1.2 percent of the survey's total respondents admitted to using it.)

The shift of meth from localized production in California to big-time assembly lines in Mexico didn't go unnoticed by enforcement agents in the United States. But the eventual crackdown brought another unforeseen consequence: as California tightened its border in response to both drug smuggling and illegal immigration in the nineties, the drug runners gradually moved east. "The eastward expansion of the drug took a particular toll on central states such as Arkansas, Illinois, Indiana, Iowa, Kansas, Missouri, and Nebraska," noted the 2006 National Drug Threat Assessment. The Midwestern methedemic, as it came to be dubbed, was born.

The war on drugs is often characterized as the product of a reactionary, possibly racist, series of administrations. But it's important to remember that in the eighties, the feds were responding to intense political and cultural pressure. American conservatives have a long history of the defense of individual liberty, and they've generally been opposed to both prohibition and the expansion of the federal government needed to regulate and outlaw drugs. However, the modern religious right, whose long-term goal is to shape the government into an institution that promotes Christian virtue, has demonstrated a keen willingness to sacrifice personal freedom for moral correctness. Its political rise began following 1973's *Roe v. Wade* decision. By the eighties, it had become a powerful player in the coalition that gave rise to the third wave of the American temperance movement.

The movement's aims were threefold: to reduce teen drug use, to raise the drinking age, and to stop drunk driving. Newly formed organizations and educational programs such as National Families in Action (founded in 1977), PRIDE (Parent Resources and Information on Drug Education, 1978), D.A.R.E. (Drug Abuse Resistance Education, 1983), the Just Say No Club (1985), and the Partnership for a Drug-Free America (1986) worked toward the first goal. MADD, or Mothers Against Drunk Driving, perhaps the most visible and influential member of the movement, worked toward the second and third.

Just as a century before, it was women who led the charge against immoderation. Candy Lightner, a resident of suburban Fair Oaks, California, whose daughter Cari was run over by a drunk driver in 1980, founded the twentieth-century equivalent of the Woman's Christian Temperance Union: a media-savvy organization that was quickly wielding substantial influence over lawmakers. MADD pressure on states and the federal government led to some notable successes. Penalties for drinking and driving were increased, blood-alcohol levels defining intoxication were lowered, and the national drinking age was boosted from eighteen to twenty-one. Nowadays, it's difficult to imagine that drunk driving once went on with little in the way of afterthought or recrimination. Just a few decades ago, cops were as likely to help you home as they are today to lock you up, sometimes for serious stretches of time.

Like those who led the American temperance movement in earlier eras, shifting its goal from mere moderation to out-and-out prohibition, MADD and its allies quickly broadened their aims. By 1985, many activists wanted to make a criminal of anyone who drove after drinking anything at all. Lightner herself began to worry that what she had created had "become far more neo-prohibitionist than I had ever wanted or envisioned. I didn't start MADD to deal with alcohol. I started MADD to deal with the issue of drunk driving." Typically, American idealism could brook no compromise.

In true eighties fashion, the fight went Madison Avenue: the Partnership for a Drug-Free America (PDFA), a campaign launched by the American Association of Advertising Agencies, produced one of the decade's indelible images with its 1987 public service announcement depicting a frying egg. And in true American fashion, many big-time drug, alcohol, and tobacco producers allied themselves with the movement. The PDFA's major—and, for a time, private—donors included Philip Morris, Anheuser-Busch, and R. J. Reynolds. After their involvement was exposed, in 1997, the Partnership dropped the booze and smokes sponsors, but it retained plenty of pharmaceutical funders: the Pharmaceutical Research and Manufacturers of America, the National Association of Chain Drug Stores Foundation, the

Consumer Healthcare Products Association, Purdue Pharma, the Bristol-Myers Squibb Foundation, the Procter & Gamble Fund, the Bayer Corporation, GlaxoSmithKline, Kimberly-Clark, Pfizer Inc., Endo Pharmaceuticals, Hoffmann-La Roche, Merck & Co., King Pharmaceuticals, Reckit Benckiser Pharmaceuticals, Walgreens.

For Big Pharma and other substance pushers, allying yourself with the ostensible enemy makes good political sense: it's better to be on the side that seems to be winning, and you might even earn a legislative loophole or two for your willingness to help out.

Throughout the eighties, with Senator Joe Biden taking a vocal lead, Democrats in Congress and state governments around the country increased prison sentences for drug offenses, coming down particularly hard on crack. In 1986, Congress instituted mandatory-minimum sentences for powder and cocaine. To trigger the powder minimum, a dealer needed to possess 500 grams. For crack, just 5 grams. Two years later, the law was extended to anybody who was associated with the dealer—girlfriends, roommates, what have you.

In 1991, Michigander Allen Harmelin argued that his life sentence for possessing roughly a pound and a half of cocaine is cruel and unusual. The Supreme Court ruled that it is neither. California enacted its three-strikes law in 1994—three felonies equals a minimum of twenty-five years—and the feds one-upped the state, declaring a third felony to result in life without parole. Twenty-three more states enacted three-strikes laws by 1995.

In 1984, just over 30,000 people were in prison for drug crimes; by 1991, the number had soared to more than 150,000. The Department of Justice found in a study of the prison population that the average length of a federal stay drastically increased between 1986 and 1997. If you walked into prison in 1986, your average stay would have been twenty-one months. In 1997, it was forty-seven months. For weapons offenders, the rise was from twenty-three to seventy-five months, and for drug offenders, it was from thirty to sixty-six months. Not all criminals could expect such increased time behind bars, however: a bank robber could expect seventy-four months in 1986 and only eighty-three months a decade later.

Three-strikes laws and lengthening prison sentences explain what appears to be a contradiction: U.S. crime rates are falling while U.S. incarceration rates are rising. It stands to reason that if fewer people are committing crimes, then fewer people would be locked up. But the combination of locking up fewer people every year and putting them away for much longer causes the prison population to mushroom.

The result is that more than one out of every one hundred Americans is currently in prison. If you're a black male between twenty and thirty-four, there's a better than one in nine chance that you're imprisoned. To keep all of these people behind bars, states spent a combined $44 billion in 2007.

For a hot minute in the early nineties, however, it looked as if the lock-'em-up-forever approach might be shelved. President Bill Clinton selected as his drug czar Lee Brown, who had a background in law enforcement, sociology, and criminology and told his staff to rethink some basic assumptions. The first one was the militarized approach being used in Latin America, aimed at increasing the cost of drugs.

Brown's people began passing around a study by a private think tank, the RAND Corporation, that came to some hopeful conclusions: An overwhelming proportion of drug use is done by a small but dedicated group of users. Therefore, getting that small group to reduce its use—even to a small degree—can reap big dividends. RAND estimated that the United States, for instance, could decrease cocaine use by 1 percent either by spending $34 million on drug-treatment programs or by spending $783 million going after drugs at the source. Fiscally, the choice seems obvious.

Rolling Stone reporter Ben Wallace-Wells, who wrote an in-depth feature in 2007 called "How America Lost the Drug War," has characterized Brown's time as drug czar as a window of opportunity that never fully opened. "When I worked as an undercover narcotics officer, I was living the life of an addict so I could make buys and make busts of the dealers," Brown told Wallace-Wells. "When you're in that position, you see very quickly that you can't arrest your way out of this. You see the cycle over and over again of people using drugs, getting into trouble, going to prison, getting out and getting into drugs again. At some point I stepped back and asked myself, 'What impact is all of this having on the drug problem? There has to be a better way.'"

Brown's 1994 drug-control budget sought to cut spending on Latin American military efforts, to emphasize treatment over incarceration for small-time offenders, and to dedicate $355 million toward treating the core group of addicts. A Democratic Congress emphatically rejected it, sending Clinton a budget that instead prioritized the same old militarized approach. The next year, Newt Gingrich and his Republican revolutionaries ran the show. Despite Gingrich's public support of medical marijuana in the early eighties, he and his colleagues had little appetite for anything but the hard line. More than 80 percent of their drug budget went toward enforcement and interdiction.

Even if the GOP had been open to drug-policy reform, the Clinton administration was by then no longer interested. Famous for the strategy of triangulation—undercutting your opponent by agreeing with him on a crucial issue—Clinton increased his emphasis on crime fighting following the 1994 Republican revolution. During his 1996 State of the Union address, Clinton made it official: Brown was out and the war would be rejoined in earnest, under the leadership of retired U.S. Army general Barry McCaffrey. McCaffrey was enamored of the theory that marijuana is a gateway drug, and that attacking it was the best way to beat drugs back.

Consequently, meth was off the federal radar. But the real-world consequences of meth addiction in the heartland would soon enough create a grassroots movement determined to undermine the enforcement-heavy approach that Clinton had embraced.

Gene Haislip, a revered DEA figure, is credited with crushing Quaaludes in the early eighties by persuading every company that made the necessary precursors to halt production. He tried to do the same thing with meth in 1986, but his effort was stymied by the pharmaceutical lobby. He'd hoped to strictly regulate all ephedrine-related precursors, but after two years of negotiations, he'd succeeded only in regulating the sales of bulk powders.

Mexican cartels, however, had no problem buying bulk product from nations such as China and India. And American producers could still get unlimited quantities of legally marketed pills, which were exempted from the Haislip agreement and could easily be crushed into a precursor-laced powder.

In 1990, the federally funded *Monitoring the Future* report first began asking about "crystal methamphetamine" or "ice." Use slowly rose over the decade, ticking dramatically upward after NAFTA was implemented. Arrests and convictions rose, too, but the prison industry couldn't keep up, creating a strong incentive at the local level to find alternatives to incarceration.

When meth is described in media accounts, it's sometimes spoken of as creating a nearly incurable addiction. "You have a better chance to do well after many types of cancer than you have of recovering from methamphetamine dependence," psychiatrist Martin Paulus told *Time* in 2007. But meth users, it turns out, respond to treatment just as well as, if not better than, other addicts. "Claims that methamphetamine users are virtually untreatable with small recovery rates lack foundation in medical research. . . . [S]everal recent studies indicate that methamphetamine users respond in an equivalent manner as individuals admitted for other drug abuse problems," a group of ninety-two prominent physicians, treatment specialists, and researchers wrote in a 2005 open letter to the media.

State legislators who needed a cost-effective way to deal with drug addiction have been much more willing to take a chance on that "equivalent manner" than anyone in Congress. Indeed, meth addiction has helped build a nationwide system of local drug courts that divert offenders from incarceration to treatment. The trend began in response to cocaine, with the first drug court established in Miami in 1989, but it rose in tandem with meth use and continued upward even after the numbers for speed began to decline. By 2005, there were more than 1,500 drug courts in operation. By 2008, there were nearly 2,500.

In 2000, California voters approved a program to provide drug treatment, rather than prison time, for nonviolent drug-possession offenders. A study of the law found that it saved the state $1.3 billion over its first six years, and that for every tax dollar invested, California saved $7 thanks to reductions in crime and health-care costs. Oregon, also hit hard by meth, factored in savings on prison costs and health and welfare spending and found that treatment returned $5.62 on every dollar spent. Maryland, Texas, and Utah followed by passing their own treatment-over-incarceration laws.

A two-year study, published in the journal *Addiction* in 2008, found that those parts of the country that turned to enforcement instead of treatment fared poorly. Researchers looked at several counties in Arkansas, Kentucky, and Ohio that had tightened laws around meth in an effort to curb supply. They discovered that when confronted by a shortage of their favored drug, meth users simply switched to snorting coke. Overall, such areas saw a 9 percent increase in cocaine use after their meth laws were enacted.

As the local movement toward treatment gained strength, it finally received some notice in Washington with the 1994 institution of the federal Drug Court Program. But the way the program was structured and funded indicates the movement's grassroots nature: it created no nationwide effort aimed at establishing a system of drug courts, but rather allowed localities to apply for federal grants for whatever it is they're doing. In 2007, the entire federal program was cut a check for $10 million—at $200,000 per state, that's about as paltry a sum as Washington can conjure.

As meth use rose nationwide, Clinton's law-and-order drug czar had little interest in either the drug or the drug courts. Of more pressing concern to McCaffrey was the November 1996 passage of ballot initiatives in California and Arizona to legalize medical marijuana. In typical drug-warrior style, the Clinton White House became determined to go after Americans' changing attitudes toward drugs at the source—so much so that it had no qualms about covertly placing antidrug messages into popular prime-time TV shows such as *Beverly Hills 90210* and *ER*.

Just after the elections in California and Arizona, McCaffrey called a meeting that included the head of the DEA and three other DEA staffers, White House advisers, and people from the FBI and the Departments of Justice and Health and Human Services. The private wing of the war on drugs was represented, too, by eight senior executives from, and the president of, the Partnership for a Drug-Free America. Drug-reform organizations got word of the meeting and went to the press about it. Reporter Daniel Forbes broke the story for *Salon.com*.

The consensus at the meeting was that medical marijuana was a spike that could be driven into the heart of drug prohibition, and that the legalization movement knew it. "Need to frame the issue properly—expose this as legalizers using terminally ill as props" was the thinking of James Copple, then president of the Community Anti-Drug Coalition of America, according to the minutes. Maricopa County district attorney Richard Romley, representing the Arizona delegation, suggested that "[e]ven though California and Arizona are different props, the strategy of proponents is the same. It will expand throughout the nation if we all don't react." His remedy: "Need to go state by state. $ to do media."

Two approaches were settled upon to prevent the medical-marijuana movement from spreading to other states: ramping up a national antipot PR campaign and threatening doctors with the loss of their licenses if they recommended marijuana to patients. The latter strategy was announced in a press conference a month later and led to the lawsuit that eventually uncovered the minutes of the meeting. The doctors won, claiming a First Amendment right to recommend whatever legal remedy they believed would be effective.

The PDFA's president threw out an idea of how much the PR component of the effort might cost: "$175 million," he suggested, according to the minutes. "Try to get fedl $." That's exactly how much the drug czar later requested for the new media campaign, and Congress helpfully tossed in another $20 million. The effort, which grew within a year into a billion-dollar public-private partnership, became mired in an accounting scandal and then ran afoul of public opinion when its strategy to pay TV networks as well as film producers for propagandist portrayals of drug use was exposed. And it certainly didn't slow the medical-marijuana movement.

With the federal government fighting this losing battle, meth use was slowly increasing in rural America, mirroring the rise of cocaine in urban areas that had accompanied the federal war on pot a decade earlier. With it came local dealers' and addicts' efforts to supplement the already plentiful supply of Mexican speed. The government has figures for meth-lab seizures beginning only in 1999, but some states' records go back further. Kansas recorded 4 seizures in 1994 and 7 in 1995. The number peaked at 846 in 2001. In 2004, the national number topped 17,000.

A year later, Congress finally succeeded in overcoming pharmaceutical-lobby objections and tightly controlled pseudoephedrine distribution with a law tied to the Patriot Act. It went into effect the first day of 2006. "It was almost like throwing a switch," Larry Rogers, an Iowa narcotics cop who's been chasing drugs since the seventies, told me. Statewide, the number of labs seized fell by more than 50 percent from 2005 to 2006, and then dropped another 60 percent or so in 2007, down to just 138. I asked Rogers if that reduced the availability of meth. "No," he said, "even at the peak of our meth-lab problem, most of the meth that we were dealing with—80 to 90 percent of the meth we were dealing with—always has been imported."

The 2006 National Drug Threat Assessment found as much. Citing DEA and other federal data, the report concluded that "Mexican criminal groups are the predominant wholesale methamphetamine distributors in the country—even in the Northeast and Florida/ Caribbean Regions—supplying various midlevel distributors, including other Mexican criminal groups, with powder methamphetamine and, increasingly, ice methamphetamine."

That doesn't mean that the pseudoephedrine regulations were completely useless, however. "The labs just presented a unique risk for us in terms of being first responders," Rogers said. "They presented environmental risks in terms of exposure, not only for the responders but for the people living at the location—children, spouses, the people actually involved. Fires, explosion—these were the ancillary problems associated with meth labs. We're glad to see them go, because now we don't have to deal with that risk. But . . . the majority of meth has always been imported."

Seizures fell by 50 percent nationally, too, down to fewer than 6,000 in 2005. The government often bandied the large seizure numbers about, in order to create the impression of a serious problem, but the labs that were typically busted weren't massive enterprises. "A lab can be something as small as somebody trying to cook something up in a milk jug," DEA spokesperson Steve Robertson told me.

That's what they mostly found in Iowa. "Most of the labs we dealt with here were small labs, capable of generating an ounce or less per cook," said Rogers. "Not the superlabs you hear so much about in Mexico and the Southwest United States. They produce meth by the pounds. We haven't ever dealt with labs on that level." In fact, few American police forces have ever had to deal with superlabs. Only around 250 were busted in 2001, according to federal data. In 2003, Canada restricted bulk pseudoephedrine exports, and the next year the number fell to 55.

As the Iowa cops easily understood, wiping out meth labs in the United States did almost nothing to reduce meth supply. It only strengthened the hand of the Mexicans. Ever since the U.S. crack-down in Colombia, which led to the death of Pablo Escobar in 1993 and the arrest or killing of many other narco-leaders, the Mexicans had gradually been taking control of drug trade. During the same decade, one-party rule in Mexico was coming to an end, as the Institutional Revolutionary Party (Partido Revolucionario Institucional, or PRI) began to lose its decades-long grip on power. By 1997, it had lost the legislature, and in 2000, for the first time in more than seventy years, it lost the presidency. Democracy was the open door through which drug traffickers walked to take control of the Mexican state.

They were inadvertently aided by the United States' launch-ing of its international drug war. From 1969's unilateral Operation Intercept—an attempt to choke off the importation of marijuana and other drugs at the U.S.-Mexico border, widely protested in Latin America—to such subsequent collaborative efforts as Operation Cooperation and Operation Condor, American antidrug measures in Mexico have had the effect of simply spreading out the drug trade. High-volume smugglers such as Ramón Arellano Félix, Joaquín Guzmán, and Amado Carrillo, who had all been regional traffick-ers in the Pacific Coast state of Sinaloa, scattered throughout the country and went to war with one another, creating the cartel struc-ture that exists today. "That was when the drug trade really began to expand," reporter Javier Valdez Cardenas told New Yorker writer Alma

Guillermoprieto in 2008. "Because the few traffickers who remained here were killed, but all the rest of them emigrated. Now they're all over the country."

Just as the cartels were rising in power, Mexico was democratizing. And running for democratic office—in a contested race, that is—costs serious money. The all-pervasive, all-powerful PRI hadn't needed to raise money to win elections. But today in Mexico, a simple campaign for the legislature can cost between $10 and $20 million. Naturally, that money comes from the people who have it: the traffickers, who now control untold numbers of politicians and are even said to have infiltrated the Mexican embassy in Washington, D.C.

In late 2006, Mexican president Felipe Calderón vowed to go to war with the cartels. Backed by a $1.4 billion investment in arms from the U.S. government, his effort has touched off violence that was once thought unimaginable in North America. Modeling their behavior after al-Qaeda insurgents in Iraq, Mexican cartels have begun beheading opponents and posting the videos on YouTube. Signs of gruesome torture are routinely found on dead bodies. Upward of five thousand people were killed in drug-related violence in 2008 alone, and the blood has begun to run in the streets of Mexico's tourist towns—the kind of thing that gets international attention.

In 2007, Phoenix, Arizona, set up a special task force to address the flood of violence coming across the border as cartel-related murders, home invasions, and kidnappings spiked. In Arizona, as in Mexico, cartel soldiers have disguised themselves as law enforcement, dressing in SWAT gear in order to raid homes and murder those inside. "It wasn't uncommon to have a new kidnapping case coming into our offices on a daily basis," Lieutenant Lauri Burgett of the Phoenix Police Department's violent-crimes bureau told a CBS News investigative team in November 2008.

The 2009 National Drug Threat Assessment names Mexican drug-trafficking organizations—DTOs in governmentese—"the greatest organized crime threat to the United States," warning that the "influence of Mexican DTOs over domestic drug trafficking is unrivaled. In fact, intelligence estimates indicate a vast majority of the cocaine available in U.S. drug markets is smuggled by Mexican DTOs across the U.S.-Mexico border. Mexican DTOs control drug distribution in most U.S. cities, and they are gaining strength in markets that they do not yet control."

In response, the U.S. and Mexican governments have stepped up combat, vowing to go even harder after the cartels. But south of the border, the government and the cartels are often one and the same. As a retired PRI man told the *New Yorker*, "When you see what amounts to a military parade in these towns, in which the Army is trooping along on the main avenue while on the side streets people are killing each other . . . when I see how these [traffickers] are climbing up right into the very beard of the state, I think, Holy fuck! This country could really collapse!"

The drug war has brought the Mexican government to the brink of collapse, making the prospect of a failed state on America's southern border a very real possibility. Meanwhile, the war costs billions of dollars to wage at home and in Mexico and has swelled the U.S. prison population, bursting state budgets at the seams. It would be one thing if this were merely collateral damage in an otherwise successful effort to reduce drug use. But an estimated 30 percent of Mexico's arable land is currently being used to grow illegal drugs— and the U.S. appetite for such crops remains undiminished. The party rages on.

Meanwhile, the media have gone on focusing on the ravages of meth, even as its use began to decline. According to federal survey data, American meth use began to tail off by 2002. Another sign that the peak had come and gone was that the media finally caught on. *Newsweek* ran a 2005 cover story titled "The Meth Epidemic: Inside America's New Drug Crisis." In March 2006, the *Washington Post* ran an equally hysterical piece headlined "The Next Crack Cocaine?" describing a meth epidemic about to sweep the nation's capital. I called the law-enforcement folks quoted in the article, as well as a few others, and got a much different story.

"It's funny—the *Washington Post* guy asked me that, but we haven't per se seen any increase in meth possessions here," Sergeant Shawn A. Urbas, a spokesman for the Anne Arundel County, Maryland, police department, told me. The *Post* had cited his county's three lab seizures as evidence of a trend, despite his having said otherwise.

"It's not that big of a deal, but we're keeping it on the radar," said Kristine Vander Wall, an intelligence analyst with the Washington/Baltimore bureau of the federal High-Intensity Drug Trafficking Area Program, which has looked extensively at meth-usage and -arrest data. "Sometimes the media has a tendency to sensationalize certain drugs. They did it with PCP a year or two ago. My director came to me and said, 'Kristine, we need to get on top of this PCP,' and I said, 'Whoa, let's analyze this first and see if it's actually a problem.'"

Captain Mary Gavin, a vice narcotics commander with the Arlington County, Virginia, police department, told me that although she had seen some meth arrests in her jurisdiction, they were less frequent than those for marijuana, cocaine, and heroin. "I'd say it has not hit us hard here," she said. I asked her to name any drug that was less of a problem than meth in the county. "Steroids," she said. After a long pause, she added, "And LSD. We don't see much of that."

CHAPTER 8

Kids Today

Kids today—they just don't get high like they used to. Starting around 2001, teen use of pot and psychedelics, which had been on the rise for roughly a decade, began to fall off. That year, 37 percent of high-school seniors said they'd smoked pot, up from 22 percent in 1992. By 2008, the number was at 32 percent. Ecstasy use dropped from 9.2 percent in 2001 to 4.3 percent in 2008. LSD use, of course, tumbled as well, falling by three-quarters between 2001 and 2006. Over the same period, the use of hallucinogens dove from 9.1 to 4.9 percent.

How to account for the downturn? Federal authorities have two explanations: random student drug testing and the drug czar's antipot media campaign. There's good evidence, however, that the real causes have little to do with enforcement policies or publicity efforts: more likely they relate to a shift in drug supply from the street to the doctor's office and a dramatic change in the way kids interact with one another.

Drug testing of the American public exploded under the Reagan administration, as, first, federal employers and, then, corporate America were called to serve in the war on drugs. It now encompasses some forty million people—soldiers and journalists, teachers and truckers, grocery-store cashiers and middle- and high-school students. In 1988, Congress passed the Drug Free Workplace Act, which requires companies to drug-test employees as a condition of receiving federal contracts. The act was made possible by a 1975 high-court ruling that created an "administrative search exception" to the Fourth Amendment, declaring that the state's interest in a strong military outweighs the privacy concerns of individual soldiers. The administrative-search exception became the legal basis for all future drug testing, even that done on kids whose uniformed combat is limited to the football field.

The drug testing of student athletes actually got under way a couple of years before the *Monitoring the Future* report recorded the D.A.R.E. generation's upswing in use. In the late eighties, when middle- and high-school drug use was relatively low nationwide, teachers in the small, middle-class town of Vernonia, Oregon, began to notice, according to court documents, "a sharp increase in drug use" among their students. A longtime English teacher told a *Seattle Times* reporter that "I got all kinds of essays from kids who described their drug addiction. A lot of them were football players and wrestlers. I'd be in the middle of a lesson, and somebody would stand up and sing 'Jesus Loves Me.' Suddenly I had a class I could not control." At Vernonia High School, an athletics coach attributed various mistakes on the gridiron and a "severe sternum injury" on the wrestling floor to student drug use. The "state of rebellion" among students systemwide resulted in a dramatic upsurge in disciplinary actions, including several suspensions. School officials tried to quell it with special classes and presentations, and then a drug-sniffing dog, all to no avail.

In 1989, the Vernonia school system hit upon an idea that has had an incalculable impact on U.S. drug policy as it relates to minors: it would drug-test students, including those not suspected of drug use. Under the new, parent-approved policy, the Vernonia schools required all interscholastic athletes to submit to a drug test before participating in a sport, and then to undergo weekly tests randomly, accompanied by an adult monitor instructed to "listen for normal sounds of urination." Administrators argued that the policy—which prescribed a therapeutic combination of parental intervention, counseling, and athletic suspension to any student who failed his or her tests—would protect athletes from injury. Perhaps it would stop the student insurrection, too. The kids, by most accounts, submitted readily. "We didn't mind the testing," one recent graduate told the *Times* in 1995. "The kids all thought it was a good thing—except for that one boy."

That one boy, twelve-year-old football-team hopeful James Acton, rebelled in a way unprecedented among his student-athlete peers. He was backed by his parents, who, in 1991, refused to sign a urinalysis consent form. His mother, Judy, argued that there was no need to drug-test her son, because he'd told her that he wasn't taking drugs. His father, Wayne, suggested to the *Times* that "[s]uspicionless searches are . . . simplistic, demagogic solutions," and that "[s]ociety works better without them." Backed by the American Civil Liberties Union, the Actons went to court—and lost.

In 1995, in *Vernonia School District in Oregon v. Acton*, the Supreme Court upheld the suspicionless drug testing of student athletes, ruling that because athletes are supervised by the state during school hours and at sporting events, they already have lower expectations of privacy than adults. In 2002's *Earls v. Tecumseh Public School District*, the court expanded the scope of random student drug testing, approving it for any student who participates in an extracurricular activity. In his opinion for the majority, Justice Clarence Thomas found that "individualized suspicion" isn't necessary before testing because a school has a custodial responsibility for its students, that participation in nonathletic extracurricular activities diminishes the expectation of privacy, and that Tecumseh's demand that students pee in cups doesn't invade their privacy because an administrator stands outside the stall and the results aren't forwarded to police.

Vernonia High principal Randall Aultman must have been pleased: the year of the *Vernonia School District in Oregon v. Acton* decision, he had admitted that his district hadn't dared to expand drug testing beyond the locker room "because we were afraid we'd be sued to hell if we went to all students."

In its fiscal year 2009 budget, the Bush administration made increasing the use of student drug testing its highest antidrug priority.

It seems like common sense that if students are warned that they could be caught getting high any given day in school, they'd be less likely to risk it. Plus, principals and the drug czar's office argue, this constant threat "gives kids a reason to say no." But a student who chooses to do drugs already has more than a random chance of getting caught: Adults and other potential snitches are everywhere. Someone could smell smoke, see bloodshot eyes, or wonder just what the hell is so funny. And because most schools test only students who do something more than just show up—join an after-school club, park on campus, or play a sport—kids can avoid those activities rather than quit puffing.

According to two major studies, drug testing might not change much more of student life than that. "[D]rug testing still is found not to be associated with students' reported illicit drug use—even random testing that potentially subjects the entire student body," determined the authors of one study. The first, published in early 2003, looked at 76,000 students in eighth, tenth, and twelfth grades in hundreds of schools between the years 1998 and 2001. It was conducted by Ryoko Yamaguchi, Lloyd Johnston, and Patrick O'Malley of the University of Michigan, which also produces the *Monitoring the Future* report. Johnston is considered something of a dean of drug-trend analysis.

The Michigan study compared the rates of drug use, as measured by *Monitoring the Future,* in schools that did some type of drug testing to those in schools that did not. The researchers controlled for various demographic differences and found across the board that drug testing was ineffective: there was no statistically significant difference in the number of users at a school that tested for drugs and a similar school that didn't. The White House criticized the study for failing to look at the efficacy of random testing. So Yamaguchi, Johnston, and O'Malley added the element of randomness and ran their study again, this time adding data for the year 2002. The follow-up, published later in 2003, tracked 94,000 middle- and high-school students. It reached the same conclusions as its precursor.

Even if drug testing is done randomly and without suspicion, it's not associated with a change in the number of students who use drugs of any kind—with one exception: in schools that randomly tested students, twelfth graders were more likely to smoke marijuana.

At a December 2004 joint press conference with Johnston and drug czar John Walters, the czar was asked why random testing was being funded if Johnston and his colleagues had demonstrated that it's bogus. Walters told the assembled media that the jury was still out: "We don't have detailed pre- and post-random-testing data."

Not quite true, countered Johnston. "We looked at schools doing any kind of testing, mostly for cause, and didn't find any statistically significant differences in drug-use rates between schools that tested and those that didn't," he said. "We also looked at schools that did random tests of student athletes, which was allowed by the Supreme Court in 1995, and again there were no significant differences in the rates of marijuana use or illicit drug use in general."

Results like these would mean budget cuts or death for some government programs. The White House has devised its own system, known as the Program Assessment Rating Tool (PART), to help it cull failed initiatives. In 2002, PART deemed "ineffective" the Safe and Drug Free Schools State Grants program, the umbrella for school drug testing. The Office of Management and Budget, which runs the PART evaluations, discerned, "The program has failed to demonstrate effectiveness in reducing youth drug use, violence, and crime." The PART evaluation didn't single out drug testing, which is a small part of the overall state grants program, but if you combine those findings with those of the Michigan studies, student drug testing would appear to be taking a bureaucratic pounding.

Workplace testing is in retreat, too. "I think what a lot of companies saw was that the White House rhetoric didn't match up. There was no reduction in workplace absenteeism or any other benefit," a lawyer with the ACLU's Drug Law Reform Project told me. "Your own eyes and budget line will tell you to turn away from that program." That hasn't stopped President Bush from sounding an upbeat note, however. "I proposed new funding to continue our aggressive, community-based strategy to reduce demand for illegal drugs," Bush declared in his 2004 State of the Union address. "Drug testing in our schools has proven to be an effective part of this effort."

Meanwhile, the evidence—or lack thereof—continues to come in. A 2007 report by the American Academy of Pediatrics affirmed that random student drug testing doesn't reduce drug use. A 2006 survey published in the *Journal of Adolescent Health* found that 83 percent of pediatricians opposed in-school testing, citing the tests' complexity and propensity to produce false positives.

At least one report did find random testing of student athletes to reduce drug use, but its results show why the program isn't likely to be effective in the long run. The study, published in a 2003 issue of the *Journal of Adolescent Health*, compared one school that randomly tested athletes and one that didn't. The tested athletes got high less frequently but drank just as much as their nontested counterparts. The testing also seriously influenced their attitude toward drugs: the drug-tested athletes, according to their survey responses, believed drugs—now under regular discussion as part of a school-mandated activity—to be less dangerous than did their counterparts who were not tested. Less surprisingly, they also had a much poorer view of their school than they did before it began random testing.

That view was turned into action in 1997, when a group of students at the Rochester Institute of Technology founded the Rochester Cannabis Coalition. The RCC was denied a charter from the school, despite having been approved by a student board, and its founder was expelled in what appeared to be retribution from the administration, but the group has since grown to become Students for Sensible Drug Policy, a national organization with 50,000 members and chapters at more than 130 colleges and a handful of high schools. One of its principal goals: ending forced student drug testing.

Like Bush and Walters, the $766 million drug-testing industry isn't ready to give up on testing students, for which it charges between $14 and $30 per cupful of urine. Melissa Moskal, executive director of the 1,300-member Drug and Alcohol Testing Industry Association, pointed me to a preliminary study that she likes better than Michigan's and that Walters also frequently references. The study was funded by the Department of Education and produced by the Institute for Behavior and Health, and its lead author is Robert DuPont, a former White House drug official. DuPont is also a partner at Bensinger, DuPont & Associates, which specializes in, among other things, "workplace drug/alcohol prevention services." His firm boasts corporate offices in four cities and more than 1,200 branch offices.

DuPont told me that Bensinger "doesn't have anything to do with drug testing." But the company's Web site states, "BDA offers a range of products designed to help employers establish and manage work-place drug and alcohol testing programs." These include "[m]edical review of urine and hair drug tests," "turn-key administration of random testing programs," and evaluation of "new and existing on-site testing devices for reliability, sensitivity, and reaction to major adulterants." DuPont's study, which he called "descriptive," chose nine schools that met certain criteria, the first of which was "student drug testing program's apparent success." Rather than gathering information from students and analyzing it, DuPont relied on a questionnaire that asked administrators how effective they believe their random drug-testing program to be.

DuPont isn't concerned about any flaws in this methodology—and he's not worried about neutrality, either. "I can't quite get the argument that [drug testing] wouldn't work," he said. He's now working on an evaluation of eight schools. The results aren't out yet, but let's venture a prediction: random student drug testing will come out looking good.

It had better, because workplace drug testing of adults has been in steady decline since 1996. It's no surprise that BDA and similar companies have a strong interest in expanding their services to a new market. In a 1999 publication titled "Drug Testing: A Bad Investment," the ACLU noted that in 1990, the federal government spent $11.7 million to test 29,000 workers in 38 agencies. Only 153, or 0.5 percent, tested positive for drug use. For many private companies, such a cost-to-benefit ratio just doesn't make sense. In 2004, according to a study by the American Management Association, only 62 percent of U.S. companies drug-tested employees, down from a peak of 81 percent eight years earlier.

In the summers of 2007 and 2008, Walters focused his PR efforts on expanding student drug testing, traveling to school districts to pitch the model and hosting regional summits on the idea. Those journeys represent a culmination of sorts. Each year of the Bush administration, the emphasis on drug testing grew. By 2008, to the consternation of career drug warriors who'd become disenchanted with the practice, expanding student drug testing was officially made the number one priority of the White House's national drug-control strategy.

The practice needed that extra push. In 2007, the state of Hawaii announced that the random-drug-testing net would be cast around teachers as well as students. The teachers, with the help of the

ACLU, beat the policy back, and in 2008, the state board of education rescinded it. In March of that year, again following a challenge by the ACLU, the state neighboring the one that had begun suspicionless random testing of students struck it down. The Washington State supreme court ruled that such testing of students who participate in extracurricular activities was unconstitutional, citing the state document's Privacy Clause: "No person shall be disturbed in his private affairs, or his home invaded, without authority of law." Call it the revenge of James Acton.

What about the antipot ad campaign? Since 1998, the federal government has spent more than $1.5 billion on ads designed to dissuade teens from using marijuana. You've seen them: while high, stoners commit a host of horrible acts, including running over a little girl on a bike at a drive-through window.

The drug czar's office and the National Institute on Drug Abuse (NIDA), the arm of the federal government that funds research on drug abuse and addiction, partnered to study the campaign's effectiveness. The White House provided the funding, and NIDA contracted with a research firm, Westat, which gathered data between November 1999 and June 2004. The report Westat produced cost the government $42.7 million. It shows that the ad campaign isn't working. Instead of reducing the likelihood that kids will smoke marijuana, the ads increase it. Westat found that "greater exposure to the campaign was associated with weaker anti-drug norms and increases in the perceptions that others use marijuana." More exposure to the ads led to higher rates of first-time drug use among certain groups, such as fourteen- to sixteen-year-olds and whites.

NIDA and the White House drug office sat on the Westat report for a year and a half beginning in early 2005—while spending $220 million on antimarijuana ads in fiscal years 2005 and 2006.

The Government Accountability Office's Nancy Kingsbury, managing director for applied research and methods, told me that her office encountered serious resistance from NIDA and the White House when it insisted that it was entitled and mandated by Congress to review the publicly funded Westat study. Kingsbury thought the drug czar's obstruction had to do with the study's unfavorable results. "I'll be really surprised if it didn't," she said.

In the beginning, said Kingsbury, the drug czar "was touting this evaluation as an important study that would demonstrate the efficacy of this program, and they kind of got a ride in their appropriations for a couple of years because they were willing to put this evaluation on the street." Indeed, the drug warriors continuously justified funding for the lavish ad campaign based on the notion that the program was being scientifically evaluated. Walters promised in Senate testimony that he would "show results within a year or admit failure," reported *Government Executive* magazine, and Congress subsequently agreed to extend the campaign through 2003. As long as the jury was out, the money could continue to flow.

The GAO has company in its frustration with the drug czar's foot dragging. In July 2006, the Senate subcommittee that oversees federal drug funding vented about the lack of cooperation from the White House drug office. Angry committee members wrote:

> The Committee is extremely displeased with the performance of [Office of National Drug Control Policy] staff regarding their communication with the Committee and their responsiveness to congressional inquiries. ONDCP's lethargy and the inadequate information provided severely impacts the ability of the Committee to conduct its oversight and make budgetary decisions in a timely manner. This kind of unresponsiveness on the part of ONDCP results in an unnecessary waste of time and energy; numerous follow up communications are required in almost every instance. The Committee is particularly concerned that ONDCP has attempted to prevent the Committee from meeting with the directors of ONDCP programs. Therefore the Committee has reduced the salaries and expenses budget to more closely reflect actual performance.

When news of the Westat results finally broke, the White House argued that the study should be ignored. Why? Because the data were more than two years old.

Yet the conclusions of the study are in line with other research that casts doubt on the effectiveness of drug education. So far, at least, it appears to be pretty much impossible to warn kids away from drugs with an ad campaign, no matter how cautious or nuanced an approach you take. Beyond the D.A.R.E. program, a project in Montana that sought to reduce methamphetamine use by plastering the state with gruesome photos of the consequences of addiction backfired; it has been associated with an increase in use and a decrease in the perception of the risk of using meth. A youth drug-prevention program called ALERT was found to be equally useless by a 1993 study.

Talking about drugs seems to give enough young people the idea of trying them that drug-education efforts are frequently counterproductive.

If it's not the fear of a drug test or scaremongering that's dissuading kids from using marijuana, what is it? Available survey and seizure data indicate that the supply remained plentiful—excluding LSD — which means that there was indeed a downturn in demand, probably due to cultural factors.

Pot smoking among teenagers tumbled after September 11, 2001, and perhaps that's not a coincidence. Former LSD king Leonard Pickard speculates via a letter that the decline isn't real, arguing that "conservative political climates, e.g. post-9/11, can account for failure to self report." That might be part of it, but a conservative political climate could also lead a kid to fail not only to divulge, but also to indulge. The feeling of patriotism and national unity that pervaded the nation during the time following the attacks was very deep and very real. George W. Bush's approval rating hit 90 percent. Comic Bill Maher lost his job for saying that the terrorists weren't cowards. A protest against globalization that had been planned for late September, expected to attract tens of thousands, was canceled. A replacement antiwar demonstration drew only a few thousand.

To the extent that pot smoking is a rebellion against, or a rejection of, authority, it might have become less attractive during a time when many Americans believed that a certain amount of authoritarianism was necessary for their nation's survival, Criminal Justice Policy Foundation president Eric Sterling, former counsel for the House Subcommittee on Crime, told me. "For young people who are experimenting and rebelling, [drug use] is a wonderful opportunity for a kind of rebellion that is unique in our society. There are very few ways that you can rebel in a cultural way," Sterling said. "I mean, you can rebel against your parents politically, or you can act out sexually. But culturally, drug use remains. I suppose you can become an Islamic terrorist, or you can become a kind of drug user. So at age sixteen, seventeen, eighteen, nineteen—put on the pot leaf, adopt the old clothing of the late sixties and early seventies."

That identity became less appealing as the country banded together following "the attack and the visual horror of that attack and the idea that we were going to mobilize," claimed Sterling. "The drug-using hippie is a cultural model of rebellion that's available [for a teen to adopt]. At a time when you're going to take on a cultural model of the patriot, the defender—and it's appropriate and it fits in with a value—that is implicitly going to lead to a rejection of styles, activities, behaviors that carry rebellious or anticultural, antisocietal elements."

For the political climate to have such an impact on kids, one might suggest, they first would have to understand it. Do they?

Psychologists Adrian Furnham and Barrie Stacey, in their 1991 book *Young People's Understanding of Society*, cite one 1977 study of political literacy among British schoolchildren that determined that "[m]ost of the political knowledge which they do have is of a rather inert and voyeuristic kind and of little use to them either as political consumers or political actors." Subsequent research, the authors write, upholds the basic conclusion that kids tend to have little genuine awareness of political figures, political parties, or the political process.

But how much more ignorant are kids than the general population? Not much, it turns out. Furnham and Stacey point out repeatedly that "there is no evidence to suggest that an enfranchised adult population actually knows more than our teenage respondents." National political moods, it seems, happen without national political awareness. Just because a kid—or, indeed, an adult—doesn't know what the Patriot Act says doesn't mean that he can't get caught up in a wave of patriotism.

Howard Kaplan, writing in a 1985 issue of the *Journal of Drug Issues*, presented findings he culled from more than 9,000 survey responses. He found what Sterling later surmised, that rebellious teens embrace drug use as a symbol of "attacks upon the worth of the values according to the standards of which the youth was judged unworthy; by permitting intrapsychic or interpersonal withdrawal from the conventional value system according to the standards of which the youth was a failure, or by permitting the substitution of new (deviant) standards that are more easily achieved than the earlier conventional ones." Translation: For some teens, the identity of the achiever is not an easy one to don. It requires being able to hit a baseball cleanly and/or a lot of homework, among many other challenging things. It's easier to pull on a tie-dye and puff on a joint.

But in times of deep patriotism, deviance becomes less attractive. For kids, it actually becomes easier to achieve that elusive conventional ideal—and all it takes is a flag.

Furnham and Stacey note that children as young as four can recognize their national banner. I was working in a middle school in 2001 and 2002, and I saw the red, white, and blue appear on backpacks and clothes practically overnight after 9/11. The nationalist sentiments brought to the surface by the attacks lingered as America went to war in Afghanistan and then in Iraq. Recall that drug use receded during the two world wars and drinking began to plummet amid the national fervor of the War of 1812. It should be unsurprising that the latest major assault on our shores could cause a similar reaction.

But could it be that simple? What else was going on around the turn of the millennium?

Whatever the political climate, weed consumption is typically a social act: someone's got a bag, leading some friends to get together somewhere discreet, sneak a few puffs, drop in some Visine, and head back home. The ritual can be as much about exploring boundaries with friends as it is about getting high.

To smoke together, kids need free time, preferably right after school lets out, when the grown-ups are still at work and the world belongs to the young. That window of opportunity, however, is getting smaller. Psychiatrists Alvin Rosenfeld and Nicole Wise wrote about this trend in their book *Hyper-Parenting: Are You Hurting Your Child by Trying Too Hard?*, published in 2000. The book suggests that as more women have entered the workforce, and as the number of hours we all work continues to increase, parents have turned to schools, churches, and other local organizations to do some of their parenting for them. Rosenfeld found that over the past twenty years, "structured sports time" has doubled and "unstructured children's activities" have declined by 50 percent among children in all socio-economic groups. It's probably not a coincidence that as kids have had less time to smoke pot, they've smoked less pot.

I asked Rosenfeld if he believes that overscheduling could diminish teen drug use. He didn't think so. In an e-mail, he wrote:

> I have no idea why use has declined . . . but I suspect that the connection is far more complex. Athletes use more alcohol than other students and they often are the most highly scheduled. Why is that the case if scheduled activities cause less substance abuse?
>
> As a child psychiatrist, I consider psychology—and the family dynamics from which it emerges—the crucial issue. What makes one kid smoke pot and the other say no thanks? What makes one kid get involved in after school programs and makes the other drop out? What makes one kid play French horn and the other become a tackle? As to socialization, I would suspect (with little objective evidence) that teenagers who have one best buddy are less likely to use drugs; those who feel angrier, more depressed and anxious, isolated and socially awkward might be more prone. Furthermore, I think any teenager can make an opportunity if they really want to—motivation is at least as important as opportunity.

The assumption that teenagers who use drugs all do so to escape their misery—or because they are "depressed and anxious, isolated and socially awkward," or, as Kaplan suggests, because they're compensating for some perceived failing to live up to conventional values—is rooted in a rather simplistic understanding of young people. Kids, first of all, are not all the same. Some are natural conformers and/or achievers and some will rebel no matter what and some are everywhere in between. The notion that only kids who are messed up in some way use drugs isn't supported by the research. In a chapter in the 1987 book *Drug Use and Psychology*, teen-drug-use researcher Michael Newcomb wrote that teen drug users often have a "self-perception of maturity and adult-likeness which is then validated by their drug-using peers and confirmed by the respect from their non-drug-user classmates." In other words, rather than being failures or socially awkward and depressed loners, many teen drug users are popular and successful students.

"The respect," Newcomb offered, "is not so much based on drug use per se, which many nondrug users will disdain and reject, but by the accouterments of other desired adult behaviors exhibited by the drug users (e.g., precocious sexual involvement, independence)." For some kids, then, *not* using drugs can lead to a feeling of having failed to live up to a set of conventional values—those created by their peers.

Rosenfeld is right about one thing, though: a true pothead will make the time. The number of kids who say in the surveys that they smoke daily has remained more or less steady, even as casual use has declined dramatically. In 1999, 6 percent of seniors said that they smoked on a daily basis. In 2000, 5.8 percent did, and that number stayed constant until it ticked down to 5.6 in 2004 and 5.0 in 2005. Rosenfeld is also right that it's not merely a tight schedule that's at work here. In recent years, the free time that kids do have has been vanishing into an abyss of technology, and their new drug habits reflect that.

For decades, smoking pot had been a classically American way for teens to socialize, one that created an informal network of mostly casual users. For such users, friends, not some dealer on speed dial, are typically the best source for illegal drugs. If one kid has a bag, the four friends he meets up with after school also have access to pot. If that one kid stops smoking for any reason, those four kids have also lost their primary source, through no choice of their own. Trends among casual users feed or starve themselves in this way, and they can be seen moving in waves throughout the standard surveys.

If a kid has a bag but doesn't leave the house, that won't do much for his friends, either. At the turn of the millennium, as socialization drifted online, new modes of hanging out rose to prominence:

AOL Instant Messenger (1997), gaming consoles that allow networked interaction (2000), Friendster (2002), MySpace (2003), Second Life (2003) Facebook (2004), YouTube (2005), and Twitter (2006). The Pew Internet Project began measuring the reach of the Internet in 2000. It found that on an average day that year, 51 million Americans were online. By 2004, the number was 70 million. Of those millions, the bulk were young people. A 2005 Pew study found that 87 percent of twelve- to seventeen-year-olds were online, the highest percentage for any age group. Kids were also much more likely than other groups to play online games, use instant messaging, or download videos or music. Pew didn't ask about the youngest demographic in its earliest research, but it did break out eighteen- to twenty-nine-year-olds, who in later data trailed the youngsters just slightly in Internet usage.

By 2005, according to the tech-slanted Forrester Research, 83 percent of teens were using instant messaging, and more than 75 percent had a mobile phone. Eighty-three percent of boys ages twelve to seventeen owned a game console; so did 63 percent of girls. A 2008 study by the market-research firm OTX revealed that although teens prefer "real friends" to "online friends," prefer romances with school acquaintances to romances with folks encountered on the Internet, and prefer going to bricks-and-mortar stores to shopping on the Web, they would also rather go without TV than go without Internet access, would rather get their information from online sources than from traditional media, and would rather have their lockers vandalized than have their online profiles vandalized. Fifty-four percent preferred IMing friends to calling them. Ninety-five percent of teens belonged to a social-networking site, and many belonged to more than one.

Dating and trips to the mall aside, as kids took to meeting online rather than in person, the casual-user network collapsed. That left many teens without ready access to marijuana, but it doesn't mean that they had no access to drugs at all.

Throughout the nineties, use of prescription drugs by both adults and children grew steadily, as did abuse. Between 1992 and 2002, U.S. prescriptions for controlled substances—stimulants such as Ritalin, narcotics such as OxyContin and Vicodin, and benzodiazepines such as Xanax and Valium—grew by 154 percent, though the American population increased by only 13 percent. The diagnosis of attention-deficit/hyperactivity disorder (ADHD) and similar ailments among children rose dramatically during roughly the same period. One study found a 250 percent increase between 1990 and 1998; another found a 657 percent increase between 1979 and 1996. U.S. production of methylphenidate, the generic form of Ritalin, jumped to meet the demand, from 1,768 kilograms annually in 1990 to 14,957 kilograms in 2000, according to the Drug Enforcement Administration. The United Nations concluded in 1999 that the United States manufactured and consumed 85 percent of the world's methylphenidate.

The number of people estimated to abuse prescription drugs roughly doubled between 1992 and 2003, from 7.8 million to 15.1 million. In 1999, savvy entrepreneurs saw an opening and established the first online pharmacies. Five years later, the National Center on Addiction and Substance Abuse released a report showing that hundreds of pharmacies were in operation online and that the vast majority of them didn't require a prescription or anything else that could get in the way of obtaining pills. The DEA estimated in 2006 that controlled substances make up 95 percent of such pharmacies' business, whereas their brick-and-mortar competitors make only 11 percent of their living slinging such pills. Regulation and enforcement of this trade is difficult at best: prescription-free sites can open and close and disappear in a matter of weeks. Most studies find that kids are unlikely to order drugs directly from the Internet—many don't have credit cards or a place to mail their purchases without their parents finding them—but the flood of pills available online makes it that much easier for kids to find someone older who might be willing to part with a few.

"Pharmies," pharmaceutical narcotics like Vicodin or Percocet used illicitly, have skyrocketed in popularity among recreational drug users, including children. In 1997, when pot smoking started to flatten and turn slightly downward, use of "other narcotics"—which excludes heroin—was at 6.2 percent annually among high-school seniors. By 2004, it was up to 9.5 percent, more than a 50 percent jump. OxyContin use wasn't measured until 2002, but it rose steadily over the next four years among all ages. Sedative use went from 5.1 to 7.2 percent between 1997 and 2005; use of tranquilizers such as Xanax climbed from 4.7 to 6.8 percent. The increases among kids who reported popping pills in the past thirty days were even higher, meaning that not only were kids experimenting more with pills, they were also using them with more regularity.

A recent DEA publication titled "Stimulant Abuse by School Age Children: A Guide for School Officials" warns administrators of the many ways that kids can divert meds during the school day: by taking them from teachers' desks, sending a nonusing surrogate into the nurse's office, and hitting up ADHD-diagnosed friends on the bus. Amphetamines or pharmies that can't be begged, bartered for, or bought at school can be found in the home medicine cabinet or on one of the hundreds of sites selling them online.

For wired-in teens, pill popping is an especially attractive activity. It fits well into a solitary afternoon. There's no social ritual involved—just a glass of water and a pill. Amphetamines are perfect for a long night of interactive gaming or Web surfing. (Pharmies are, too, although they induce a more zonked-out experience.) Online journaling, too, can be enhanced by pills. "Kids who live in remote areas can develop a camaraderie online of drug-abusing kids," Carol Falkowski of the Hazelden Foundation, an addiction treatment and research center, told USA Today for a June 2007 feature. "They can share stories about drug experiences." The rather alarmist piece is headlined "Teens use Internet to share drug stories," and it no doubt introduced some adult readers to an unnerving instant-message acronym: "POS," for "parents over shoulder."

Some kids have learned the hard way exactly who's standing behind them. In 2006, members of the Northwestern University women's soccer team were suspended—and all were required to complete a community-service project and an educational program— after pictures of hazing rituals that included lap dances, bondage, and simulated sex were posted online. Officials at schools nationwide have trolled students' Facebook profiles for evidence not only of sexual misconduct, but also of underage drinking and drug use, especially by athletes. At Vassar in 2006, a member of the Student Athlete Advisory Committee warned her classmates by e-mail that the head of athletics "looks through our Facebook accounts every Monday morning to see how the weekend went." In May 2008, the University of Iowa announced that it would be implementing an old-school policy in response to all of this newfangled social-networking technology: the random testing of student athletes—or at least of their online personae. Instead of peering into a cup in search of illicit activity, the powers that be would be peering into a Web browser. "We believe in trusting our student-athletes," one administrator told the *Daily Iowan*. "But the ball is in their court."

Around the same time the Northwestern soccer team was stripping down for its digital portraits, the drug czar's office took a break from cheering the decline in marijuana use to notice that kids were still getting high in roughly the same numbers—only now many of them were abusing pharmies instead of pot. The czar warned that every day, 2,500 kids between the ages of twelve and seventeen were abusing a narcotic for the first time. "Though overall teen drug use is down nationwide," an ONDCP statement noted, "more teens abuse prescription drugs than any other illicit drug, except marijuana; more than cocaine, heroin, and methamphetamine combined."

The never-ending game of Whac-A-Mole continued, as the White House announced a new nationwide campaign against teen abuse of prescription drugs. The effort, though, was more of the same, relying almost exclusively on old media and virtually ignoring the new one through which the phenomenon was spreading. The $30 million effort launched with a Super Bowl ad and also included two print ads in fourteen national magazines, open letters to health and school officials in trade publications, open letters to parents in forty-three national and regional newspapers, and a "tool kit to help community groups implement local prescription drug abuse prevention efforts."

The campaign isn't entirely offline, however. A Web site set up by the White House, TheAntiDrug.com, includes a "virtual tour" of a typical home so that parents can identify "danger zones." Of course, if those parents' more Web-savvy children take the tour instead, they'll come across numerous suggestions from the drug czar as to where they might be able to find pills, including "Mom's purse," "Bedside table," and "Trashcan."

CHAPTER 9

YouTrip

T he first time I went to visit Leonard Pickard, I left Los Angeles
early in the morning, driving ninety miles to a federal prison
complex built into the moonscape desert near the broken-
down town of Victorville, California. Without the facility, the area
wouldn't be even remotely viable economically. The San Bernardino
Valley as a whole is an impoverished place, but this section of it made
some of the towns along the way look downright pleasant.

The maximum-security compound appeared on the horizon as a
surreal mirage. I had been inside prisons before, most often a squalid
joint in Jessup, Maryland, that housed a friend who was doing time
for selling cocaine. Even with its crumbling brick, lack of air con-
ditioning, and broken windows, it was nothing compared to this site
in terms of sheer intimidation. The guard at the front desk told me
that visitation had been canceled for the "indefinite future" following
a riot that morning. Pickard told me in a subsequent letter that one
gang member had kicked off the scrum by knifing another and that
"blood droplets" were splashed about the place.

Pickard had told me more than once that when I came to visit
him, I had to be sure that nobody had smoked pot near me for several
days. In addition to a metal detector—which roundly fails to keep out
metal—the Federal Bureau of Prisons uses mass spectrometers that can
detect microscopic amounts of drug residue. Drug use is still rampant
inside the prison walls, Pickard said, but he would lose all visitation

rights for thirty days if I was swabbed and found to have recently been close to someone getting stoned—something that nearly half of all Californians do on a regular basis, in many cases legally.

For my second attempt, I drove down the coast just after leaving Burning Man, an annual subcultural gathering of artists and techies and the sort in the Nevada desert. Hardly anybody exiting that event had a stitch of clothing that wasn't covered in some sort of illegal residue. So on my way, I stopped at a Wal-Mart and bought a new shirt, pants, socks, and shoes. At the prison, a guard quickly stopped me. "No white shirts," he said. White had been adopted as a gang color inside the prison, he said, and was now banned. Miles from the Wal-Mart, I headed into town to look for a new shirt, but each store I pulled up to turned out to be out of business. After an hour of looking, I finally found a place that sold T-shirts. No one, as far as I knew, had gotten high near the one that I chose.

I had come to this retail-deprived wasteland to try to get a better understanding of the 2000 bust that I had described in print as the main reason for the disappearance of LSD. I'd already obtained copies of court transcripts and tracked down Carl Nichols, the Drug Enforcement Administration agent who led the investigation into Pickard and took part in his arrest. Both confirmed something that Pickard had told me in a letter from prison: that the feds never seized 90.86 pounds of LSD from him. Instead, Pickard had dumped out buckets of some liquid that might have weighed approximately that. Nichols was watching him from a distance at the time, but he said that Pickard wouldn't have known that he was under surveillance.

No one except Pickard can say for sure what was in those buckets, but there's virtually no way that it could have been pure acid. Pickard wasn't wearing a protective suit or even gloves, and no chemist with decades of experience would fail to shield himself against the possibility of spilling a couple of thousand doses on his arm—do that, and you might as well block off the next week or so, because nothing's getting done. And because Pickard didn't know that he was being watched, there's no reason that he would have dumped millions of dollars' worth of anything into the Kansas soil.

Pickard also told me in letters—and claimed in court—that he was a simple academic who had gotten out of the LSD game by the time of his arrest. He was framed by another member of the acid-distribution ring, he maintained, although it's very hard to find anyone seriously interested in psychedelics who doesn't chuckle at this suggestion.

Jon Hanna, the organizer of the annual psychonaut gathering Mind States, is as well connected as anyone in the acid universe. At the 2007 conference in Costa Rica, he told me that there is no doubt in his mind that Pickard had been producing the vast majority of the nation's LSD—not that there was anything wrong with that. Pickard had to deny it, Hanna said, because his case is still on appeal. Rick Doblin, founder of the Multidisciplinary Association for Psychedelic Studies, a nonprofit organization dedicated to sponsoring "scientific research designed to develop psychedelics and marijuana into FDA-approved prescription medicines," told me, "Leonard really was the major producer."

At Burning Man, I had asked Hanna if he had any questions for Pickard. "Ask him when he'll stop appealing his case," he replied.

As long as Pickard is working on his appeal, he'll continue to deny any involvement in LSD production or distribution. During our interview, he invariably preceded answers to my questions with "Well, I understand from my academic research that . . ." At one point, he apologized, saying that he hoped someday to be able to speak freely.

The biggest question behind Pickard's arrest, of course, isn't exactly how much of exactly what he dumped out, or even whether he was in fact LSD's top U.S. producer. It's how his bust—no matter how neatly it overlapped with the demises of Jerry Garcia, Phish, and the outdoor rave scene—could have presaged such a complete collapse of the acid market.

One day, it seemed, LSD was there for the taking; the next, it wasn't. Why, after the drug vanished, did no one step up to meet the demand of the nation's legions of suddenly deprived acidheads?

The answer lies in the tight-knit nature of the LSD-producing community. The Brotherhood of Eternal Love, organized in the late sixties in Laguna Beach, California, to control the acid trade, is celebrated by some as a powerful and pervasive operation. Two books about the Brotherhood, Stewart Tendler and David May's *The Brotherhood of Eternal Love: From Flower Power to Hippie Mafia— the Story of the LSD Counterculture* and Dick Lee and Colin Pratt's *Operation Julie: How the Undercover Police Team Smashed the World's Greatest Drugs Ring*, characterize the group as a bunch of surfers struggling, often in vain, to find the necessary precursor chemicals.

In fact, members of the Brotherhood didn't even produce LSD for the first several years of its existence, but rather served as middlemen. The syndicate became famous thanks to the arrival in its orbit of media darling Timothy Leary—whom the group later paid the Weather Underground to break out of prison. Eventually, the Brotherhood did make copious amounts of LSD, but several other producers were at work before the group, and those producers remained at work after the feds busted the Brotherhood, in 1972.

The reality is that LSD producers have historically had a much looser syndication, one known as the Family—or, more accurately, the Families. Pickard has always been a controversial figure in the acid underground, but widely respected by his peers and adversaries alike as a talented chemist. "He's one of the few we know of who has ever synthesized mescaline," Nichols told me, referring to a process that's far too difficult and expensive to be profitable. One of the few others known to have accomplished the feat is Alexander Shulgin.

"Pickard is a charlatan," blotter artist, blotter-art collector, and unofficial Family spokesperson Mark McCloud told me. He and many others warned me not to take anything that Pickard said at face value. Within the several Families, Pickard is known as someone who can't be trusted, and for good reason: facing decades in prison following a 1988 conviction for running an LSD lab, he cooperated and had his sentence drastically reduced, according to news reports from the time. (He denies any collaboration.) Many in the syndicate suspect that his cooperation with the feds dates back even farther, to the sixties or the seventies.

At Shroomery.org, where the psychedelic community meets online, it's generally assumed that Pickard is a longtime informant who intensified his snitching after his most recent arrest. The psychedelic underground is infested with paranoia—indeed, not entirely unfounded. Pickard may never once have cooperated with federal authorities, but the suspicion that he had was enough to send psychedelia tripping. One post to the site, allegedly from a respected member of the Family, describes the aftermath of his takedown:

> After his bust there was a mad scramble in N. Cal. The feds were everywhere they shouldn't have been. The precurser market (the link that ties every one together) was exposed and i'm told quite a bit of [ergotamine tartrate] ended up in the Pacific ocean by family that was totally freaking out. A lot of heat came down on people who didn't work with Pickard but knew him. It's possible that someone Pickard had working for him talked, or maybe Pickard himself. Nobody knows, but it's evident that someone was giving out a lot of information that is highly guarded. This is why Every family stopped any activity.

That activity included LSD distribution as well as production, so even if a non-Family-affiliated manufacturer had continued to crank out doses, it would have had no easy means of selling them on a large scale. Foreign producers probably stayed away because acid isn't exactly a moneymaker. LSD's traditionally rock-bottom retail price might be a good thing to those eager to spread the psychonautical gospel, but it's a con for anyone weighing the rather inconsequential economic benefit of selling the drug against the significant risk of transporting it across international borders. And because acid isn't habit-forming, the potential for market growth is severely limited.

With the Families hunkered down, the marketplace was left with an unmet demand for a particular kind of mind alteration. The conventional wisdom is that Ecstasy took LSD's place. However, Ecstasy use began to decline in 2000, not increase. That drug was in its ascendancy a few years earlier. The largest federal survey estimates that about 500,000 people tried Ecstasy for the first time in 1996, about double the rate of two years earlier. The survey shows another doubling of first-time users by 1998 and a further doubling by 2000, when two million new people tried the drug. By 2000, Ecstasy was dominating the market, even before Pickard was arrested. But it didn't replace LSD: the number of first-time acid users slowly increased over the same period, hovering at around one million new heads per year.

A 2002 change in *Monitoring the Future*'s methodology makes it impossible to judge whether there was a significant increase in the rate of psychedelic-mushroom use following acid's disappearance, but the survey makes it clear that use did not decline: use of "hallucinogens other than LSD" remained steady. Further evidence that significant demand for psychedelics persisted into the early years of this century is the post-Pickard rise of fake LSD. Consider the final Phish show, a two-night affair held in the summer of 2004 in Coventry, Vermont. Whenever I heard someone muttering, "Doses, doses," I'd buy one. After three transactions, my wallet was lighter but my mind as firmly tethered to the ground as ever. Others I spoke to had the same experience.

I had tried the same experiment a few months earlier at the massive, jam-band-friendly Bonnaroo festival in Manchester, Tennessee, and I'd also gone looking for LSD at the national Rainbow Gathering in northern California's Modoc National Forest. Both events yielded similar results. Before the bust, a con artist selling fake doses at a Phish concert was a rarity. Real acid came with a promise that there's something beyond ordinary life—a plane of existence governed by love, trust, and peace. The bogus stuff suggested something much more prosaic: good old-fashioned greed.

Faced with a dire shortage of LSD, American heads found new ways to trip. Google searches offered easy access to research chemicals, and the number of above-ground suppliers grew from just a few to dozens. Ayahuasca, a natural hallucinogenic brew, rose in popularity. Salvia, a powerful psychedelic plant still legal on the federal level and in most states, was also easy to buy on the Internet after the Families closed ranks. A federal survey estimated that by 2006, more people had used the formerly little-known plant in the past year than had tried LSD— 756,000 to 666,000. Another 104,000 did "DMT, AMT, or Foxy"— research chemicals that the feds started asking about that year.

As research-chemical use grew, the use of a natural hallucinogen picked up, too, although federal surveys don't ask about it. Ayahuasca brew, a combination of two plants that grow in South America, has long been known to the readers of Beat literature as yage. It first came to the attention of Western scientists in 1851, but Amazonian tribes have probably used it as a medicine and religious aid for centuries. One of the plants in the brew, *Psychotria viridis*, contains dimethyl-tryptamine—or DMT—which is listed as a Schedule I drug. By itself, though, it has no real effect. Indeed, many common plants contain DMT; so does the human body, though the brain is wired to neutral-ize it. Thus the second plant in the brew, *Banisteriopsis caapi*, which knocks down the brain's ability to neutralize DMT.

Without reliable survey data, it's impossible to know for sure to what extent ayahuasca use might be growing in the United States. But anecdotal evidence points to a rise. Beginning around the turn of the millennium, folks unable to find acid in their hometowns— or just looking for something new—started hopping flights to Peru, Ecuador, or Brazil, hoping to experience an ayahuasca journey, as the experience is known. "Before 2001, I never saw an American come down," a Peruvian shaman I met in New York told me.

Such psychedelic tourism grew so quickly that ayahuasca jour-neys are now offered in Latin American countries that have no native tradition of using the brew. Tommy Thomas is a farmer who lives in Costa Rica. A Washington, D.C., real-estate developer who moved to the country more than two decades ago, he'd hoped to earn a liv-ing growing hallucinogenic plants. The market turned out to be less lucrative than he'd imagined, so he now grows mostly traditional crops, dedicating only a small portion of his farm to mind expansion, on a four-acre plot he calls an "ethnobotanical garden." As we toured it, he told me that he first noticed the ayahuasca trend take a major upswing in 2005. The local version of the ceremony involves flying in a Peruvian, Ecuadorian, or Brazilian shaman, because their Costa Rican counterparts never used ayahuasca.

"It kind of pisses them off," Thomas said of the native Costa Ricans, "but it's good money." Indeed, the retreats, mostly organized by Americans, can cost thousands of dollars per head.

Another sign that ayahuasca vacations have hit a critical mass is media exposure. *National Geographic* and a number of other outlets have run chronicles of their writers' mind-blowing excursions to

South America, complete with harrowing bus/plane/boat rides, stays in mosquito-ridden camps, and much vomiting. But there's really no need for Americans to travel to go on an ayahuasca journey. In the nineties, the Peruvian shaman told me, he brought his brew to places such as Spain, Italy, and India, but not to the United States. "I didn't even consider coming to America," he said. "I didn't think the people would be open to it." He eventually met a few Americans who persuaded him to come to San Francisco. Today, he goes almost nowhere but the United States. There are more towns asking him to come than he has time to accommodate.

Two ayahuasca-using churches with Brazilian roots have recently grown in membership and public prominence in the United States, as well. The Santo Daime church, founded in 1930 by a rubber tapper who experienced a vision of the Virgin Mary after drinking ayahuasca (or Daime), is perhaps the oldest formal institution to offer the brew to non-tribespeople. The Centro Espirita Beneficiente União do Vegetal was established in 1961 by another visionary rubber tapper. Its New Mexican branch battled the feds over the church's central tenet of ayahuasca consumption, arguing that religious liberty allows the church to use the drink. In 2006, the Supreme Court upheld the União do Vegetal's right to trip in *Gonzales v. O Centro Espirita Beneficiente União do Vegetal*, although it remanded the case to lower courts for further review.

I met Coco Conn, a Santo Daime member and Web innovator at the forefront of the social-networking movement, at the Mind States conference in Costa Rica, where she told me that ayahuasca had allowed her to give up drinking and other drugs. Conn explained what the União do Vegetal had to do to demonstrate that it offered a sincere religious ceremony: "They had to show it isn't fun. If it's fun, American courts will rule it's not a religious experience. Ayahuasca's no fun, that's for sure," she said laughingly, referring to the often harrowing four-to-six-hour trip the União do Vegetal's sacrament induces.

"I was a vomiting snake," early adopter Allen Ginsberg wrote of one ayahuasca journey. "I vomited with eyes closed and sensed myself a Serpent of Being . . . covered with Aureole of spiky snakeheads miniatured radiant & many colored around my hands & throat—my throat bulging like the Beast of Creation, like the Beast of Death."

• • •

The organized ayahuasca churches make up only a tiny fraction of American users. Most tend to imbibe no more than a few times a year, in a friend's living room guided by a traveling shaman, or in a joint like the industrial Brooklyn warehouse I traveled to in early 2007. I'd been asked not to reveal the name of the place because of "complexities of the legality." Every few weeks, on Fridays and Saturdays, a shaman flies up from South America to lead ayahuasca sessions. "The Journey Room is down and to your left," said a bearded man in his twenties as my wife, Elizan, and I filed in. Plastic pitchers—vomit buckets—were stacked on a small table to the right.

I grabbed a blanket from another stack, plopped down on a dilapidated mattress, and waited, the bucket in my lap. On a futon to my left were Zito and Eric, both from New York. They had been there before and suggested that writing while on the journey will be difficult at best. "You should probably just go with it. Just let it happen," said Eric. The woman near them was also from the city. She'd never done ayahuasca, she said, but was there for "exploration."

The owner of the warehouse found me on the mattress to talk about a mutual friend who had vouched for me. Her first ayahuasca journey, he said, was here, and shortly after it she sent him an e-mail from Peru, where she was doing a weeklong ayahuasca retreat. The owner, the veteran of several ayahuasca journeys, then gave me a brief résumé that included both porn production and investment banking. He had quit caffeine, alcohol, meat, and anything that's been cooked. He mentioned that he'd been fasting for the past three days because doing so can help bring on a "light" journey. "The dark ones are good, too, but whoa," he said, shaking his head and shuddering.

The first time that he took ayahuasca he had a magical, euphoric experience. He credited his healthy lifestyle and general goodness. "I thought it was a sign of how well I was living my life that I could handle it like nothing," he said. "Then, the second time, I went straight to hell. Oh god, it was awful. But wonderful, of course." He reminded us to relax, to let go, and to remember to breathe. "Good luck," he concluded, finding a place against the wall. The warehouse now held twenty-five people, each of them having paid $200 cash for this gourmet psychedelic experience. There were a middle-aged couple, a group of three women in their twenties dressed in pajama pants and sleeveless camis, and a frat guy with a magazine-worthy physique who'd already removed his shirt.

Between the couple and the women was a makeshift shrine. The shaman, who comes up from Peru every few months with his metal thermos of ayahuasca, walked toward it and pulled out his guitar. He looked to be in his late twenties—and, as I'd later learn, he was born in Spain. He set down rules (no talking; no making noise that could interfere with someone else's journey) and offered advice (relax, let go, breathe). He said that there might be moments in which we feel that time is frozen, unable to move forward. We might feel as if we'll be on ayahuasca for eternity. He promised that these feelings would go away and that in several hours we would feel just the way we do now—perhaps even better.

I'd heard talk similar to this before and had even used it once myself to ease a woman through a bad trip at a Phish show: "You've taken a chemical substance and it feels like you'll be tripping forever, but the chemicals are working their way through your body and you will eventually return to normal. But the next few hours are going to suck."

One by one, the shaman summoned us to him. He poured a muddy beverage from his thermos into a metal shot glass. I downed it as he said, "God bless you." I thanked him and walked back to my dingy mattress to wait, bucket ready. A slow wave of vomiting began to roll around the room. It wasn't looking good for the turkey sub I'd had at a rest stop on the way to the city, or for the bag of barbecue chips.

In the spring of 2008, Hebrew University professor Benny Shanon, who claims to have used ayahuasca at least 160 times in the early nineties, speculated that Moses was on a variant of the brew created from plants available in the Middle East when he encountered God with fear and trembling. "In advanced forms of ayahuasca inebriation," Shanon writes, "the seeing of light is accompanied by profound religious and spiritual feelings." At about a half an hour in, Elizan pointed out that I was shaking. And I was—as if I were in a T-shirt in fifteen-degree weather.

"Breathe," she said. The shaking stopped, but whenever I didn't focus on submitting to the ayahuasca, it came back, sometimes gaining strength and moving not just my arms but my entire body. "Jesus," said Elizan. Next to us, Zito started shouting: "Yes!" He was dragged out, wailing incoherently.

In high school and college and shortly after, I'd probably eaten either acid or mushrooms more than fifty times, and some of the experiences had been out-of-this-world powerful. But nothing had prepared me for ayahuasca. I had never been so far from reality. I could get back to the ground, sort of, by finding Elizan. I tried to tell her that I was on another planet, but words were extremely hard to form. "I'm getting more," she said. As best I could, I begged her not to, wondering what would happen if both of us became this lost. She promised not to and got up anyway, but I didn't realize it until hours later.

In the meantime, I was having conversations with people I know. The talks were so real that I didn't even step outside of them to note how strange it was to be hallucinating an entire conversation. I just participated. Mostly, the people lectured me about my life, telling me about obligations and consequences.

Then it got worse. I started to experience the things I'd been reading and writing about as a political reporter: I was in a firefight in Baghdad, explosions and dead bodies all around. I was swept away by Hurricane Katrina, then trapped in a baking attic as the festering water rose.

The suffering gave way to a conversation on power. I thought back to confrontations that I'd had with people at or near the top of the congressional and administrative ranks and the stories I'd written that had made life difficult for them. This is serious stuff, my unknown interlocutor told me. This is not a game. You're playing with some of the most powerful people on the planet, and I promise, if you keep this up, they'll crush you.

All trips lend themselves to melodrama, but for what seemed like an eternity, I felt as if I was being tortured by the power that I'd found myself reporting about, now unquestionably malevolent. Are you really up for this? Are you willing to be ground to pieces by the machine? No, I finally conceded, I'm not. I vowed to switch careers and move to the suburbs if I made it back to D.C., a promise I recanted immediately after the torture ended.

I saw colors and objects and serpentlike demons and prayed to God that there is actually no God and no heaven, because the thought of this experience lasting forever seemed unbearable. It was frightening to the bone. I would rather never have lived, I reasoned, than live a full, happy life followed by this in the afterlife. I prayed that when we die, we just die.

And, finally, I was down. I leaned over to Elizan and told her, "I think I've decided I like drugs that are fun."

I didn't have a bad trip. I had an ayahuasca journey—and they're almost all bad. Elizan and I did feel phenomenal for several days afterward, though.

Charles Grob, a professor of psychiatry and pediatrics at UCLA's School of Medicine, speculates that the antidepressant effect of aya-huasca has to do with the way it relates to serotonin, a chemical cru-cial to our mood and state of mind. The typical antidepressant works by boosting serotonin, bombarding the brain with happiness. The bombardment can, however, make neural receptors less sensitive to normal levels of serotonin. Grob studied União do Vegetal mem-bers in Brazil and found that they have a greater sensitivity to lower amounts of serotonin because their nerve cells had created more receptors. In other words, ayahuasca users need less serotonin to be happy. "Ayahuasca is perhaps a far more sophisticated and effective way to treat depression" than Prozac and similar drugs, he concluded.

Despite its potential benefits, ayahuasca is something I haven't had the courage to do again. I have company in my reluctance to experi-ence more psychotherapeutic terrors, including Ann Shulgin, who tried the brew at a ceremony hosted by a friend. "There were all kinds of lights and rattling and a train was barreling right at me. I was afraid for my life," she said. "I consider myself pretty experienced, but holding on and trying not to get hit by that train was not a pleasant experience. . . . A voice said, 'Don't come here again.'" Her husband, she said, had a different but equally bad experience. Sitting next to her, he nodded in agreement, raising his eyebrows to indicate the beating he took.

The next day, said Ann, her friends held another ceremony. Not to be rude, she and Sasha took part again, this time risking only half a dose. "And here came that train again. The voice said, 'Didn't you hear me last time?' I have not taken ayahuasca since, and I'm not going to."

Salvia offers a similar experience—but in a more manageable five- to fifteen-minute version. Search YouTube for "salvia," and you'll quickly realize why this once obscure member of the mint family might well become the next banned drug in America. In thousands of clips, young people film themselves puffing salvia and then laughing uncontrollably or writhing on the ground in apparent agony. Users report out-of-body experiences and otherworldly hallucinations—not the kinds of things that are typically legal in the United States. The same medium that has spread the word about salvia—the Internet and, specifically, YouTube—will probably be the one that makes it illegal, as recently enlightened politicians inevitably call for a ban. Of course, the plant is exceedingly easy to grow and will likely prove exceedingly difficult to eradicate.

Unlike other hallucinogens, *Salvia divinorum*, as the plant is properly known, doesn't target serotonin, but rather neurotransmitters known as opioids. An understanding of how salvia works could give insight into how to treat disorders of mood, appetite, and tissue healing, among others, and research toward those ends is now under way at a number of universities. The plant is one of several psychedelics traditionally used by the "Mazatec Indians for ritual divination and healing," according to the DEA.

Salvia's rise as a recreational drug has coincided not only with the shrinking of the LSD market, but also with the growth of the Internet. The plant was barely mentioned in the media before 2000. Then, in 2001, salvia became a blip on the nation's radar screen. A Nexis search turns up 35 mentions of *Salvia divinorum* that year. By 2005, it pops up 67 times. By 2007, 271.

Salvia extract can be purchased easily and legally online, and a single trip shouldn't cost more than five dollars or so. Head shops and some herbal-remedy establishments tend to carry it, as well, but it was by word of e-mail, blog posts, and Web videos that salvia use spread. Folks began taping themselves and their friends zoned out on the stuff and uploading the videos to YouTube. By the summer of 2008, a search for "salvia" on the site pulled up 3,830 videos, many with hundreds of thousands of views.

"Trippin on Salvia—First Timer—Soo Funny" (507,510 views) and "Crazy Ass Salvia Trip" (411,019) are typical of the genre. Young men—though there are plenty of women in the videos, too—smoke salvia extract and go nearly catatonic or laugh hysterically while their friends giggle around them. The user might roll around on the ground or otherwise appear to be having a nervous breakdown. One YouTube video, "Salvia Sandwich," attempts to prove that users wouldn't possibly be "dumb enough to drive a car when they can't even make a sandwich." The video shows a chubby, scruffy-looking guy pulling hits of salvia extract through a device labeled "Hell Bong."

"This right here is James," says his buddy. "James is going to do some salvia and then attempt to make a peanut butter and jelly sandwich." In front of James are two slices of bread, a knife, and jars of peanut butter and jelly. He stares helplessly at the objects as a friend assists by opening the jelly. A little more than two minutes in, he drops the knife and leans back on the couch. It's clear that the sandwich will have to wait.

"This is probably the most awful example possible, and may appear to be a reason to schedule this drug," explains the narrator. "I digress, though, and point out that salvia's effects last between five to twenty minutes, depending on the potency, and the hallucinogenic effects are not harmful. Though it's used by idiots today, *Salvia divinorum* is a shamanistic drug, and has never been the cause of suicide. For longer than a thousand years, people have been smoking and drinking salvia. Then one kid, having had contact with it at some point in his life, kills himself—while taking other medication proven to lead to depression and suicide. Media fucking frenzy."

That's essentially true. In early 2006, Delaware teenager Brett Chidester committed suicide. His family found an essay in which he wrote that salvia showed him that "earthly humans are nothing" and that "existence in general is pointless." The essay came to be understood by lawmakers and the media as a suicide note—even though Chidester wrote a real note, which his mother hasn't made public. *Salvia divinorum* was eventually listed by the chief state medical examiner as a contributing cause to Chidester's death—never mind that most users so thoroughly lose control of their bodies for the few minutes of the experience that successfully completing a suicide attempt would be close to impossible.

Still, Delaware passed "Brett's Law" in the spring of 2006, banning salvia and attracting national attention. As early as 2002, Representative Joe Baca, a Democrat who represents Pickard's San Bernardino Valley, had introduced a bill to place salvia and its active ingredient, salvinorin A, into Schedule I, meaning that they would become completely illegal, with no legitimate medical use. Researchers would need a difficult-to-obtain license to work with the drug. The bill died in subcommittee, but in December of that year, the DEA listed salvia among its "drugs and chemicals of concern," alongside such unscheduled substances as anabolic steroids, the analgesic tramadol, and Southeast Asian coffee relative *Mitragyna speciosa Korth*, long used in that region for its psychoactive effects.

The DEA doesn't need congressional authority to move salvia into Schedule I. It can do so immediately with an "emergency scheduling." Rogene Waite, a spokeswoman for the agency, said that the administration is in the process of studying the plant to determine whether to ban it. "Our Office of Diversion Control is looking at the drug, and it would need to gather a significant amount of information before any decision could come forward," she said. "There would have to be an imminent hazard to public safety."

In April 2008, Nebraskan Kenneth Rau, a bottling-plant worker with an interest in herbalism, became the first person arrested for salvia, charged under a new state law with intent to distribute. Police found a stash he had purchased for thirty-two dollars on eBay. The local CBS 12 news story published about the bust appeared directly opposite Google ads for salvia—meaning that CBS itself was guilty of conspiracy to distribute. Rau, who said he had no idea that it was illegal, faced twenty years in prison but refused a plea agreement, vowing to fight the charge.

If the United States does schedule salvia, this nation would join at least nine other countries—Australia, Belgium, Brazil, Denmark, Estonia, Finland, Italy, Spain, and Sweden—in regulating it. In the meantime, state legislators are moving forward without the feds. In 2005, Louisiana banned the purchase or sale of salvia; Missouri banned it the same year. Tennessee and Oklahoma followed Delaware's passage of Brett's Law with their own legislation in 2006. Bills proposing regulatory controls have been introduced in more than a dozen states since, and bans are now in place in Florida, Illinois, Kansas, North Dakota, and Virginia. In July 2008, Florida state representative Mary Brandenburg told *U.S. News & World Report* that "YouTube seems to have been an influence" on the spread of salvia use. "I guess if you're foolish, then you might think the videos of people high and doing stupid things is cool."

Of course, old-media coverage has probably helped increase the number of salvia users, too. In its June 2007 issue, GQ ran a feature story on salvia. "Have you tried the new hallucinogen? It's stronger than LSD and it's legal (for now)," advertised the cover. Author Christopher Ketcham wrote:

> I at first felt nothing and was waiting for the thwack of the drug, pulling bedcovers over my head, when I heard a groan—Dios—and looked up and saw [my guide and transla- tor] Jonas had stripped naked and wrapped himself in sheets of yellowed cotton. Then he crashed to the floor and against the bathroom door and rolled across the room, chirping and clicking, and I thought this was hilarious and went into a fit, until I abruptly remembered the warning of the shaman, who said that the madness of the abuser begins with a foolish laugh. So I shook it off and stood up and went to make sure Jonas was all right. I had come down to the Sierra Mazateca, in the Mexican state of Oaxaca, for an experiment: to see what happens when fatheaded Americans get their hands on a sacred consciousness-altering plant and abuse it.

Ketcham calls salvia "perhaps the most powerful naturally occur- ring hallucinogen known to man—approaching the potency of the epically powerful lysergic acid diethylamide. Fittingly, the kids in the States had dubbed it the 'legal acid' and smoked it in bongs, chattering about the high afterward on their laptops, how they left their bodies and traveled in time or saw the future or spoke with demons." He also points out how the Internet has taken salvia global, beyond Mexico to "Denmark, Germany, France, Britain, Australia."

Maine state representative Chris Barstow, who authored a bill to restrict salvia in late 2006, has been complimentary of the piece. "I thought it was a very good article and very timely. I shared it with advocates of my ban," he told me. In committee, Barstow's bill, now law, was amended to prohibit use only among those under eighteen. Adults can still use salvia legally in the state. Barstow claimed that he introduced his legislation to correct the hypocrisy he sees in a federal system that bans marijuana but doesn't regulate salvia, a much more powerful drug. "If you are going to keep salvia legal, we need to examine whether marijuana should be illegal," he said.

Ketcham told me that he knew the piece would provoke some kind of governmental reaction. "Whenever the media reports effectively and honestly, it ultimately leads to the backlash and prohibition," he said. "I knew this was only going to contribute to the hysteria of the dimwits running our country. It may be that our society is not destined to be mature enough to be able to handle a drug like salvia."

Following the *GQ* story, WJLA, a local news outlet affiliated with *Politico*, the online publication that I write for, ran an investigation into salvia. The piece's producers asked if I'd be willing to trip on camera. I declined, so they anchored the story to YouTube clips instead.

CHAPTER 10

Blowback

The uprising began slowly, with a several-mile march from El Alto to La Paz. It had taken thousands of cocaleros, campesinos, miners, and other protesters about a week to hike to La Paz. The miners had brought their dynamite, which they tossed here and there throughout the day. Occasionally, a bomb of serious weight rocked the city.

I had come to Bolivia to discover the impact on the country of the coca trade and American efforts against it, and I had arrived just as tensions were rising. The specific issue that had galvanized these marchers was control of the country's natural-gas resources. But it was Evo Morales, then the head of a cocalero union, who led the march. Without him and the coca growers, the protest would likely have been nothing more than a marginal demonstration leading to a few speeches and a natural-gas law written by oil companies.

An Aymara, the charismatic Morales is revered among the Indians who make up more than half of Bolivia's population. He's a leftist of the purest man-of-the-people stripe, a coca grower who, like many of his followers, grew up in poverty and imagines a future in which Bolivia's native resources—natural gas, oil, and, yes, coca—will benefit native Bolivians at least as much as they do foreigners. "Since coca is a victim of the United States, as coca growers we are also victims of the United States," Morales told the *Observer* in 2003, "but then we rise up to question these policies to eradicate coca. Now is the moment to see the defence of coca as the defence of all natural resources."

The day after protesters arrived in La Paz, I accompanied about two thousand Aymara on a smaller march. Along the way, they methodically smashed the windows of stores and cars, often with the passengers still inside. "¡Cabrón! [Asshole]" shouted one minibus driver as glass poured over his riders.

The march ended in a standoff with police a block away from the presidential palace. I was with a group of four journalists when a miner tossed what looked to be a stick of dynamite at us. It exploded a foot behind me. The force rocked me forward, but it was all air—just a blasting cap.

Bottles started to fly, followed by rocks. The police raised their riot shields and held their ground. Then another explosive was tossed at the feet of three soldiers, who blocked its effects with their shields. Then they raised their guns, and we ran up the hilly streets to safety, no easy task at 13,000 feet above sea level. I saw tear-gas canisters fly by, but soon there was little visibility. I could hear the hiss of gas as it filled the street. A rubber bullet hit me in the back.

A block away, the police fired tear gas again. There was more running. I snapped a picture of a crowd coming toward me, turned, and was punched hard in the back. I pretended it didn't happen and kept my pace. Surrounded by angry Indians and painfully aware of my whiteness, I ducked down an alley and there managed to avoid any more random blows.

Within a few blocks I became separated from Christian Parenti, a journalist friend with whom I was traveling. I stumbled blindly through the streets.

"Ryan?" said a voice through the haze. "Ryan, are you okay?"

"Lucia?"

"Sí. ¡Ven conmigo!" The voice belonged to the secretary of a man Christian and I had met earlier in the day, Senator Antonio Peredo. A leader in Morales's party, he's the younger brother of Inti and Coco Peredo, who with Che Guevara hoped to spark a socialist revolution in Bolivia in the sixties. The CIA chased them around the jungle, ultimately catching and killing Guevara. "I was too young too join them," Antonio had told us in his office, which was decorated with no fewer than three portraits of Che.

Lucia took me to her apartment, where she gave me a cigarette—the first I'd had in thirteen years. On the news the night before, I'd seen a public-service announcement reminding Bolivians that cigarettes waved before the face are the best remedy for tear gas. My eyes and lungs quickly cleared up.

I headed back into the streets and managed to meet up with Christian. In Plaza San Francisco, La Paz's main square, a protester shouted at us: "¡Gringos se culpa! ¡Gringos se culpa!"

"Sí, sí, we're guilty," Christian said, not quieting the man down. A police officer—one in a line of ten—walked our way. The protester turned to the cop and launched a brick-sized rock at him, hitting him in his face mask. The cops raised their weapons, and I heard myself yelling at them not to shoot. A second later, I realized that I wouldn't be able to reason with them. As Christian dove to the ground, I turned and ran as well as I could. The spent tear-gas canisters I'd been collecting weighed me down, and I felt a little absurd securing them in my pocket while fresh ones were flying around us.

A canister rocketed by my left arm, its trail spreading slowly around us. I ducked behind a wall and peered over. All around me, Indian men and women were stoically gushing tears and passing a cigarette back and forth. Those who tried to run had canisters and rubber bullets fired their way.

La Paz was designed in the 1500s to withstand attacks from outside, and there are only a few ways to get in. There are also, much to the chagrin of some former heads of state, very few ways to get out. Several thousand protesters can slow the city significantly; tens of thousands, as there were in the spring of 2005, can bring it to its knees.

After vowing not to resign, President Carlos Mesa stepped down on June 6. A few days later, Bolivian legislators took flight from the besieged capital to select a new president in Sucre, nearly five hundred miles to the southeast. But demonstrators had other ideas. Blockades were lifted so that truckloads of protesters could race to Sucre to prevent parliament from naming right-wing senate leader

Hormando Vaca Diez, Washington's friend in La Paz, as the successor to Mesa. The mayors of El Alto and La Paz announced hunger strikes to oppose Vaca Diez, who, a poll revealed, was supported by only 16 percent of Bolivians.

Parliament's morning session was canceled as miners, coca growers, and other protesters battled police in Sucre's streets. According to news reports, several legislators urged the cancellation of the session so that they could fly out of Sucre before demonstrators took over the airport. They didn't move quickly enough. In protest of Vaca Diez, airport workers went on strike. Now stuck in Sucre, parliament met again around midnight, and then gave in. Vaca Diez resigned his constitutional right to ascend to the presidency, as did the next in line, Marlo Cossio. At 11:47 p.m. on June 10, the man whom protesters had been demanding as a caretaker president, Supreme Court leader Eduardo Rodriguez, was sworn in, with elections scheduled for several months later.

Protest leader Morales swept the elections, becoming president on January 22, 2006, and quickly aligning himself with Washington enemies Hugo Chavez, Fidel Castro, and the Sandinista Daniel Ortega. He'd carried a coca plant through crowds of supporters on his way to vote, and he soon went on an international tour to promote the crop. Before the United Nations General Assembly, he called coca criminalization a "historical injustice." "The coca leaf is symbolic of Andean culture, of the Andean environment, and of the hopes of peoples," he argued. "It is not acceptable that the coca leaf be legal for Coca-Cola and illegal for medicinal consumption not only in our country but throughout the world."

Morales wasn't calling for the worldwide legalization of cocaine, but in the eyes of some American drug warriors, he might as well have been. Morales is probably overstating it to call himself "America's worst nightmare." But he does present a significant challenge to the U.S. government's long-held policy of overseas eradication, and to the notion that America's drug problem is the world's drug problem. When our moral resources, as President Richard M. Nixon described them, collide with someone else's natural resources, we can have a very different kind of problem. In September 2008, Morales kicked the Drug Enforcement Administration out of the

Chapare, and Bolivia joined Venezuela and Myanmar on a short U.S. list of countries that refuse to cooperate with the drug war.

The idea that the Mafia or some other underworld syndicate is in glamorous command of the world drug market is held not just by the HBO-watching public and the media, but also by law enforcement and the federal government. If only a big enough kingpin could be brought down, they all assume, the whole intricate structure would topple.

The truth is much less romantic. The international drug trade, involving countless users, producers, distributors, agents, and middlemen, is, after all, merely a marketplace. It's moved, above all, by economic realities, not by the whim of cartel leaders—or, conversely, by the will of federal governments. To the great benefit of drug producers—and the great detriment of drug warriors—the market as a whole is extremely resilient and extremely flexible. Interdiction is invariably met with innovation, whether it's consumers shifting to a new high or producers shifting to a new precursor. The people most affected by interdiction are those who profit least from the drug trade—those who, like Morales's cocaleros, are as much raw materials of the drug trade as their crops are.

In the Chapare province of Bolivia, where coca has been grown for centuries, Christian and I met a woman who had been shot in the back while running toward her coca field to protect it from eradication. Several years later, she was still growing—our jeep was forced off the road to drive around her drying crop. For the small farmers who produce the raw materials for much of the world's drug supply, violence is less of a threat than poverty. The woman's husband, who stood outside their splintering, dirt-floored shack, didn't seem very political. He's a member of Morales's party because he, like a U.S. autoworker, is required to be. But he doesn't often attend meetings. What does he think of the natural-gas issue? "I cook with wood," he said in Spanish. "Why would I care about gas?"

Naturally, some of the principal risks associated with an illegal enterprise are that the owner or his employees can be shot, arrested, jailed, have their assets seized, or experience some other interference from law enforcement. The greater the size of an operation, the higher the risk, and therefore the more expensive the enterprise, because that risk must be accounted for. Employees must be paid commensurate with their risk, otherwise they might take an equally well-paying job in a less perilous trade—if such a job is available.

In Bolivia in the mid-nineties, growing fruit netted a small farmer several hundred dollars less per acre than growing coca. At the time, about 10 percent of the country's work force was involved in the drug trade in some way, with more than 6 percent of the gross domestic product resulting from cocaine trafficking. Today, some of that business has shifted to Peru and Colombia, but coca remains the backbone of the peasant economy.

The seeds of Morales's leftist uprising were sown a few years before. In 1988, in response to long-standing U.S. disapproval of local coca cultivation, the Bolivian government put a cap on the amount of the plant that could be grown legally, vowing to wipe out the illegal portion of the crop. In 1997, President Hugo Banzer developed a national plan for crop destruction—Plan Dignidad, or the "Dignity Plan."

Washington contributed hundreds of millions of dollars to the effort, which succeeded not only in reducing the number of coca plants grown in Bolivia, but also in lowering the already low standard of living among the country's peasant farmers. An $800 million attempt to introduce alternative crops such as pineapple, animal feed, and tea faltered along with the Bolivian economy. Prices for those alternatives were simply too low for growers to bother, thanks in part to U.S. subsidization of domestic farmers.

The food-price spikes that began in 2008 could alter the calculus, however: prices more than tripled that year in Afghanistan, causing some farmers there to switch from poppies to wheat.

Risk is the reason the drug market is decentralized. The bigger an operation, the greater the need for expensive cautionary measures such as payoffs to law-enforcement officials and politicians. Trafficking high volumes is also risky, because one seizure can result in losses large enough to threaten the viability of the entire organization. Witness the enormous seizures of cocaine in Mexico, Central America, and the Caribbean in 2007, which were likely the result of tips to law enforcement from warring cartels. If the entire U.S. cocaine import in a given year is around 500 metric tons, then the one-time loss of more than 20 metric tons means a significant drop in someone's revenue.

Prohibition also puts pressure on a company's cash flow and access to credit. Because banks can't be used with impunity by illegitimate businesses, employees and agents must be trusted to carry large amounts of cash—and, of course, to skim some off the top. And larger amounts of cash are proportionally more difficult to transport. In the spring of 2007, Mexico seized more than $200 million in one raid. That's a massive loss even to a legitimate multinational corporation. The legitimacy of a drug operation's cash is an issue, too. Money laundering is a service: clients pay a fee to make dirty money clean. Above-board corporations get quite different economic treatment, with banks and other investment agencies paying for the privilege of holding the company's money.

More important, perhaps, is that it's tough for an illegal enterprise to get a loan. Certainly there are lenders out there—most of them illegal themselves—willing to take a risk on a bookie or a drug producer or distributor. But their increased risk is accounted for in the borrower's paying higher interest rates than a business with auditable books could expect from a bank—and for smaller amounts of capital, too. And a cartel can't go public with shares of its business to raise fresh funds. Without access to credit and capital markets, an organization must grow by reinvesting its profits. That's not impossible in a lucrative industry, but it's a relatively slow road to riches.

When a distributor can break out of the credit trap, the results can be dramatic. In the early eighties, the suppliers of California trafficker Ricky Ross—known as "Freeway Rick"—began to provide him with a line of credit in the form of product that was delivered up front but paid for only when sold. Partly thanks to that advantage, Ross was able to spread his crack-cocaine operation throughout Los Angeles and then across the country. It's not surprising that his suppliers could afford to give him such a valuable benefit: They were representatives of the Contras, a right-wing insurgent group created and armed by the United States to battle leftists in Central America. The protection they received from the CIA—as well as the use of airplanes and landing space—enabled them to greatly cut their operating costs.

University of Maryland professor Peter Reuter notes that prohibition makes illegal businesses difficult to sell, which would limit growth to the life of the owner. In theory, a business could be taken over by a relative—or by force—and continue apace, as long as the new owner knew what he was doing. But because employee loyalty is often to the owner himself—say, Pablo Escobar—rather than to the firm, the new boss might have some trouble keeping things together.

Escobar suggests what at first seems to be a counterargument, if the man's operation was even a fraction the size of legend. In 1989, *Forbes* listed history's favorite narco-trafficker as one of the world's ten richest people. Major Mexican cartels, too, don't seem to find it hard to grow a business. Just two days after that $200 million seizure in Mexico, the U.S. Coast Guard intercepted a ship carrying 43,000 pounds of coke, which was visible in an aerial photo of the Panamanian-flagged vessel. The DEA estimated the seizure was worth $300 million. Somebody's doing some business on a large scale—although it's clearly not Bolivian coca growers.

Rather than refute Reuter's theory, such spectacular examples support his notion that legal risk is the greatest limiter of firm size. In Colombia and Mexico, where the governments are exceptionally corrupt and a major dealer has only a small chance of getting busted, the market can be taken over by a few strong players. The bigger an operation in a corrupt country, the less likely it is to be busted because of its political power. Smaller firms are more likely to be taken down, both as a favor to the larger cartels and as a sign to Washington that the country is serious about pursuing the drug war.

Profit margins are so high in the drug trade that producers can lose large portions of their product and remain in the black. The British government has estimated that, at best, 20 percent of the world drug supply is seized, whereas somewhere around 80 percent of it would have to be nabbed for the business to become unprofitable. Even under the best of circumstances for law enforcement, that's just not going to happen. Government agents might as well be looking for a bale of cocaine on a snow-covered mountain. The high value of drug imports belies their relatively small size—something around 15 tons for heroin and 400 to 500 for cocaine, which is vanishingly puny compared to overall American imports.

• • •

Prohibition helps create the very conditions that make prohibition ineffective. Attempts to disrupt the drug supply face all kinds of problems because that supply is the product of a decentralized market. The easiest market players to go after domestically are small-time dealers, and the easiest on the world stage are small-time farmers. In both cases, those who bear the brunt of the penalties are the lowest-level personnel in an operation.

In the United States, mandatory-minimum sentences implemented in the eighties, under which someone caught with 5 grams of crack must face the same prison term as someone busted with 500 grams of powder cocaine, have all but assured that most of those locked up are easily replaceable cogs. Gauging the level of a person's involvement in an enterprise based on the quantity of drugs he or she is carrying makes about as much sense as assuming that the driver of an armored car is the CEO of the bank, anyway. Lock up the driver, and the bank will find another one for the same price.

Lewis Rice Jr., special agent in charge of the DEA's New York Field Division, told Congress roughly the same thing when he testified on Ecstasy enforcement in June 2000. It cost a smuggling organization in the Netherlands, he said, $200 per trip to recruit somebody to be a courier of between 30,000 and 45,000 pills. When the United States caught one, the five-year mandatory minimum sentence for drug possession would apply. So the state would shell out at least $100,000 to imprison this pawn, while it cost the dealer $200 to find a new one. Extrapolate this disparity across the spectrum of the drug war, and we begin to see how relatively small players are able to confound the multibillion-dollar efforts of the world's only superpower.

As the United States has intensified its drug war abroad over the past two decades, overseas casualties, too, have come disproportionately among the small-time.

The typical Bolivian cocalero grows a relatively tiny crop of coca. Throughout the fifties and up through the eighties, left-wing organizations were organizing these and other Bolivian peasants, often with the aid of the Soviet Union. Among them were miners who worked extracting the nation's rich tin deposits, an activity that once accounted for 40 percent of Bolivian exports but became dramatically unprofitable as the price of the metal tumbled on the world market in the mid-eighties. In 1985, under the guidance of Senate president Gonzalo Sánchez de Lozada, Bolivia became a testing ground for a "shock therapy" cure of its various economic ills, including a massive national debt and 24,000 percent hyperinflation. State subsidies were discontinued; industries were privatized. Inflation was indeed halted, but thousands lost their jobs in the process.

As the unemployed flooded into the Chapare in search of land to grow coca—for many, the only moneymaking option available—the United States launched its Bolivian drug war, funding the military unit Unidad Móvil de Patrullaje Rural ("Mobile Rural Patrol Unit"), or UMOPAR, which was tasked with the destruction of illegal coca crops. Morales and the cocalero unions organized to defend themselves against the onslaught. At the time, both left-wing insurgents and right-wing paramilitaries were involved in the Latin American drug trade. Given that the latter were protected by the CIA, that agency's mission tended to collide with that of the DEA. In 1982, the Reagan White House issued an order that the CIA was not required to disclose to the DEA when it was working with a suspected drug-smuggling operation.

But the DEA has had a tougher fight against the forces of economics. Take the agency's one major success: the spraying of massive Mexican poppy fields with pesticides greatly reduced the flow of opium and heroin into the United States in the mid-seventies. But American demand for those drugs was then met by Afghanistan and Southeast Asia, and the Mexican growers adapted by moving to smaller, better hidden locations. Within about five years, their country was once again a major supplier. The Afghan and Southeast Asian crops were both encouraged by the CIA, which was happy to see its bands of local anti-Communist warriors with a steady stream of income. The Afghan crop initially supported the U.S.-backed mujahideen, who battled the Soviet Union. Today, it still supports an insurgency against an occupier, only this time that occupier is the United States. Once again, eradication is the favored policy.

Wiping out any crop is nearly impossible, even under the best of circumstances, and on an international scale, it's fraught with political difficulty. The small farmer struggling to feed his family can plainly see that were it not for American demand for his harvest, he'd have no reason to be in the business. Resistance to eradication in Afghanistan is fierce, and the Taliban uses it as its strongest political tool: Uncle Sam wants to destroy your crops, it correctly warns poppy farmers. We'll protect you and your livelihood. The cost of that protection is political allegiance and a stiff tax, which the Taliban uses to wage its insurgent effort.

Attempts to take out coca in South America have faced similar intransigence. The DEA managed in the early part of this century to reduce the number of acres of the plant grown in Bolivia and Peru, but the crop just shifted to Colombia—and Bolivia elected a coca-grower president. When the U.S. and Colombian governments sprayed coca fields in Colombia, growers moved their operations to national forests, where spraying isn't allowed. Still, acreage known to be under coca cultivation has declined by about a third in South America since 2000. But the decline hasn't been accompanied by any significant disruption in production, according to the 2007 World Drug Report produced by the United Nations. This is largely due to another adaptation to U.S. policy: producers' increasing the yield of the coca plant.

Despite the high price the United States pays politically, eradication does essentially nothing to stop the flow of drugs into America. The cost of coca or poppies is a negligible fraction of the final price of cocaine or heroin, so drug producers are willing to pay farmers relatively well to compensate for the risk of growing. It costs about $300 to buy the coca leaf needed to make a kilo of coke, which retails for more than $100,000 in the United States. Doubling or tripling a farmer's pay won't have much impact on either the producer's bottom line or the farmer's quality of life—but it will encourage the planting of more coca.

The Bolivian example highlights the political hurdles the United States faces when attempting to destroy a drug crop. While Christian and I were in the Chapare, we had an interview with two regional mayors. Both were members of Morales's party, Movimiento al Socialismo ("Movement toward Socialism"), or MAS. In response to a question about the consequences of the war on drugs, the mayor of Villa Tunari, Feliciano Mamani, lifted his pant leg, revealing a star-shaped scar on his shin. He was hit by a tear-gas canister during a 2000 demonstration. It is a human-rights violation to fire canisters directly at people rather than bouncing them off the ground. My experience in La Paz and the wound on Mamani's leg indicated that that rule wasn't a high priority for Bolivian soldiers.

"It just stopped pussing a few weeks ago," he said in Spanish. Though the 2000 protest had been over water rights, it is instructive that Mamani first and foremost blamed the American drug war. American power in Bolivia was seen to be behind every effort to control the countryside. That suspicion was not without merit, given that the United States had funded and trained the Bolivian military and propped up several American-educated presidents. The American government also cut monthly checks to Bolivian judges and prosecutors, payments laughably known as "anticorruption bonuses."

Mamani and Shinahota mayor Rimer Agreda, both cocaleros, came up through the MAS party ranks during the eighties and nineties. "The war made the American government's intentions clear to the people of Chapare," said Mamani. "Behind the war on drugs there are other interests. Interests in natural resources, and in dismantling the [MAS] unions in the Chapare." Agreda added, "There was a reaction of the people, and they decided to oppose this until they reached their goal." The calculus is quite simple: Coca is what allows the people of the Chapare to survive; therefore, an attack on coca is an attack on the people.

Jaimie Rojas, a seventy-four-year-old newspaper vendor and college student in Villa Tunari, had been in the Chapare longer than almost anyone else. He arrived as one of the early settlers in the fifties, and he'd known Morales and the other MAS leaders since they were in their early twenties. I asked him when he noticed Morales's leadership skills. "When UMOPAR came to Chapare and Evo spoke out against it," he said. "He was able to unite the people and have them all turn back UMOPAR."

I spoke with Evo himself at the Cochabamba airport—just before warily boarding a small plane with the leftist leader—and asked him if the U.S. drug war had contributed to his rise to power. "In the beginning, yes, but now we are much bigger," he said in Spanish. Through a translator, he added that coca eradication and U.S. imperialism, which are one and the same thing as far as he's concerned, are so unpopular that they allowed his union to form and his movement to grow. He stressed that his supporters now encompassed more than just coca producers, an assertion that would be proved correct several months later, when he captured almost 54 percent of the vote, beating the Washington-backed candidate in a 25-point landslide.

It's one thing for MAS leaders to believe that they came to power because a majority of Bolivians oppose the U.S. war on drugs. But even those charged with fighting the war say the same thing.

Christian and I visited a military base in Chimoré to take a DEA-sponsored helicopter ride and meet with the base commander, but he was nowhere to be found. Bolivian soldiers played a lively game of soccer while we were distracted with a tour of the base's piss-stained prison and the DEA's coke museum. Afterward, Christian pulled out his bag of coca leaf, which he had bought in La Paz and we'd been chewing steadily. Combined with a touch of baking soda, which almost all Bolivians carry around in a small vial, coca leaf gives a caffeine-like buzz and numbs the mouth and stomach. Personal possession of the plant is legal under Bolivian law, which makes the U.S. effort to uproot it that much more difficult. It's often chewed by UMOPAR soldiers while they're doing their eradication.

Christian offered me some. The soldier minding us got a shocked look on his face. "¿Desde La Paz?" he asked, pointing to the bag.

"Sí."

The soldier smiled: La Paz coca is supposed to taste better than the Chapare variety, which it was his charge to destroy.

"¿Por favor?"

Christian nodded, and the soldier stuffed a handful in his mouth, then stashed another in his canteen bag. "Quita el hambre," he said. "It takes away the hunger."

His mouth numbed by coca, the soldier warmed up to us. He told us he wasn't unhappy in his job. He was poorly educated, he said, so his lot could have been worse. He's paid roughly $130 a month by the Bolivian government and a little extra by the United States. Plus, he admitted with a smile, he likes the uniform.

After a long silence, he asked us in Spanish why it was that we were allowed to come to his country and tour the military bases, but he couldn't get a visa to visit our country. "It's called imperialism," Christian said in English, a statement no one translated.

While still waiting for the base commander, we were taken in to see the subcommander. Before we asked a question, he told us how committed he is to *derechos humanos*, "human rights." UMOPAR has had a history of corruption and human-rights abuses, just like almost every effort that relies on the poor to staff a unit dealing with large amounts of cash, funded by a foreign government, and opposed by the local people. The operation is similar in style and substance to many others around the globe, and its transgressions have included disappearances, political assassination, seizure of land, and other methods of terrorizing the local populace.

The subcommander is so committed to human rights, he said, that he recently took a course on them with the Ministry of Justice. To prove it, he handed us a certificate: "Major Fernando Plato has successfully completed the course Human Rights and Sexually Transmitted Diseases."

"What does that mean?" Christian whispered to me. "They teach them to wear condoms when they're raping detainees?"

Plato told us that the human-rights abuses associated with the antidrug campaign of the eighties and nineties sparked fierce resistance among the people of the region, which MAS channeled to build its organization.

As Plato filibustered, it looked less and less like we'd be getting a helicopter ride. We were brought bread and three-liter bottles of Coke and, finally, Colonel Dario Leigue. He's sorry, we were told, but he can't meet with us without the permission of the commander-in-chief, Admiral Luis Aranda, who was in a meeting. Seeing our skepticism, Leigue told us to call his commander ourselves. He gave us a cell number, but the admiral didn't answer. (A few weeks later, he was in the news denying that he was plotting a coup. I called him up again, but he didn't answer then, either.)

At the checkpoint outside the base, a woman was selling coca. "Prohibido Orinar," said a sign on a crumbling wall behind her. "No urinating."

CHAPTER 11

Conflicts of Interest

Douglas Farah was in El Salvador when the *San Jose Mercury News* broke a major story in the summer of 1996: the Nicaraguan Contras, a confederation of paramilitary rebels sponsored by the CIA, had been funding some of their operations by importing cocaine into the United States. One of their best customers was a man named Freeway Rick—Ricky Donnell Ross, then a Southern California dealer who was running an operation that the *Los Angeles Times* dubbed "the Wal-Mart of crack dealing."

"My first thought was, Holy shit! because there'd been so many rumors in the region of this going on," said Farah twelve years later. He had grown up in Latin America and covered it for twenty years for the *Washington Post*. "There had always been these stories floating around about [the Contras] and cocaine. I knew [Contra leader] Adolfo Calero and some of the other folks there, and they were all sleazebags. You wouldn't read the story and say, 'Oh my god, these guys would never do that.' It was more like, 'Oh, one more dirty thing they were doing.' So I took it seriously."

The same would not hold true of most of Farah's colleagues, either in the newspaper business in general or at the *Post* in particular. "If you're talking about our intelligence community tolerating—if not promoting—drugs to pay for black ops, it's rather an uncomfortable thing to do when you're an establishment paper like the *Post*," Farah told me. "If you were going to be directly rubbing up against

171

the government, they wanted it more solid than it could probably ever be done."

In the mid- to late eighties, a number of reports had surfaced that connected the Contras to the cocaine trade. The first was by Associated Press scribes Brian Barger and Robert Parry, who published a story in December 1985 that began, "Nicaraguan rebels operating in northern Costa Rica have engaged in cocaine trafficking, in part to help finance their war against Nicaragua's leftist government, according to U.S. investigators and American volunteers who work with the rebels."

Only a few outlets followed Barger and Parry's lead, including the *San Francisco Examiner* and the lefty mag *In These Times*, both of which published similar stories in 1986, and CBS's *West 57th* TV series, which did a segment in 1987. A Nexis search of the year following Barger and Parry's revelation turns up a total of only four stories containing the terms "Contras" and "cocaine"—one of them a denial of the accusation from a Contra spokesperson. Stories popped up here and there over the next decade, but many of them make only oblique reference to a couldn't-possibly-be-true conspiracy theory.

Then came the *San Jose Mercury News* piece, a 20,000-word three-parter by Pulitzer Prize–winning staffer Gary Webb published under the title "Dark Alliance." "For the better part of a decade, a San Francisco Bay Area drug ring sold tons of cocaine to the Crips and Bloods street gangs of Los Angeles and funneled millions in drug profits to a Latin American guerrilla army run by the U.S. Central Intelligence Agency, a Mercury News investigation has found," the story begins.

The series initially received little attention from major media outlets, but it was eventually transported across the nation by the Internet and black talk radio. The latter put its own spin on the tale: that the U.S. government had deliberately spread crack to African American neighborhoods to quell unruly residents. The *Post* newsroom was bombarded with phone calls asking why it was ignoring the story, the paper's ombudsman later reported.

In response, the *Post*, the *New York Times*, and the *Los Angeles Times* would all weigh in with multiple articles claiming that Webb's assertions were bunk. His career was effectively ruined, and even his own paper eventually disavowed "Dark Alliance," despite having given it a cutting-edge online presentation complete with document transcriptions and audio recordings.

The big papers had been pushing the same line for years. In 1987, *New York Times* reporter Keith Schneider had flatly dismissed a lawsuit filed by a liberal group charging that the Contras were funding their operations with drug money. "Other investigators, including reporters from major news organizations, have tried without success to find proof of aspects of the case," he wrote, "particularly the allegations that military supplies for the contras may have been paid for with profits from drug trafficking."

In These Times later asked Schneider why he'd rejected the Contra–coke connection. He was trying to avoid "shatter[ing] the Republic," he said. "I think it is so damaging, the implications are so extraordinary, that for us to run the story, it had better be based on the most solid evidence we could amass."

The American republic, of course, is an idea as much as it is a reality. That idea is of a nation founded on freedom and dedicated to the progress of human rights around the globe. It's most certainly not of a country that aids the underground drug trade — even if it does.

If Webb didn't have ironclad proof that the CIA had knowingly done just that, he did have a stack of circumstantial evidence leading to that conclusion. He based his series on court records and interviews with key drug runners. One of them, Danilo Blandón, was once described by Assistant U.S. Attorney L. J. O'Neale as "the biggest Nicaraguan cocaine dealer in the United States."

Webb had been unable to get Blandón to talk, but the cocaine dealer testified at a trial shortly before "Dark Alliance" came out. Blandón wasn't on trial himself, wasn't facing any jail time, and was in fact being paid by the U.S. government to act as an informant — in other words, he had no obvious incentive to lie to make the United States look bad. Nevertheless, in sworn testimony, he said that in 1981 alone, his drug operation sold almost a ton of cocaine — worth millions of dollars — in the United States, and that "whatever we were running in L.A., the profit was going to the Contra revolution."

Blandón's boss in the operation was Norwin Meneses, the head of political operations and U.S. fund-raising for the Contras. Meneses was known as Rey de la Droga—"King of Drugs"—and had been under active investigation by the U.S. government since the early seventies as the Cali cocaine cartel's top representative in Nicaragua. The Drug Enforcement Administration considered him a major trafficker, and he had been implicated in forty-five separate federal investigations, Webb discovered through government documents. Regardless, Meneses had never served any time in federal prison and lived out in the open in his San Francisco home.

In 1981, Blandón testified, he and Meneses traveled to Honduras to meet Colonel Enrique Bermúdez, the military leader of the Contra army and a full-time CIA employee. "While Blandon says Bermudez didn't know cocaine would be the fund-raising device they used," Webb wrote, "the presence of the mysterious Mr. Meneses strongly suggests otherwise." The reporter drew on court documents and government records to show that anyone remotely involved in, or familiar with, the drug world at the time knew exactly how Meneses went about raising revenue.

Blandón sold the Contras' product to Ross for prices well below what other dealers could command, allowing him to expand his business throughout L.A., then to Texas, Ohio, and beyond. Ross told Webb that he owed his rise to Blandón and his astonishingly cheap coke. "I'm not saying I wouldn't have been a dope dealer without Danilo," Ross said. "But I wouldn't have been Freeway Rick."

Webb had uncovered a direct link between the Contras and street-level crack cocaine. His story also repeatedly highlighted the facts that the Contras were a CIA-directed entity and that the drug runners avoided prosecution despite mountains of evidence implicating them. Webb never explicitly stated that CIA brass or other Washington bigwigs condoned smuggling drugs into the United States, but the facts of his story strongly implied it.

As shocking as that might have been to Webb's readers and colleagues other than Farah, they were hardly unprecedented in American history. The United States' global drug policy had long taken a backseat to more important foreign-policy concerns, in this case toppling Nicaragua's socialist Sandinista National Liberation Front.

Since at least the 1940s, the American government has founded and supported insurgent armies organized for the purpose of overthrowing some presumably hostile foreign regime. In Italy, the United States pitted the Corsican and Sicilian mobs against Fascists and then Communists. In China, it aided Chiang Kai-shek's Kuomintang in its struggle against Mao Zedong's Communist Party of China. In Afghanistan, it backed the mujahideen in their fight against the Soviet Union.

All of these and other U.S.-supported organizations profited heavily from the drug trade. One of the principal arguments made by the DEA in recent years in support of the global drug war is that the drug trade funds violent, stateless organizations. The administration is referring specifically to al-Qaeda and the Taliban, but the same method of fund-raising has long been used by other violent, stateless actors the United States has befriended.

Foreign critics are quick to blame the global drug trade and its attendant problems on the voracious demand of American drug users, who get high at rates many times greater than those of users in the rest of the world. Stop snorting so much coke, they tell us, and our farmers will stop growing coca. American drug warriors, meanwhile, treat the trade as a foreign threat that needs to be eradicated in root countries and stopped at the border. Stop growing so much coca, and we'll stop snorting it.

But both sides miss—or ignore—a crucial fact: Americans' involvement in the international drug market extends well beyond our appetite to get high. For decades and for a variety of reasons, the United States has been an important link in the global supply chain, protecting and often funding major drug-running organizations. The government has denied it for just as long. Anyone who believes it is labeled a conspiracy nut. And the American media, Webb discovered the hard way, can tie itself in knots trying to avoid discussing it.

In the forties, Americans may well have fought a "good war," but that doesn't mean we waged it like angels. In its effort to defeat Hitler, Mussolini, and Tojo, the U.S. government forged relationships with a host of other criminals, some of whom would make it very difficult for the feds to succeed in another militarized conflict: the war on drugs.

The conflict in Europe and Asia had disrupted global supply routes to such an extent that by the end of the thirties, heroin addicts had great difficulty finding their drug of choice and substituted all manner of intoxicants in its stead. Meanwhile, Mussolini's war on the Italian mob, which had begun in 1924, was going well, with La Cosa Nostra a shell of its former self and its leaders exiled to Canada and the United States. Mafia kingpin Charles "Lucky" Luciano was in prison in upstate New York, locked up since 1936 after being convicted of running a massive prostitution ring.

For the previous two decades, Luciano and his partner, Meyer Lansky, had dominated not only the Manhattan call-girl market, but also the U.S. heroin trade, modeling their business, Lansky claimed, on John D. Rockefeller's Standard Oil Trust. Cuba was used as the drop-off point for heroin manufactured in Sicily, which also allowed the Mafia to build the island nation's gambling industry. But it all began to unravel during the war, and Luciano was left controlling his threadbare syndicate from prison.

Luckily for Luciano, the feds had use for him. The government was deeply concerned about infiltration and sabotage at American ports, which Mafia-connected unions controlled, and it was equally worried about a strike that could shut the docks down. Communist organizers had been making inroads against the corrupt mob unions, so Luciano had good reason to cooperate with the feds. The mob gave U.S. Naval Intelligence operatives access to its docks and instructed its people to ferret out any German spies. In return, the government allowed the mob to battle the radical union organizers threatening to shut the ports with impunity. Between 1942 and 1946, more than two dozen dockworkers and organizers were killed, their murders left unsolved.

Luciano also opened up channels of communication between exiled Sicilian mobsters and those still at home, yielding intelligence that would be used during the U.S. invasion and occupation of Sicily. The United States expressed its gratitude by installing mobsters as the leaders of occupied Italy, where they went about murdering Communist opponents and restarting the heroin trade.

On May 8, 1945, V-E Day, a petition was filed for Luciano's early release. Supported by U.S. intelligence officials, it cited his contribution to the war effort. Luciano was freed in January by New York governor Thomas Dewey, the same man who had locked him up in his first major case as "special rackets prosecutor," as the *New York Times* described Dewey in a story on the commutation, one of a handful of items the paper printed about the mobster's release. That minimal coverage contrasted with the breathless, wall-to-wall reporting the *Times* had offered when Luciano had been taken down a few year earlier.

Dewey, in ordering Luciano's release, explained that his "aid was sought by the armed services in inducing others to provide information concerning possible enemy attack. It appears that he cooperated in such effort though the actual value of the information procured is not clear." Sourcing Luciano's attorney, the *Times* reported that Luciano's intelligence "led to the locating of many Sicilian-born Italians who gave information of military value on conditions in Sicily" and that he "aided the military authorities for two years in the preliminaries leading to the invasion of Sicily."

More than five hundred Italian-born mobsters would follow Luciano back home over the next five years, solidifying the Italian–American drug connection.

Heroin addiction in America rose through the late forties and early fifties as U.S. intelligence continued to find a useful purpose for its Italian friends: teaming up with the CIA to thwart the Communist Party in the 1948 Italian elections.

Closely linked to the Soviet Union, the Italian Communists hoped that a win at home would give Stalin's regime a toehold in Western Europe—exactly what the United States feared most. The effort on the U.S. government's behalf by the Mafia was voter intimidation at its most direct: offices were burned, candidates and activists were assassinated, and demonstrators were gunned down. Coupled with simple ballot stuffing, it had the desired effect: the Communists were defeated, in what historians of Europe consider a pivotal postwar moment.

The CIA struck up a similar partnership with Corsican mafiosi in the French port city of Marseilles. The mobsters battled a coalition of Communists and Socialists who had vowed to root out mob influence. The mob prevailed with the help of CIA weapons and agents—a development that would prove very damaging to the cause of American drug warriors.

In 1950, U.S. Federal Bureau of Narcotics head Harry Anslinger persuaded Italy to stop a major pharmaceutical firm from selling heroin legally to Luciano. In response, the boss formed an alliance with the Corsican mob—which had just taken over Marseilles. The vaunted French Connection, which supplied the vast majority of America's heroin over the next two decades, was born. Not a single major bust was made of French Connection folks between 1950 and 1965. It wasn't for lack of evidence: a 1976 Department of Justice report concluded that on repeated occasions, charges against Corsican drug runners were dropped at the insistence of the CIA for national security reasons. It's another case of drug policy riding in the backseat, driven by more important concerns.

The dots were there for anybody who wanted to connect them, but the only people to make much of a case for U.S. involvement in the global heroin trade were Dewey's opponents, who included Tennessee senator Estes Kefauver. The Democrat had national political aspirations: he twice sought his party's presidential nomination, in 1952 and 1956, and he was Adlai Stevenson's running mate in 1956. The Republican Dewey, a popular governor who had run for president in 1948 and 1952, was a ripe target.

In the early fifties, Kefauver held fifteen months' worth of hearings on organized crime. It was the first televised congressional drama to be watched by millions, and it started the nation's love affair with the workings of the Mafia. Here's how *Life* magazine described the public reaction: "[T]he week of March 12, 1951, will occupy a special place in history. . . . [P]eople had suddenly gone indoors into living rooms, taverns, and clubrooms, auditoriums and back-offices. There, in eerie half-light, looking at millions of small frosty screens, people sat as if charmed. Never before had the attention of the nation been riveted so completely on a single matter."

Kefauver called in armed-forces representatives who told the committee that Luciano was back in Sicily running a drug operation and had contributed essentially nothing to the war effort. The dual charge called Dewey's commutation into question. Lucky didn't take kindly to the attacks on his prosecutor-cum-liberator: Dewey "pardoned me from a fifty-year sentence he imposed on me earlier," an "indignant" Luciano told the Associated Press, saying that the attackers had "political motives." He threatened that shortly after the 1952 election, he would reveal "certain stories which will make everybody in the United States take notice" and "put an end to all the dirty speculation about me." Luciano also pointed to his wartime service. "I got my pardon because of the great services I rendered the United States," he said, "and because, after all, they reckoned I was innocent." (Those "certain stories" were never publicly told by Luciano.)

In a memoir published after Dewey died, Dewey expressed similar indignation at the charge that "there might have been something crooked about my action." He knew that whatever the actual value of Luciano's contribution, the armed services had indeed approached him, and they did have a hand in freeing him, despite the self-protective testimony they'd given in the Kefauver hearings.

Dewey knew he wasn't the only one who'd gotten tangled up in the heroin trade. If the military was going to take him down, Dewey must have figured, he'd drag it with him. So the governor commissioned a study of Luciano's role in the war. New York Commissioner of Investigations William Herlands finished his report in 1954. Herlands pulled together 2,883 pages of statements from 57 major witnesses, including Luciano right-hand man Lansky, Luciano attorney Moses Polakoff, and racketeer and wartime Naval Intelligence collaborator Joseph "Socks" Lanza. Herlands also talked to 31 U.S. Navy personnel.

Rear Admiral Carl Espe, then director of naval intelligence, called the study "thorough" but asked that Dewey suppress it. Public disclosure "might jeopardize operations of a similar nature in the future," he warned, foreseeing the likes of the mujahideen and the Contras. He added that "there is potential for embarrassment to the Navy public relations-wise." Dewey consented and a détente was reached; the report stayed secret, and he was no longer accused of shady dealings with the mob.

The report didn't see public light until researcher Rodney Campbell found a copy in the late Dewey's papers and used it to write the 1977 book *The Luciano Project: The Secret Wartime Collaboration of the Mafia and the U.S. Navy*. The media, however, barely took notice. The *New York Times* wrote about the book just before it came out and mentioned it again when Campbell died decades later, saying that his exposé had garnered "widespread attention."

That isn't exactly true: a Nexis search for *The Luciano Project* turns up just eighteen stories written over more than three decades—a portion of them about entirely unrelated construction projects.

Postwar, the U.S. government continued to finance or turn a blind eye to known drug traffickers who were on the American side of the Cold War. Involvement in the drug trade was not merely an evil that the CIA accepted as a cost of allying itself with the right forces; often, the drug trade was what made such forces possible, given that congressional funds didn't always flow freely to potentially useful organizations.

U.S. involvement in the drug trade wasn't always sanctioned at the top levels. The desire to make money and get high knows no cultural, socioeconomic, or political bounds—and therefore seeps into the ranks of the drug warriors even when the overall policy is opposed to drugs. In 1968, before the DEA was created, the IRS stumbled on knee-deep corruption in the Federal Bureau of Narcotics. More than three dozen agents were helping to import and distribute drugs. It's a hazard that the government runs into: the drug trade doesn't produce any immediate victims, so there's no one to call the police. Therefore, the cops rely on deception to become part of the trade themselves. Inevitably, some realize that they can't stop it, so they might as well make some money off of it. The economic argument for a drug enforcement officer in any country can be overwhelming. The United States was no different, even after those dozens of cops were fired.

Forty years later, little had changed. In early 2006, the Web site NarcoNews.com—founded by former Associated Press reporter Robert Parry, who broke the original Contra-cocaine story—published a memo by Thomas Kent, then an attorney for the office of wiretaps in the Narcotic and Dangerous Drugs Section of the Justice Department, calling for an investigation into DEA corruption. It outlined pervasive corruption in the Bogotá station and warned that informants were being systematically killed off. "Each murder [of an informant] was preceded by a request for their identity by an agent in Bogotá," wrote Kent, who still works for the Justice Department.

The media largely ignored the memo, but the AP did file a 332-word story early in the morning of January 14, 2006, headlined, "U.S. Official: DEA Agents in Colombia Allegedly Involved in Drug Trade." Twelve hours later, it published precisely the same story, in time for the Sunday papers, but this time called it, "Probe of DEA Agents Finds No Wrongdoing." No other major paper touched it.

Stateside cops still aren't immune to the temptations. In December 2008, the FBI charged fifteen Chicago-area officers with protecting drug runners. "When drug dealers deal drugs, they ought to be afraid of the police—not turn to them for help," said U.S. Attorney Patrick Fitzgerald during a news conference announcing the charges—in between nabbing Dick Cheney chief of staff Scooter Libby and Illinois governor Rod Blagojevich, his more prominent victims.

During the Vietnam War, U.S. intelligence made friends with a number of known drug traffickers in Southeast Asia, including the Laotian smack smugglers who used CIA-owned civilian airline Air America to transport their product. Although the affair was slapsticked and sensationalized in the 1990 Mel Gibson movie *Air America*, it received more sober treatment in Alfred W. McCoy's 1972 book *The Politics of Heroin in Southeast Asia*, which amassed substantial evidence and concluded that "American diplomats and secret agents have been involved in the narcotics traffic at three levels: (1) coincidental complicity by allying with groups actively engaged in the drug traffic; (2) abetting the traffic by covering up for known heroin traffickers and condoning their involvement; and (3) active engagement in the transport of opium and heroin."

The agency continued to deny knowledge of what its allies had done or were doing, but by May 1980, two Carter administration officials had had enough. Drug-policy advisers David F. Musto and Joyce Lowinson took to the *New York Times* op-ed page, frustrated at their inability to get through to Carter or to the media, and tried to blow the whistle on the long-standing practice of colluding with drug runners. "We worry about the growing of opium poppies in Afghanistan and

Pakistan by rebel tribesmen," they wrote. "Are we erring in befriend-ing these tribes as we did in Laos when Air America (chartered by the CIA) helped transport crude opium from certain tribal areas?"

"We live in a dirty and dangerous world," *Washington Post* publisher Katharine Graham told a gathering of CIA recruits in 1988. "There are some things the general public does not need to know, and shouldn't. I believe democracy flourishes when the government can take legitimate steps to keep its secrets and when the press can decide whether to print what it knows."

Webb apparently made the wrong decision, and Graham's paper was instrumental in discrediting his story. On October 2, after "Dark Alliance" had gained some traction on black radio and online, renowned *Post* media reporter Howard Kurtz weighed in, heading off the most damning of the piece's implications. "The series doesn't actually say the CIA knew about the drug trafficking," Kurtz acknowl-edged, quoting an interview with Webb in which the reporter points out that "This doesn't prove the CIA targeted black communities. It doesn't say this was ordered by the CIA. Essentially, our trail stopped at the door of the CIA. They wouldn't return my phone calls."

Kurtz hammered Webb for not getting an official denial. But he also noted, "The fact that Nicaraguan rebels were involved in drug trafficking has been known for a decade," assuring his readers that "the Reagan Administration acknowledged as much in the 1980s, but subsequent investigations failed to prove that the CIA condoned or even knew about it." This formulation raises a ridiculous question: If the White House knew about the Contras' participation in the drug trade, how come the CIA didn't?

"I wasn't an expert on drug trafficking or South America," Kurtz told me years later, saying that he "looked up what had been reported in the past, and my recollection is I found a number of stories about drug trafficking and Nicaraguan rebels. So the question is, How much of that did the *Washington Post* and other big papers report? I don't know; I'd have to look into it."

He wouldn't have had to look very hard, because the *Post* reported very little pre-Webb. In April 1989, when Senator John Kerry completed a two-year investigation finding that contractors connected to the Contras and the CIA were known at the time to be running drugs but were not prosecuted, the *Post* reacted with a 703-word piece by Michael Isikoff tucked away on page 20.

When the Barger and Parry duo broke news of the Contras' connection to cocaine in 1986, the *Post* declined even to run the wire story. It mentioned the allegations two days later, when Democrats demanded that President Ronald Reagan respond to the charges. His refusal to do so appeared in a 515-word story on page 38 written by Thomas Edsall, now of the *Huffington Post*.

After "Dark Alliance" was published, the *Post* went after Webb only grudgingly. The paper's preferred method of dealing with the series would have been to ignore it, according to veteran *Post* national security reporter Walter Pincus. "Originally, I didn't do anything about it because I checked it out and didn't believe it to be true," Pincus told me. "If you go look at the chronology, I didn't write about it until the Black Caucus took it up as a serious issue."

Black radio hosts and audiences had met "Dark Alliance" with an I-knew-it-all-along reception that didn't dull their outrage. The Congressional Black Caucus, led by Los Angeles Democrat Maxine Waters, demanded an investigation. (Waters even traveled to Nicaragua to conduct her own.) The head of the CIA traveled to South Central Los Angeles to meet with hundreds of residents packed into a huge community meeting, where he denied angry accusations that his agency had purposely caused the crack epidemic.

Kurtz "initially got into this because black radio hosts and others were seizing on the Gary Webb series and making claims that went far beyond what he had actually reported," he told me. "And the person who agreed with me on that was Gary Webb. . . . He considered me always to be fair to him." The *Post* reporter explained that his effort was meant to be in defense of the media: "In the pre-blogging age, it was this surreal environment in which the mainstream media were being accused by critics of covering up or ignoring allegations involving the CIA that weren't actually made by the San Jose Mercury News."

•   •   •

On October 4, 1996, about five weeks after the *Mercury News* report, the *Post* published a five-piece package dedicated to discrediting "Dark Alliance." The paper seemed genuinely frightened by the black community's response to Webb's series, perhaps imagining that it would spark a riot similar to the one that had swept through D.C.'s Hispanic Mount Pleasant neighborhood a few years before, after a police officer shot and wounded a reportedly unarmed man during a Cinco de Mayo celebration. As the *Post's* editorial board explained in a piece that appeared five days after the initial anti-Webb salvo, "the shock of the story for many was not simply the sheer monstrousness of the idea of an official agency contributing to a modern-day plague—and to a plague targeted on blacks. The shock was the credibility the story seems to have generated when it reached some parts of the black community."

The *Post* offered an explanation of why African Americans had gotten so riled up: a "history of victimization" that had led to "outright paranoia." The October 4 assault included not one but two stories intended to counteract this process. "Whatever makes the truth slide into rumor and then plummet into myth, it isn't new," wrote Donna Britt in an essay titled "Finding the Truest Truth." "Nearly 50 years ago, Howard University surgeon Charles R. Drew—the renowned director of America's first Red Cross blood bank—died after a car accident in rural North Carolina. Within hours, rumor had it that Drew, 45, had bled to death because a whites-only hospital had refused to treat him. The tragic story, repeated in newspapers, documentaries, even in an episode of TV's M*A*S*H, is an outrage—and entirely false."

She suggested that Webb's piece would probably end up plummeting into myth, too—and perhaps already had. "It doesn't matter whether the series' claims are 'proved' true," she wrote. "To some folks—graduates of Watergate, Iran-contra and FBI harassment of Malcolm X and Martin Luther King Jr.—they feel so true that even if they're refuted, they'll still be fact to them." Britt's story ran on the front page of the Metro section. For readers who might not make it that far into the paper, the *Post* ran a strikingly similar piece by Michael Fletcher on page A1. Blacks' skepticism, Fletcher duly notes, is rooted in a "history of victimization . . . [that] allows myth—and, at times, outright paranoia—to flourish." He cites the Drew story—"a man who had benefited medicine for all races died because of anti-black attitude"—and concludes that "[e]ven if a major investigation into the allegations is done, it is unlikely to quell the certainty among many African Americans that the government played a role in bringing the crack epidemic to black communities."

Nonetheless, the *Post* quelled the best it could, going after the portions of Webb's story that most explicitly suggested a racist conspiracy against American citizens. In the process, it authored a myth of its own: that everything in "Dark Alliance" was wrong.

The October 4 package's lead piece, "CIA and Crack: Evidence Is Lacking of Contra-Tied Plot," was written by Pincus and national-desk staffer Roberto Suro, who rejected "the idea that Blandón and Ross alone could have launched the crack epidemic." Webb hadn't reported exactly that, but he did note that cocaine "was virtually unobtainable in black neighborhoods before members of the CIA's army started bring it into South Central in the 1980s at bargain basement prices."

Farah, who's now a consultant on the drug trade with the Department of Homeland Security, speculated that the *Post's* proximity to the corridors of power made it beholden to whatever the official line was at the time. He said that he saw a "great deal of weight on what the official response was, whether it was Haiti or El Salvador death squads. There was so much Washington influence that it ends up dominating the story no matter what the reality on the ground was."

Farah said that his reporting on Webb's trail led to one of the biggest battles of his career. "There were maybe, in my twenty years at the *Post*, two or three stories out of however many hundreds or thousands I wrote, where I had this kind of problem, and this was one of them. I wasn't in general in confrontation with my editors but this thing was weird and I knew it was weird," he said. "I did have a long and dispiriting fight with the editors at the *Post* because they wanted to say ultimately—their basic take was that I was dealing with a bunch of liars, so it was one person's word against another person's word and therefore you couldn't tell the truth. But it was pretty clear to me."

The official response was provided to national-security reporter Pincus, who had at one time served in the U.S. Army Counterintelligence Corps. "One of my big fights on this was with Pincus," Farah remembered, "and my disadvantage was that I was in Managua and he was sitting in on the story meetings and talking directly to the editors. And we had a disagreement over the validity of what I was finding. At the time, I didn't realize he had been an agency employee for a while. That might have helped me understand what was going on there a bit."

Pincus, who said that his involvement with the CIA several decades before was overblown, remembered it differently. "To be honest, I can't remember talking to Doug at the time," he said. "To me, it was no great shock that some of the people the agency was dealing with were also drug dealers. But the idea that the agency was then running the drug program was totally different."

Pincus said that Webb's core story about the Contras and cocaine didn't resonate not because it didn't have any truth to it, but because it was obviously true. "This is a problem that came up—it's probably a question of how long you cover these things," he said. "It came up during the Vietnam War, where the U.S. was dealing with the Hmong tribes in Laos and some of the people that were flying airplanes that the agency was using were also [running] drugs."

Calling him a CIA stooge, added Pincus, does little to advance understanding of the story. "Anytime somebody wants to object to something I've written about, they go back to quote my connection with the agency, all of which they can prove because I wrote about it," he said, claiming that he didn't know a front group that he was involved with was connected to the CIA and that he declined an offer to join the agency.

Pincus told me that trying to draw lessons about the media from the Webb saga is pointless, just as it was to try to ascribe motives to the entire band of Contras. "This is sort of like saying the media is liberal," he said. "The media is made up of—what?—five thousand different people, and some of them are far-left and some of them are conservative, but that doesn't stop some people from making generalities. And when you say 'the Contras,' you're talking about a whole bunch of different leaders, some of whom were good, some of whom were bad."

Both the good and the bad, however, would get a pass at the *Post*. "I thought my story was really cool," recalled Farah, noting that Nicaragua was in the middle of an election and all the players he needed to talk to were in Managua. "I had an amazing run of luck where I had rounded up everybody I needed to see in twenty-four hours and got to see Meneses . . . I got all this stuff. I thought it was going on the front page, and I got a tagline or something on the front-page story and my story buried away. And I remember that they cut it down. I don't remember how long it ran, but they cut it down considerably." (Run on page 18, it was cut to 948 words; the Pincus piece, which contradicted it on the front page, ran at 4,048 words.)

Farah's reporting, he concluded, confirmed the largest parts of Webb's story. "The contra-drug stuff, I think, was there," Farah said. "Largely, I think it [Webb's story] was right." The cuts and the editorial push-back, however, discouraged Farah from pursuing a further investigation into the Contras' drug-running history. "I was really sort of disappointed at how things had run there at the *Post* on that story, and there wasn't much incentive to go forward after that," said Farah. (The *Post*'s top editor at the time, Leonard Downie, told me that he doesn't remember the incident well enough to comment on it.)

Although Pincus said that he didn't have a role in neutering and burying Farah's story, he did admit that he sympathized with the reporter. "I was writing about there being no weapons [of mass destruction] in Iraq, and it was put in the back of the paper," he said. "I've been through the same thing."

In its modern-day-plague editorial, the *Post* declared, "For even just a couple of CIA-connected characters to have played even a trivial role in introducing Americans to crack would indicate an unconscionable breach by the CIA. It is essential to know whether the agency contributed to this result or failed to exercise diligence to stop it."

More than a year later, when the CIA's inspector general finished an investigation conducted in response to the Webb series, that knowledge somehow seemed much less essential—or at least that's what the *Post*'s handling of the story suggests.

Before the CIA made its findings public, it leaked word to Pincus and a few other national-security reporters, assuring them that the report, to be released the next day, would exonerate the agency. Pincus, relying on anonymous officials, repeated this assertion in the paper—possibly without having seen a copy of the report. (He told me that he doesn't remember whether he was given a copy or only briefed on its contents.) The next day, the CIA pulled the football away. For national-security reasons, it said, it had decided not to publicize the report after all.

It was a good move. The report, when it finally did come out, in January 1998, determined that the agency "did not inform Congress of all allegations or information it received indicating that contra-related organizations or individuals were involved in drug trafficking." It also found that the CIA had intervened in a California drug bust, that it had ignored a narcotics-for-arms trade by the Contras, and that Meneses and Blandón did indeed meet with agency asset Bermúdez, who suggested to them that drug-running would be an acceptable means of raising funds for the Contras. The *Post* ran a page 4 story by Pincus with the misdirecting headline "Probe Finds No CIA Link to L.A. Crack Cocaine Sales."

Two months later, readers of another Pincus dispatch would learn that CIA inspector general Frederick R. Hitz testified before Congress that "dozens of people and a number of companies connected in some fashion to the contra program" were involved in drug trafficking. "Let me be frank," Hitz added, "there are instances where CIA did not, in an expeditious or consistent fashion, cut off relationships with individuals supporting the contra program who were alleged to have engaged in drug-trafficking activity or take action to resolve the allegations."

Hitz discovered, too, that high-ranking Reagan administration officials were aware of Contra drug trafficking. "The inspector general also said that under an agreement in 1982 between then Attorney General William French Smith and the CIA, agency officers were not required to report allegations of drug trafficking involving non-employees, which was defined as meaning paid and non-paid 'assets,' pilots who ferried supplies to the contras, as well as contra officials and others," Pincus reports. "[T]his policy was modified in 1986 when the agency was prohibited from paying U.S. dollars to any individual or company found to be involved in drug dealing." That same year, Congress approved $100 million in funding for the Contras, meaning that the group no longer needed to rely on drug money.

Where were these bombshells printed? Page 12. In October 1998, the inspector general released another report. The *New York Times* pushed it to page 7. James Risen, confirming the underlying assumptions of "Dark Alliance," wrote:

> In all, the report found that the C.I.A. received allegations of drug involvement by 58 contras or others linked to the contra program, including 14 pilots and two others tied to the contra program's C.I.A.-backed air transportation operations. The report indicates that information linking the contras to drugs began to emerge almost as soon as the contras came into existence, and before it became publicly known that the C.I.A. was supporting their effort to overthrow the Marxist-led Government in Managua.

Yet the writer made sure to take a swipe at Webb: "The first volume of the C.I.A. inspector general's report, issued in January, dealt primarily with the specific allegations raised by the *Mercury-News* series and dismissed its central findings."

Pincus covered the report the next month, November 1998, in a 1,566-word piece on page 4. It was his final attempt to reconcile the new findings with the notion that Webb had been wrong:

> Although the report contradicts previous CIA claims that it had little information about drug running and the contras, it does not lend any new support to charges of an alliance among the CIA, contra fund-raisers and dealers who introduced crack cocaine in the 1980s in south-central Los Angeles. Those charges created a national sensation during the summer of 1996 when they were published in a series of articles by the *San Jose Mercury News*.
>
> The allegations, which were not substantiated by subsequent reporting by other newspapers, prompted a year-long CIA inquiry that produced two reports, including the one

released last month. The first report found that there was no evidence to indicate that the CIA had any dealings with the California drug traffickers. The classified version of the second report, sent to Congress earlier this year, concluded that there was no evidence that the CIA "conspired with or assisted contra-related organizations or individuals in drug trafficking to raise funds for the contras or for other purposes."

However, the unclassified report provides a wealth of anecdotes indicating that the CIA routinely received allegations about drug trafficking links to the contras. Although the report does not specify in most cases whether the allegations proved accurate, it suggests that in many cases the charges were simply ignored or overlooked because of the priority to keep the contra effort going.

After nine months of backing Webb, the *Mercury News* finally recanted. And when it did, it made bigger news than when it broke the initial story. The *New York Times* ran a notice on the front page, and its editorial board congratulated *Mercury News* editor Jerry Ceppos for his courage. Kurtz mentioned several times to me that when Webb's own paper stood down from the story, it ended the debate over which parts of "Dark Alliance" were factual and which were conjecture. "The Mercury News looked into its own work and concluded that the series had fallen short," he said. "So now . . . instead of having Gary Webb versus the critics, you had Gary Webb versus his own editors."

Ceppos wrote a front-page editorial suggesting that the paper's most significant error was failing to report that Blandón stopped sending money to the Contras in 1982. He also noted that "Dark Alliance" "oversimplified" the way that the crack epidemic spread across the country and, most significantly, that knowledge of Contra drug-running by the CIA was implied and not proved, therefore making the story bunk. "[T]hough we never said the CIA knew of, or was involved in, this Contra fundraising effort, we strongly implied CIA knowledge," wrote Ceppos. "Although members of the drug ring met with Contra leaders paid by the CIA and Webb believes the relationship with the

CIA was a tight one, I feel that we did not have proof that top CIA officials knew of the relationship."

Ceppos was given the 1997 Society of Professional Journalists' National Ethics in Journalism Award for the editorial. Webb, meanwhile, continued researching and reporting on his own, and published his work in the 1999 book *Dark Alliance: The CIA, the Contras, and the Crack Cocaine Explosion*. If he thought that his book, combined with the CIA's validation of some of his initial assertions in the article, would resurrect his reputation, he hadn't yet figured out the game that he was playing.

"Poor Gary never really could fathom why they got the knives out and slashed him to death. He foolishly believed that in the end respect for Truth made for a level playing field," e-mailed Alexander Cockburn, whose own book on the subject, co-authored with Jeffrey St. Clair, came out in 1998 and was often jointly reviewed with Webb's. Both were shredded, and not just by the mainstream media.

Cockburn recalled that his "book was savagely attacked, particularly by liberals (including a vast review in the *Nation*), almost invariably—Jeffrey and I came to this conclusion after puzzling over the weird vehemence of the attacks—because they couldn't stomach the immensely detailed and carefully sourced account of the history and role of the CIA, not as 'a rogue' agency, but as the obedient servant of the US government. They can't stand to look at Medusa's face."

Geneva Overholser, the *Post*'s ombudsman, took a look at her own paper a month after the Webb takedown and didn't like what she saw. "The Post (and the others) showed more passion for sniffing out the flaws in San Jose's answer than for sniffing out a better answer themselves," she scolds in a November 10, 1996, op-ed. "A principal responsibility of the press is to protect the people from government excesses. The Post (among others) showed more energy for protecting the CIA from someone else's journalistic excesses. Not an invalid goal, but by far a lesser one. Perhaps there is better to come."

Not for Webb, however. He was demoted and sent to a dustbin bureau 150 miles from San Jose. He resigned after settling an arbitration claim and went to work for a small alt-weekly. Over the next several years, his marriage fell apart and his meager wages were garnished for child support. On December 10, 2004, Webb was discovered dead, shot twice in the head with his father's .38. The local coroner declared the death a suicide.

Obituaries in the major papers continued to reference his "discredited" series. The *Los Angeles Times* obit recalls his "widely criticized series linking the CIA to the explosion of crack cocaine in Los Angeles," noting that "[m]ajor newspapers, including the Los Angeles Times, New York Times and Washington Post, wrote reports discrediting elements of Webb's reporting." The *New York Times* ran a five-paragraph Reuters obit that began, "Gary Webb, a reporter who won national attention with a series of articles, later discredited." It added, "The articles led to calls in Congress for an investigation, but major newspapers discredited parts of Mr. Webb's work," making no mention of the fact that those calls for an investigation were heeded, and that the investigation confirmed a great deal of Webb's reporting.

"Web of Deception" sat atop Howard Kurtz's write-up in the *Post*. "There was a time when Gary Webb was at the center of a huge, racially charged national controversy. That was eight years ago, and it turned out badly for him," Kurtz began. "The lesson," he concluded, "is that just because a news outlet makes sensational charges doesn't make them true, and just because the rest of the media challenge the charges doesn't make them part of some cover-up."

Reading the obituaries at the time, Farah recalled, was dispiriting. "Everybody, especially in the news business when you're working fast, makes mistakes," he said. "But I don't think that should stand as his final word on what he did."

Kurtz, however, stood by what he said then. "Of course it's very sad what happened to him in the end, but I just did some basic reporting on him," he said. "I wasn't going out on a limb."

CHAPTER 12

Puff, Puff, Live

A first-time visitor to Harborside Health Center might have a hard time believing he's about to enter "an extraordinary environment of medical care, honesty, and friendliness," as the place describes itself online. Situated in a nondescript warehouse just off the freeway in Oakland, California, it's labeled only with the giant digits of its street number, 1840. Two security guards in blue are posted outside, and the facility is also equipped with motion detectors, video and audio surveillance, and laser alarms. The guards are, in fact, extraordinarily friendly, offering professional smiles to those who approach. But they're not exactly welcoming, and for good reason: at Harborside, no one gets in without a medical-cannabis card or a recommendation from a doctor.

I had come with a federal medical researcher who'd recently finished a long study of medical-cannabis clubs in the Bay Area and was able to vouch for me. But it's not exactly impossible to get a card or a recommendation. Ads in alt-weeklies throughout the state advertise doctors willing to give a consultation to anyone who has one of a seemingly endless list of symptoms and illnesses that might be treatable with medical marijuana. Take the ad for Aldridge Medical Care that runs in the LA Weekly and features a man wearing a white coat with a stethoscope hanging around his neck. Walk-ins are accepted, the text states, as long as the patient suffers from "pain, migraines, cramps, anxiety, depression, ADHD, nausea, IBS, insomnia, etc."

Once you get the card, it's not much harder to find a shop. On the very same page of the *Weekly*, the Green Earth Pharmacy offers "Free Samples" to "first time patients with this ad." And for the consumer looking for choices, there's WeedTRACKER.com, which, yes, tracks the varieties of weed available at Harborside and similar centers, allowing patients to rate the quality of each establishment—a Better Business Bureau of sorts. ("[W]e carry over 50 different types of buds, plus all our edibles and concentrates. If we don't have what you are looking for, we probably have something you will like," Harborside promises.) If you're not an official medical-cannabis patient, WeedTRACKER suggests that you "click here"—which sends you directly to Google, a site almost as good at finding pot dispensaries.

We walked through Harborside's metal detector and waited for the two owners, a man named David Wedding Dress and his partner, Steve DeAngelo. They opened the center in October 2006, on a day that three other clubs in the Bay Area were raided. "We had to decide in that moment whether or not we were really serious about this and whether we were willing to risk arrest for it," said DeAngelo. "And we decided we were gonna open our doors. And we did, and we haven't looked back since. The only way I'll stop doing what I'm doing is if they drag me away in chains. And as soon as they let me out, I'll be back doing it again." After less than a year, the shop was making $1 million a month in revenue.

In the next room were a half-dozen glassed-over counters where Harborside personnel were describing the various strains of marijuana available to customers. Marijuana's major ingredient, tetrahydrocannabinol, or THC, combines with more than thirty other active agents called cannabinoids. It's not clear how the interaction of THC and cannabinoids affects the user's experience, but THC taken by itself has an effect different from that of marijuana. Different varieties of the plant also have different effects. *Cannabis sativa* provides a speedy, uplifting high. ("Good for when you want to clean out your garage," said one sales rep.) *Cannabis indica*, often recommended for pain relief, knocks you out stone-cold. Most of the pot on sale is a mix of the two, and a young woman behind one counter elaborately explained the benefits of each and whether it had been grown indoors, outdoors, in the shade, or in the open and when in its life cycle it was harvested. "Green Erkle is Purple Erkle picked before it turns purple," she offered. "It's a sativa-indica blend heavier on the sativa, with a nice fruity flavor to it."

For those without a green thumb, the shop offers classes on pot-growing, both indoor and outdoor. Would-be farmers who want a more professional-sounding degree can also enroll at nearby Oaksterdam University.

Continuing the tour, Dress pressed a finger to an electric scanner, opening the door to a back room. Three men sat in a waiting room with duffel bags full of marijuana. In the next room, two Harborside employees were sorting through the deliveries and negotiating prices with people who could reasonably be called drug dealers.

Patriotic potheads love to point out that cannabis was grown at Jamestown, that George Washington might have used hashish, and that Thomas Jefferson wrote a draft of the Declaration of Independence on hemp-fiber paper. But recent history offers more compelling reasons that marijuana is a definitively American drug: since the 1930s, it has slotted neatly into the age-old debate over chemically induced pleasure versus chemically induced pain relief. Since the 1990s, it has been at the center of a conflict between states' rights and federal authority. As of this writing, marijuana is considered by advocates and opponents alike to be the most likely of all controlled substances to change the terms of U.S. drug policy.

Of course, the medical-marijuana movement is hardly unprecedented in our national history. During Prohibition, congressional hearings were held on "medical beer," a serious effort to get around the law. There has always been some legitimacy to the medical-use argument: alcohol and marijuana can both make people feel better. But there has always been some cynicism. In March 1921, under the scare-quoted headline "Brewers Jubilant Over 'Medical' Beer," the *New York Times* dryly noted that "one physician in Chicago wrote 7,000 prescriptions for liquor, none for less than a pint, in the course of a few weeks." Marijuana Policy Project (MPP) founder Rob Kampia has conceded that he originally backed medical marijuana as the first step toward what he calls "recreational marijuana." (He has also said that after meeting hundreds of doctors and patients, he's been persuaded that medical marijuana is a legitimate end in itself.)

A committed activist, Harborside's DeAngelo has been involved for years in efforts to legalize marijuana. Trying to put him and Dress at ease during my visit, I told them that I used to work for MPP and explained the organization's long-term goal of making medical marijuana legal across the country. It was a risky thing to do. I'd forgotten about the rift that exists between the different factions of the legalization movement, and I didn't know where the Harborside owners stood.

Kampia "has presented MPP as if they're a policy group, that they don't use drugs—Oh no, not us," NORML's Keith Stroup told me, typifying the disdain many in the movement hold for an organization that they see as arrogant, domineering, and too beholden to its primary benefactor, Progressive Insurance head Peter Lewis. "Rob is a whore, if you wanna know what I think," Stroup added. "I don't think he has any principles at all. But he's a talented whore. He sucks up well to rich people, so he's got his role. But he's routinely hated in the movement, not just at NORML."

The haters aren't waiting for progress in Washington—they've just gone ahead and done it. California-based Americans for Safe Access (ASA) and other grassroots groups rely on contributions from patients and pot clubs for funding and take a more movement-oriented approach. ASA, which claims to be "the largest national member-based organization of patients, medical professionals, scientists and concerned citizens promoting safe and legal access to cannabis for therapeutic use and research," has brought the California Highway Patrol to court over medical-marijuana confiscations and worked with local governments to develop regulations for pot dispensaries. "Well, I'm glad we don't have to wait for MPP," said DeAngelo, an ASA member. "We hope to get it done much sooner than that."

Indeed, the clubs have come a long way since the August day in 1996 when Dennis Peron heard boots pounding up the stairs of his Cannabis Buyers Club in San Francisco's Castro district and thought he was being robbed. His club had been openly selling marijuana to the ill—and, allegedly, the non-ill—since at least 1991. That year, San Francisco voters passed Proposition P, which made enforcement of laws against medical marijuana the city police's lowest priority. Within days of Peron's arrest—which was made with a deliberate lack of assistance from local authorities—four more clubs had opened.

"Repression isn't used to that reaction," suggested DeAngelo. "Repression is used to bringing down the hammer and having a ripple effect. Instead, all they did with Peron was cut off the head, and now the four managers needed somewhere to go. So they started their own clubs."

A few months after Peron's arrest, the voters of California legalized medical marijuana with Proposition 215. The people who had opened the state's first shops quickly found themselves overwhelmed by demand. "The first dispensaries were started by activists, really well-intentioned people who didn't have any business experience, who didn't have any capital, who didn't know how to manage or run a business, who often didn't really know that much about the cannabis business because they were activists, not dealers," said DeAngelo, who proudly keeps detailed accounting records at Harborside. "There were so many patients flocking to them. They found themselves, without even trying to, in the middle of these very lucrative businesses bringing in millions of dollars a year."

In a pattern that would repeat itself in cities across the state, a second wave of entrepreneurs entered the fray. In San Francisco, pot clubs quickly outnumbered McDonald's franchises. Their owners had the same motivation as those of the Golden Arches: profit. Out went the idealism that had helped to police a business illegal on the federal level and quasi-legal on the local level. Though medical marijuana wasn't prohibited anymore, it wasn't regulated or licensed, either, with no central authority controlling zoning, licensing, or consumer protection. And despite the state law, some aggressive law-enforcement officials—including the far-right state attorney general Dan Lungren, who'd ordered the raid against Peron's club—still sought to prosecute dispensaries, citing federal law as justification.

"[The second wave of pot clubs] was started by people, unfortunately, who were more interested in those millions of dollars than they were attracted to doing service for the community or moving the medical-cannabis movement forward," said DeAngelo. "So [their clubs] were opened quickly, often in inappropriate locations.

They weren't up to code. They were run by people that had shady backgrounds. And inevitably, problems started occurring. There were robberies, there were neighbors and nearby business that complained. Cars were double-parked. There were shootings. There were not good things happening."

In Oakland in the late nineties, as in San Francisco a few years earlier, federal raids served only to increase the number of cannabis clubs. If a club owner was jailed and his place shuttered, his former staffers often kept themselves employed by opening new clubs. Soon, downtown Oakland was being referred to as "Oaksterdam," host to at least eight pot clubs and a culture of pot smoking. Even some cafes and bars began to allow patrons to smoke on their premises.

Jeff Jones, a longtime medical-marijuana activist, opened a pot club right around the corner from Oakland City Hall—with the full knowledge of those who worked in the building. He was one of those who, like Peron, jumped out ahead of the pack without any legal protection from the state. He told me that he opened his shop in July 1996, five months before the election. City politicians, he says, had been generally supportive but were unsure of what to do next. In March of that year, the city council had set up a task force to study the medical-pot issue and passed a resolution endorsing Jones's club. "What do you want, another liquor store?" Jones said he would ask cops and council members whenever they got squeamish.

Local politicos were certain that Prop 215 would fail and that Jones would then have to close his shop. Indeed, some were actively lobbying against the legislation. Senator Dianne Feinstein, who as mayor of San Francisco had opposed the movement, said that the proposed law was "riddled with loopholes so big that it would have the effect of legalizing marijuana."

She was partly right, but 56 percent of the state didn't care. "They were blown away when we won," Jones said of city officials. "'What do we do now, Jeff?'" Oakland politicians had company in their surprise: eleven days after California passed Prop 215 and Arizona approved its own medical-cannabis law, Clinton drug czar Barry McCaffrey convened a high-level meeting to formulate a response. The opposition had been caught flat-footed. California and Arizona, he vowed, would be the last two states to legalize medical marijuana.

McCaffrey summoned two of the initiative's most vocal opponents, Orange County sheriff Brad Gates and California Narcotic Officers' Association spokesman Tom Gorman, to D.C. to plot how to thwart implementation of the law. (At this same meeting, the participants conjured up the antipot advertising campaign that led to accusations of federally sponsored payola.) McCaffrey announced that the federal government would work hard against doctors and patients involved with medical marijuana, going after the licenses of physicians who recommended it. Doctors sued, arguing that the penalty violated their First Amendment rights, and won a landmark victory.

Since then, medical-cannabis centers have spread across the state of California, and they now represent the single greatest threat to current pot-prohibition policies. In 2003, the California legislature attempted to codify the new industry with the passage of a bill designated—seriously—SB 420. If the clubs remain successful—and, as Harborside's self-image has it, "professional"—they could fundamentally alter America's cultural relationship with drugs. The backers of prohibition know this, and they've dug in against medical marijuana, making it a major target of the drug war.

In McCaffrey's defense, there was little that he could have done to beat Prop 215. The movement had been gaining strength in response to another phenomenon that the federal government had initially ignored: the AIDS epidemic. "Once AIDS came on the scene, [the movement] exploded. That's what put us over the top," said Mykey Barbitta, who runs the Compassion Care Center, a descendant of the Cannabis Buyers Club located at the same spot on Market Street as Peron's clinic. "The medical-cannabis movement was a response to a need—HIV," agreed Randi Webster, founder of the San Francisco Patients Care Collective, who lost more than thirty friends in the early years of the AIDS epidemic. "It started as a treatment for patients with extreme bone disease."

Long before the Reagan administration was taking AIDS seriously, people suffering and dying from it spread the word that marijuana could ease nausea and increase appetite, both crucial to living with the disease. Some early AIDS patients turned to a little-known

Food and Drug Administration pilot program that allowed those with legitimate medical need to get marijuana directly from the government. The program dated to 1976, when Washington, D.C., resident and glaucoma patient Robert Randall, using the medical-necessity argument, essentially forced the feds into growing pot on a farm in Mississippi. Today, a handful of surviving patients get a monthly canister containing three hundred prerolled joints.

The Compassionate Investigational New Drug program had very few initial participants. For one thing, marijuana was widely available, cheap, and of increasingly high quality. For another, the nation had a permissive attitude toward the drug, with even President Jimmy Carter calling for decriminalization. There was little incentive for a patient to apply, especially given a built-in disincentive: that your name would now be on a federal list associated with marijuana. That changed with HIV. As AIDS patients discovered pot's palliative effects, cancer patients took notice, too. In 1992, overwhelmed with applications, the feds closed the Investigational New Drug program to new members.

Two years before, the medical-marijuana movement had received a significant public-relations boost in the form of an elderly San Francisco General Hospital volunteer, Mary Jane Rathbun, who'd realized that marijuana eased the suffering of AIDS patients and allowed them to eat. Brownie Mary, as she became known, was arrested and charged with drug distribution for baking pot brownies and giving them to AIDS patients. Rathbun refused to take any plea bargain, demanding a jury trial and creating a media disaster for the district attorney. The charges were dropped, and Brownie Mary was free to help Peron open the Cannabis Buyers Club and advocate for Prop 215.

By the time that Prop 215 made the ballot, the medical-marijuana movement had some real money on its side. George Soros, an eccentric billionaire on a quest to spread freedom across the globe, had met Ethan Nadelman, a drug-policy wonk with an activist streak, in the early nineties. Soros offered to fund Nadelman's effort to reform drug policies and was soon bankrolling a large percentage of the Prop 215 campaign.

Soros's money made a difference, certainly, but without the grassroots movement behind it, the campaign couldn't have been won. By 1996, many Californians knew at least one cancer or AIDS patient who had benefited from using medical marijuana—either on the recommendation of a doctor or not. And if they didn't, they had probably heard of the charismatic septuagenarian who gave free brownies to the terminally ill. Recall that medical-cannabis clubs had opened in San Francisco even before they were legal by state standards, bolstered by the passing of 1991's citywide Proposition P, which urged that doctors "shall not be penalized for or restricted from prescribing hemp preparations for medical purposes."

Some local officials, including City Supervisor Harvey Milk and Mayor George Moscone, had openly supported medical cannabis as early as the seventies. Milk's support of Peron even while he was in prison on a separate pot charge enraged the right-wing minority trying to hold back the wave. (In fact, conservative supervisor Dan White was apoplectic about Milk's defense of a convicted criminal, and there's plenty of reason to believe that it contributed to his decision to walk into City Hall in 1978 and assassinate him and Moscone. Moscone's acting mayoral replacement, Feinstein, immediately reversed Moscone and Milk's pro-medical-marijuana policy.) As the clubs began opening post-1996 throughout the Bay Area, as well as in other parts of the state, most cities decided to work with them, and the few Southern California towns that battled the clubs generally lost in court.

But the Clinton administration and California attorney general Lungren, a McCaffrey ally then considered a possible GOP vice presidential candidate, had more political firepower than officials in the conservative rural counties that opposed medical pot. On August 4, 1996, agents carried out the raid on Peron's club in the Castro, seizing computers, 40 pounds of marijuana, and medical records. Lungren claimed that Peron had sold pot to an undercover agent for nonmedical reasons. According to Peron, the agent had claimed to be an AIDS patient intent on establishing a dispensary for other sufferers.

The attorney general's claim is noteworthy: Peron was selling to those other than medical patients. Prop 215 wouldn't be voted on for another few months, so at the time, it wasn't legal to sell pot to anyone. Public opinion, however, was such that Lungren knew that he couldn't take Peron down just for selling to patients.

That approach continues today at the federal level, with the Drug Enforcement Administration often claiming that the cannabis-club owners whom it busts had been selling to people other than patients. In 1998, the feds filed suit against and closed down Jones's club, arguing not only that the dispensary had violated the Controlled Substances Act, but also that medical cannabis had not been declared safe by the FDA, making its distribution doubly illegal. The Oakland City Council responded, somewhat desperately, by declaring the club a city agency. The case eventually made it to the Supreme Court, where, in *United States v. Oakland Cannabis Buyers Cooperative*, justices overturned the Ninth Circuit Court of Appeals and ruled that there's no medical-necessity defense in the war on drugs.

"It is clear from the text of the [Controlled Substances] Act that Congress has made a determination that marijuana has no medical benefits worthy of an exception," wrote Justice Clarence Thomas in the May 14, 2001, decision. "The statute expressly contemplates that many drugs 'have a useful and legitimate medical purpose and are necessary to maintain the health and general welfare of the American people,' but it includes no exception at all for any medical use of marijuana."

Having failed to strip the feds of the authority to raid medical-marijuana clubs, advocates have instead pleaded with them not to exercise it. It seems to be working. In the middle of my interview with Harborside's owners, DeAngelo, looking at his desktop computer, threw his hands up and shouted, "Yes!" Hillary Clinton, campaigning for president in New Hampshire, had just told a video-camera-wielding MPP employee that, if elected, she would end federal raids on pot clubs in California. That meant that all three leading Democratic candidates—including the ultimate winner, Barack Obama—had vowed as president to leave DeAngelo and Wedding Dress alone.

California is often derided as a place that is out of touch with the rest of America. "San Francisco" and "Hollywood" have become political epithets. For Californians, of course, it's the rest of the country that's out of touch. Each Supreme Court decision or thundering threat from the drug czar has only strengthened the state's position on medical marijuana. Public support for it grew even as the anarchic situation brought on by the second wave of cannabis clubs got out of hand. More than forty localities responded with moratoriums on the opening of new clubs, but reversing legalization was never seriously considered.

The California phenomenon is explained not by the state's divergence from the rest of the country, but rather by its essentially American nature. The state is pluralistic and assertive, populated by a mix of immigrants, transplants, and descendants of people who, not so long ago, picked up stakes and headed out west. California's oft-stereotyped liberalism has a deep libertarian streak, and the state has a vibrant right wing, too, with seven of its cities ranking among the nation's most conservative, according to a 2005 study by the Bay Area Center for Voting Research. In recent years, the state has repeatedly clashed with the White House, not only over medical cannabis, but also over pollution controls and the U.S. Navy's use of submarine-detecting sonar, which threatens California gray whales and other local marine mammals.

In such a place, it's apparently nothing to create a statewide system to tax, regulate, and license a billion-dollar industry that the federal government still equates with the Medellín cartel. Indeed, the Californian mix of liberal compassion and libertarian opposition to federal authority has been essential to nurturing the medical-marijuana movement.

It hasn't been one long, smooth ride, as the moratoriums demonstrate. In 2003, Oakland mayor Jerry Brown ordered an investigation of the city's cannabis clubs, hoping to clean them up before, as he had warned Jones, the feds did it for him. City Council president Ignacio De La Fuente went a step further, suggesting that Oakland needed only one medical-cannabis dispensary. The resulting regulation shut down all but a few of the shops and the whiff of pot smoke downtown subsided a bit. But the owners of the closed shops simply headed across the bridge to San Francisco, which was still a regulatory Wild West.

Soon enough, though, San Francisco was following Oakland's lead. In the spring of 2005, the city counted within its limits at least forty-three unregulated dispensaries, one of them in the same building as a center for drug and alcohol rehabilitation. Others were near schools, day-care centers, and other places that neighborhood folks justifiably tend to hold sacrosanct. In June of that year, the city council instituted a six-month moratorium that would allow it to write and review regulations covering the existing clinics. "The absence of laws has allowed adverse opportunities to emerge," Supervisor Ross Mirkarimi, who proposed the ban, said at the time.

The dispensaries were also becoming difficult for the cops to countenance. "It's a huge scam," said Captain Rick Bruce of the San Francisco police, telling the *New York Times* that dealers were hiding behind the law. "We see guys coming out of these places, and the only description I can come up with is that it looks like a Cheech and Chong movie. They are what you would call your traditional potheads; whether they have a medical condition beyond that is subject to debate."

As municipalities struggled with the details of the reality of medical marijuana, they also joined with activists in the fight against federal intervention. By 2004, another nine states had passed medical-cannabis laws, and the debate in California began to take the turn that the feds feared most. At the time, I was working with the Marijuana Policy Project as a staffer assigned to state-level policy. The organization teamed up with activists in Oakland to help organize and fund the campaign for Measure Z, on behalf of which I did marginal paper-pushing, drafting messages to MPP membership and coordinating with folks on the ground.

Measure Z sought to make enforcement of marijuana laws—all laws, not just those relating to medical marijuana—the lowest priority of local law enforcement. In that ambition, it followed in the path of legislation by several other localities that had done the same. It went a significant step further, however, by declaring that the "City of Oakland shall establish a system to license, tax and regulate cannabis for adult use as soon as possible under California law."

That objective didn't faze Representative Barbara Lee, who represented Oakland. In an op-ed supporting the measure, she adopted a quintessentially Californian stance, equating compassion for patients with resistance to the drug war:

At the state level, we have passed policies to ameliorate the federal drug war, including Proposition 215 in 1996, to allow medical marijuana, and Proposition 36 in 2000, to direct drug offenders to treatment rather than incarceration. Nevertheless, each year California still spends $150 million to arrest, prosecute and imprison marijuana offenders. The drug war has completely failed to control drug use. Since former President Richard Nixon began the drug war in the 1970s, drug use has continued, but imprisonment has soared.

Some people have asked, why Oakland? The answer is simple. Oakland has a population that has witnessed first-hand the harmful effects of the drug war. It has a serious crime problem that demands the undiluted focus of our law enforcement. It's a compassionate city that has strongly supported the rights of patients to have access to medical marijuana. And here in the Bay Area, voters have a distinguished history of leading the nation in progressive reforms. We deserve policies here in Oakland that reflect the values of our citizens, not those of Attorney General John Ashcroft. Measure Z is a good step in that direction. Vote yes.

Sixty-five percent of the city followed her advice.

By the time I got to MPP, the organization had more than twenty employees and a $6 million budget, about 80 percent of which came from Peter Lewis. MPP assiduously cultivated an image of professionalism to counter the stoner stereotype. "We're known for our accuracy," a coworker told me when I started. I would hear that mantra over and over again, although I always doubted that's what we were "known for."

MPP assisted with pushing through medical-marijuana laws in Vermont and Rhode Island, and it won a semi-victory in Maryland, where you now pay a maximum fine of one hundred dollars if you can convince a judge that your pot use was for medical purposes. It also helped win a statewide initiative to legalize medical marijuana in Montana. In 2008, it funded a successful drive in Massachusetts to make possession of less than an ounce of marijuana a hundred-dollar civil citation. The law, which passed with 65 percent of the vote, includes a clever and overlooked stipulation: cops making a small-scale pot bust can't ask to see ID. "You can tell us that you're Mickey Mouse of One Disneyland Way and we have to assume that's true," Wayne Sampson, executive director of the Massachusetts Chiefs of Police Association, griped to the *New York Times* after reading the fine print of the law with which voters had saddled him. "Not only do you not have to identify yourself, but it would appear from a strict reading that people can get a citation, walk away, never pay a fine and have no repercussion. . . . I would argue that the proponents knew these complications right from the beginning."

Legislation favorable to medical cannabis was achieved in twelve states by 2006, with Michigan making it thirteen in 2008. But despite such local successes, MPP and the rest of the medical-marijuana movement have made little progress at the federal level.

In the summer of 2005, the Supreme Court ruled in *Gonzales v. Raich* that state laws do not shield medical-marijuana growers or users from federal arrest and prosecution. A bloc of five liberal justices reasoned that in the case of medical marijuana, the Constitution's Commerce Clause gives the feds authority over the states. Notorious originalist Antonin Scalia joined them to make it six, but his fellow federalist Clarence Thomas stuck to his principles, even though he opposed the specific policy. "By holding that Congress may regulate activity that is neither interstate nor commerce under the Interstate Commerce Clause, the Court abandons any attempt to enforce the Constitution's limits on federal power," Thomas argued in his dissent.

Emotions seemed to have gotten the better of Scalia. During oral arguments, he flung himself back in his chair and nearly shouted, "There are some communes that grow marijuana for the medical use of all of the members of the communes!" His actions suggested that he had a moral objection to marijuana so powerful that it trumped his political beliefs, particularly the extension of federal power. "Scalia tends to be more interested in originalism when it fits into his Catholic social conservatism," George Mason University law professor David Bernstein suggested to me. "Or when he's using it to bludgeon the left."

"I was struck by Scalia's emotional reaction," Randy Barnett, who argued the case for plaintiffs Angel Raich and Diane Monson, told me. "I didn't know what he was talking about. Had I known he was talking about the cooperatives, I could have corrected him."

Sandra Day O'Connor, who dissented, argued that it is possible for states to allow medical marijuana without undercutting the cherished Commerce Clause, which has also been used to justify national environmental and civil rights laws. "The states' core police powers have always included authority to define criminal law and to protect the health, safety, and welfare of their citizens," she noted. Rather than accede that, however, the liberal justices took the rather dramatic step of suggesting that, if a federal law is at issue, then that law should be changed. Citing "respondents' strong arguments that they will suffer irreparable harm" if deprived of medical marijuana, the judges proposed that Congress might want to revise the Controlled Substances Act. "Perhaps even more important," wrote John Paul Stevens at the end of his opinion, "is the democratic process, in which the voices of voters allied with these respondents may one day be heard in the halls of Congress."

He was referring to the bipartisan Hinchey-Rohrabacher Amendment, which would ban the federal government from raiding medical-marijuana clinics or arresting users who live in states that have made medical pot legal. Every year since 2003, it had been voted down in Congress, falling some sixty or more votes short. The year 2005, it turned out, was no different. With the Supreme Court defeat, a lack of support on Capitol Hill, and repeated losses in Nevada, where MPP was trying to legalize what it called "recreational marijuana" for adults twenty-one and over, the "professional" wing of the medical-marijuana movement was reeling.

"At least some of us think that some of the initiatives [MPP has] launched have been ill-advised and not very well planned out, but that's more a question of competence than it is a question of differing views," said Harborside's DeAngelo. "What the poll numbers have always taught us is that you need to have about a five-percent advantage going into the initiative because you're going to lose numbers in the course of the campaign. You're not going to pick numbers up. They were five or six points down [in Nevada] and they still moved ahead." The initiative lost in 2002, with just 39 percent of the vote, and again in 2006, with 44 percent. In 2004, the campaign forgot to turn in a box of petitions and couldn't get the initiative onto the ballot, even after dumping $1 million into a legal challenge.

From the nation's capital, it looked as if the medical-marijuana movement had stalled out. Even on a local level, Washington lawmakers were hostile to the movement: In 1998, through an amendment to a District of Columbia funding bill spearheaded by Georgia Republican representative Bob Barr, Congress had blocked implementation of the district's own medical-cannabis referendum. The legislation went so far as to block counting and certification of the votes, which were later shown to be 69 percent in favor of the law. (Barr, later in his career, became a lobbyist for MPP.) "That's about when I decided that I'd been in D.C. about thirty years and I'd earned the right to come someplace where, if I went through the trouble of changing the law, that maybe it would stay changed," said DeAngelo, who helped lead the District effort. "That's what brought me to California."

The same week that I toured Harborside, in the summer of 2007, the federal government sent letters to the landlords of about 150 Los Angeles–area dispensaries. The list would eventually expand to more than 300. The letters politely informed the recipients that their tenants were operating illegal drug-manufacturing and -distribution centers, and that if they didn't boot the renters out, the feds would seize their property. Los Angeles shop owners, recalled Jeff Jones, were petrified, telling him, "'The sky is falling! I have no protection!' Well, what did you think? You never had any protection."

Jones guessed that blatant advertising in alt-weeklies and pot-focused newspapers and on the Internet brought the federal response. Oakland, he said, had been shrewder. "The city hated advertising," he said. "They were fearful of it. They said, 'It's gonna bring the feds out.' They don't want it."

Today, it's much easier to find a pot club in Los Angeles than it is in the Bay Area. In 2007, when there were close to five hundred L.A. clubs, I pushed open the door to one, prompting the tattooed owner to rush out from behind a Plexiglas wall: "Whoa, whoa! What are you doing?!" I told him I was a reporter covering the crackdown. Predictably, he consented to an interview only if I didn't identify him. "Some of these guys will sell to anybody. Kids, even," he said. "They're going after those kinds." He said that he, by contrast, checks all pot cards, doesn't sell to children, and provides only small amounts of marijuana to each customer. But ultimately, he conceded, he just prays.

Few, if any, medical-marijuana advocates saw the landlord move coming. Tactically, it was brilliant: Landlords, like most Californians, are generally sympathetic when it comes to medical marijuana. But how many are willing to lose property over it? Allison Margolin, a prominent Los Angeles pot lawyer—she calls herself "L.A.'s Dopest Attorney"—said that the landlord letters have led to a significant number of evictions and created a "culture of fear." "But there are still tons of clubs," she added. One club owner took his landlord to court to prevent the eviction and prevailed. His attorney hopes that if the feds now come after the club owner, he can argue that it was a selective prosecution and thus unconstitutional. "It's one of the better ideas I've heard," said Margolin. "I don't know if it'll work, but at least it's an idea."

In the meantime, pot clubs were becoming more and more legitimized in the Golden State. They're even becoming a significant source of above-board state revenue, which bodes well for not only such clubs' long-term survival locally, but also for their viability outside of California.

In the fall of 2006, California clarified to its cannabis dispensaries that they were, in fact, responsible for paying its 7.25 percent sales tax, and had been since 2005. (Depending on the jurisdiction, some clubs are also required to add on a bit for local and county taxes.) Some club owners, backed by ASA, had argued that, as quasi-pharmacies, their businesses were exempt, a line of reasoning dismissed by the state. Others, such as DeAngelo, initially opposed the tax but came to support it, arguing that the perennially underfunded state would get addicted to the tax dollars generated by its one thousand or so pot clubs—a number that will continue to climb absent any major federal intervention.

Harborside is charged an 8.75 percent tax. With revenue of around $1 million per month, its annual sales-tax bill comes in at something like $875,000 per year. And that's just one shop. Betty Yee, chairwoman of the State Board of Equalization, which oversees tax collection, told me that there's no way to break out exactly how much money the state is getting from pot clubs because it doesn't require them to state on their tax forms what product they sell. ("Regardless of legal status, anyone can get a seller's permit," she explained.) However, she did release the tax records of some clubs that had been raided by the federal government, noting that because they employed sizable numbers of people, they also paid state and federal income and payroll taxes. The Compassion Center, licensed by Alameda County, paid $3 million before being shuttered in October 2007 by the DEA. Nature's Medicinal, licensed by Kern County, paid close to $1 million in 2007, which included $203,000 in state and federal income taxes, $365,000 in payroll taxes, and $427,000 in sales taxes. The Compassion Center employed and provided health benefits to fifty people; Nature's Medicinal twenty-five. (The demise of the latter wasn't universally deplored by the medical-pot community, however: Its alleged affinity for high-powered weaponry didn't jibe with the pacifist vibe the industry espouses.)

It's estimated that between 150,000 and 350,000 Californians have medical-marijuana cards. (There's no comprehensive state list, for obvious reasons.) A 1999 study by Australian economists Kenneth W. Clements and Mert Daryal found that a daily marijuana smoker consumes on average 18.57 ounces of pot annually. They found once-a-week-or-more smokers toke 13 ounces; once-a-monthers inhale 1.7 ounces. (The emphasis must be on the "or-more" in the former case, otherwise those folks were puffing a quarter ounce per sitting.) Let's assume, then, that out of about 200,000 medical-pot smokers, half are daily users. That number yields nearly 2 million ounces of pot. At $400 an ounce, we're talking about nearly $800 million worth of weed. At the lowest sales tax rate, 7.25, that's nearly $60 million. If there are 50,000 occasional smokers, they'd kick in another $20 million. The monthly smokers are worth another $3 million, for a total of more than $80 million. And that's just sales tax. In the case of Nature's Medicinal, sales tax made up 42 percent of total taxes paid, suggesting that the California pot industry would pay total taxes of about $200 million per year. Even if that estimate is wildly overblown, the state is unlikely to give up easily revenue anywhere near that amount: a special notice sent to clubs by the Board of Equalization assured sellers they "may decline to provide information on products sold due to concerns about self-incrimination."

A November 2006 report by the City of Oakland's Measure Z Oversight Committee came up with similar figures. It estimated that Californians consume between $870 million and $2 billion in medical marijuana per year, generating sales-tax revenue between $70 million and $120 million. In 2004, when Oakland's clubs were thriving, it took in, according to city records, $2.3 million in taxes on more than $26 million in revenue. As the feds swept through, that dropped, in 2006, to just $477,000 in taxes on $5.5 million in revenue. Two million dollars pulled from an annual city budget of about $900 million isn't exactly spare change.

NORML and ASA estimate that medical users make up about 10 percent of California's pot smokers. But given the laundry list of conditions that qualify someone as a legit patient, it's safe to assume that we're looking at a serious growth industry here. If the system eventually encompassed all of California's pot smokers, the tax revenue would be in the range of $2 billion. As the movement evolves into an industry, the feds will find it increasingly difficult to roll it back.

The pro-pot folks found out just what power entrenched industries can wield in 2008. Drug-policy reformers campaigned on behalf of a ballot initiative that would reduce marijuana-possession charges to small infractions and divert other drug offenders into treatment instead of prison. It had the backing of the California Nurses Association, the California Society of Addiction Medicine, and the California Academy of Family Physicians. But it had stronger opponents. The California State Sheriff's Association, the California Narcotics Officers Association, the California Peace Officers Association, and the Police Chiefs of California all lined up against it. In 2007, the state declared its overcrowded prison system to be in a state of emergency. But one prison-industry group didn't quite see the urgency. California's prison guards union spent some $2 million fighting the proposition. It went down sixty to forty.

California's fiscal situation is becoming increasingly unstable, with towns, counties, and even the state teetering on the brink of bankruptcy. Maintaining the bursting prison system may be a luxury unaffordable in tough economic times. Extra tax revenue, too, is nice in good times. During bad times, it's an absolute necessity. And the nation is due for some bad times. "We're headed for the wall at lightning speed," former Treasury Secretary Paul O'Neill put it in December 2008, as the U.S. economy reeled. The movement to repeal Prohibition was given a major boost by the economic collapse of the late twenties and early thirties. Legalizing booze would create tax revenue and jobs, the argument went then. Today, as we head for the wall, opponents of the drug war make the same case, citing the billions in tax revenue and economic growth that could be generated by legalization.

The advent of the medical-marijuana industry is a crucial development in the medical-marijuana movement. But the industry's activist roots are what keep it from toppling under the weight of federal pressure. Marijuana might be good business, pro-cannabis do-gooders suggest, but it does actually help sick and dying people.

The San Francisco Patients Care Collective, founded in 1999, has a lineage stretching all the way back to Peron and Brownie Mary. It's an emphatically noncommercial venture, according to its owner, Randi Webster. "I want no mercantile terms associated with me. We don't 'buy' our supply; we 'get' it," she said, wearing a purple velvet dress, thick glasses, and a crown of pot leaves. "'Club' is like the N-word. We prefer 'facility.'"

A look around her facility confirmed that she's not profit-hungry: the clients all appeared to be in serious need of medical treatment with little ability to pay for it—no fakers here. The collective also serves as a community center. There's a small stage for open-mic night, and bingo night is also popular, said Webster. Peron's spot, which has gone through a series of names as it survived bust after bust, maintains an activist feel, too. It offers a free joint to patients with no money, free Internet access, and free video games on a flat-screen TV. A framed letter on the wall thanks the club for what it does for patients and the community. The writer thanks Peron for an offer of a tour, saying that she hopes to make it one day. Signed, Nancy Pelosi.

Pelosi wasn't yet the Speaker of the House when she penned that letter, but she wasn't the political equivalent of a nickel bag of stems and seeds, either. Pelosi's support of medical marijuana cost her nothing back at home, and it apparently hasn't cost her in Washington, either. Still, how to explain the movement's failure at the federal level?

A series of conversations I had with a number of state legislators—along with a Zogby International poll that MPP commissioned that year—explains some of it. Simply put, California succeeded in legalizing medical marijuana because it succeeded in legalizing medical marijuana. In 2004, I was sent to Salt Lake City for the National Conference of State Legislators as an MPP representative. Sitting behind the booth, my coworkers and I endured the typical jokes—"Got any samples?"; "You should be giving away brownies"— so we could have a chance to persuade lawmakers to introduce bills legalizing medical pot.

At a luncheon, I happened to be seated with legislators from Utah. With no thought that I might succeed, I laid out the arguments on behalf of medical marijuana to my meal companions. After some back and forth, each one of them ultimately told me that he would personally support medical marijuana, but he was dead certain that none of his colleagues would. Compare that attitude to the Zogby poll, which was taken in Vermont and Rhode Island and in the midst of ultimately successful legislative campaigns to pass medical marijuana bills. Seventy-one percent of Vermonters said that they backed medical marijuana. So did 69 percent of Rhode Islanders. No big surprise there; similar numbers have appeared in poll after poll across the country. But Zogby threw in an extra question: "Regardless of your own opinion, do you think the majority of people in [Vermont or Rhode Island] support making marijuana medically available, or do you think the majority opposes making marijuana medically available?"

In Vermont, only 38 percent of people thought a majority supported it—even though support was over 70 percent. Thirty-seven percent thought that a majority opposed medical marijuana, and a quarter said that they weren't sure. Rhode Islanders were also pretty sure that their fellow citizens were nowhere near as enlightened as they themselves were: Only a quarter said that a majority of their fellow citizens probably supported medical marijuana. A majority— 56 percent—said wrongly that there was no majority support, and 18 percent said that they weren't sure.

For medical-marijuana advocates, the message of those numbers couldn't be clearer: once Americans realize that they agree with themselves, then the debate is over.

To celebrate the tenth anniversary of Prop 215, MPP commissioned Mason-Dixon Polling & Research to survey all of the states that had by then enacted medical-marijuana laws. In each but one, support for the legislation had risen considerably since it initially passed. (The exception was Montana, where 62 percent of people voted for a medical-marijuana law in 2004; two years later, support was still at 62 percent.) In California, where cannabis clubs were popping up all over, 72 percent of respondents said that they supported the law, with 47 percent saying that they strongly supported it. That approval even cut across party lines, with 56 percent of Republicans saying that they agreed with the law, along with overwhelming numbers of Democrats and independents.

California, which had had its law in place the longest, saw the biggest jump in support. Other states averaged about a 10-point uptick since their legislation passed. "Real-world experience demystifies it," said MPP spokesman Bruce Mirken. "People see that, in fact, the world doesn't end, the state doesn't become awash in marijuana, their kids don't all turn into potheads. Life pretty much goes on."

The polling data and those conversations in Utah also explain why the first wave of states to legalize medical cannabis had to do so through the ballot box rather than through the legislature. Alone, with a secret ballot in hand, Americans have consistently voted yes to medical marijuana in dozens of elections. (The one exception is South Dakota, where a medical-marijuana law was voted down 52 percent to 48 percent in 2006.)

By about 2010, if the pace keeps up, more than half of the American population will live in states where it's legal to smoke pot for medical purposes—which in California means for the relief of not only glaucoma, AIDS, and cancer, but also of irritable bowel syndrome, insomnia, and that infinitely flexible catchall, "etc." Although some states originally limited medical marijuana to specific ailments, these have gradually expanded access under pressure from patients not covered by the law.

The federal government, it would seem, is up against the tide of public opinion. Nearly half of Americans polled now say that marijuana should be taxed and regulated much like alcohol. Solid majorities— from two-thirds to three-quarters—support medical marijuana. Liberals, especially the young ones who run the blogosphere, don't have the same fear of being called soft on crime that dogged their Clinton-era predecessors, and they have embraced drug-policy reform as a defining issue. Meanwhile, the religious right that helped elect George W. Bush to the presidency has become disillusioned with his administration's moral failings and once again begun to fade from politics. As it has done so, it has taken its calls for temperance legislation with it, leaving the libertarian wing of the Republican party ascendant. The feds' fear is that, if they lose ground now, they won't ever regain it. (Which, if they knew their history, they would know isn't true.)

With that in mind, Drug Czar Walters has routinely called out the medical-marijuana movement as a fraud, an attempt to legalize drugs using sick and dying people as a cover. He reiterated that take in a discussion that the White House posted online in December 2007:

> Funded by millions of dollars from those whose goal it is to legalize marijuana outright, marijuana lobbyists have been deployed to Capitol Hill and to States across the Nation to employ their favored tactic of using Americans' natural compassion for the sick to garner support for a far different agenda. These modern-day snake oil proponents cite testimonials— not science—that smoked marijuana helps patients suffering from AIDS, cancer, and other painful diseases "feel better." While smoking marijuana may allow patients to temporarily feel better, the medical community makes an important distinction between inebriation and the controlled delivery of pure pharmaceutical medication. If you want to learn more about this, we have information available that shows how medical marijuana laws increase drug-related crime and protect drug dealers.

Wedding Dress, of course, has a different way of describing what he's up to. "I still believe that our intention and what we're doing in the world is actually insulating us," he said, adding that Harborside's legit relationship with the city also helps. He offers Hope Net, a club that San Francisco police protected from the federal government, as a demonstration of the connection that a responsible pot clinic can forge with local officials. "That dispensary is still open and functioning," he said, "and no one was charged."

Not yet, at least. "I'm not as optimistic as my partner in terms of the federal threat," DeAngelo said. "The federal strategy is very difficult to read, and we don't know where they're going to hit next. Anybody who opens a dispensary has to be ready to go to federal prison."

CHAPTER 13

Cat and Mouse

I n June 2004, Fire Erowid surfed over to the *Chicago Tribune*'s
Web site, on a tip that it contained a reasonably balanced article
on the growing use of dextromethorphan (DXM), the main
ingredient in Robitussin. Americans had been getting themselves
high on DXM for decades, but the Internet had recently made the
pill form of the drug more readily available. With acid gone, "robot-
ripping" was becoming more popular, as kids swapped online
tales of out-of-body experiences and ever-increasing plateaus of
pleasure.

When Erowid typed "DXM" into the paper's search engine, it
returned three links that caught her eye. One was to a public service
announcement inveighing against the dangers of abusing the drug;
the other two were ads for places offering DXM in bulk. Erowid
was amused, given that her own drug-information site, Erowid.org,
has often been derided as encouraging psychoactive drug use, even
though it has never linked to sites that sell drugs. Of course, the
Tribune probably didn't have an intent to distribute. It was clearly
using some sort of programming code that connected searches to ads
with little regard for details of content or legality.

In the freewheeling world of the Internet, it's hard to censor
certain kinds of data while encouraging the rapid flow of others—
a phenomenon that has become frustratingly evident to the federal

government as it has brought the war on drugs online. The illegal drug trade has always adapted to interdiction, but on the Web, with its vast scale, its cloak of anonymity, and its disregard for international borders, adaptation is easier. Interdiction, naturally, is harder.

The DXM ads that Erowid stumbled across were hardly unprecedented. In the late nineties and the early years of this century, companies claiming to traffic in "research chemicals" operated with apparent impunity. They offered sample-sized packages in chat rooms and listed their wares against retina-searing psychedelic backgrounds—making it obvious exactly what type of research their products were intended to foster. Some sellers even described their goods as "psychoactive." Many companies had apparently convinced themselves that online, psychedelic-drug dealing had become a legal activity.

It's easy to see why. By the time LSD was banned, in 1966, a robust legal research industry had grown up around it. A few of the participants—the U.S. Army, the CIA—didn't immediately get out of the business, and some chemists began tweaking acid's and other drugs' molecular structures to create new substances that, though technically legal, still blew your mind. The psychedelic MDA was placed into Schedule I in 1970, but a similar compound, MDMA, now known as Ecstasy, was legal until the mid-eighties. There was nothing the government could do to stop chemists from producing such "designer drugs" other than racing to ban one substance after another.

Some of the new drugs, or analogs, had turned out to be more dangerous than acid, which has no known fatal dose. In the early eighties, a botched attempt to synthesize an analog of the opioid analgesic Demerol led to permanent Parkinsonianism in several users in California. Around the same time, analogs of the surgical anesthetic fentanyl began to cause what would eventually be more than one thousand deaths nationwide. In 1986, Congress responded with the Analogue Act, which says that a drug is illegal if it "represents or intends to have a stimulant, depressant, or hallucinogenic effect on the central nervous system that is substantially similar to or greater than the stimulant, depressant, or hallucinogenic effect on the central nervous system of a controlled substance in schedule I or II."

The law applies only to substances marketed for human consumption, not those that are used for research into what might be the next great painkiller—a qualification that online retailers were quick to exploit. Despite their often blatant hints about potential uses for their products, Web merchants shielded themselves with the research-chemical designation. In 2002, the Drug Enforcement Administration launched Operation Web Tryp, cheekily named in honor of tryptamine, a key component of many research chemicals, and targeted at folks selling drugs online. The boot came down in earnest in July 2004, when the DEA arrested ten people who ran five Web sites with names like DuncanLabProducts.com and OmegaFineChemicals.com.

DEA chief Karen Tandy hailed the takedown. "The formulation of analogues is like a drug dealer's magic trick meant to fool law enforcement. They didn't fool us and we must educate our children so they are not fooled either," she said, claiming that the busted companies were responsible for two overdose deaths and that one firm had been pulling in $20,000 a week. "Today's action will help prevent future deaths and overdoses, and will serve as notice for those dealing in designer drugs and the illegal use of the Internet."

Interdiction might have decreased access for less-committed users, but it also strengthened the core market, creating savvier salespeople and more discreet customers. The government has little chance of winning such a cat-and-mouse game. The long-standing overlap between techie culture and druggie culture means that the feds are a decade behind the users and losing virtual ground every day. Fire Erowid, for instance, was swapping information on drug use online with her peers back before DEA agents even knew how to use e-mail.

Erowid.org, cofounded by Fire with her partner, Earth Erowid, has opened up the vast store of knowledge that had been kicking around for years in the underground and run it through a rigorous fact-checking process. The site's more than 50,000 pages contain information on just about any substance that can even slightly alter the human mind. By drawing on the collective knowledge of Erowid.org's many remote and devoted users, Fire and Earth have compiled one of the world's most exhaustive and accurate collections of information on recreational drugs and their use.

The pair have done this on a shoestring budget, without paid advertising or, more surprisingly, righteous rage at drug prohibition. "Erowid does not take a stance on drug policy," Earth told me. Erowid—whose name, according to Fire, was assembled from Proto-Indo-European roots that together mean "Earth wisdom" or "knowledge of existence"—accepts that prohibition exists and that drugs also exist—and will always exist. It seeks to operate within reality while charting a course out of it.

The site doesn't sell drugs or even point potential buyers in the right direction, yet drugs are fetishized in its pages. A membership donation lands such thank-you gifts as a T-shirt reading, "So Many Schedules, So Little Time" or a silver drug-molecule pendant. Highs are described with a detail and ardor more often found in wine reviews. "[M]uch like mescaline but less sparkly," reads a write-up of 2C-T-7, aka Blue Mystic. "Lots of movement and aliveness—velvety appearance and increased depth perception." The site has even adopted a rating system: a 1 is an undistinguished trip with mild hallucinations, a 4 "a rare and precious transcendental state." The scale also allows negative numbers, representing experiences you'd rather not have.

In the Erowid entry for 2C-T-7, for example, under "Description," the site tells you simply that the drug "is a synthetic psychedelic known for its colorful visuals. It experienced a surge in popularity, due to Internet sales, during 1999–2001 before being made illegal in the U.S." Under "Effects," you can learn more—a dose's duration, whether taken orally (five to ten hours) or insufflated (three to seven hours), as well as the drug's onset period (sixty to ninety minutes orally, but only five to fifteen minutes up the nose), its plateau, and its aftereffects. Below that chart is a list of specific effects, organized into positive, neutral, and negative categories. "[I]ncreased appreciation of music" and "sense of inner peace" make it into the positive list. "[G]eneral change in consciousness (as with most psychoactives)" and "change in perception of time" are included in the neutral category. Under negative, you'll find "nausea and vomiting," "delirium (at higher doses) (potentially dangerous)," and "death."

You'll also find the basics of Blue Mystic's molecular structure, its threshold dose, instructions on drug production, and almost anything else you can think of. By following a link, readers can learn how to cook up Blue Mystic themselves, an elaborate process that begins with placing 3.4 grams of potassium hydroxide in 50 milliliters of hot methanol and ends many steps later with "spectacular white crystals." Similar information exists for nearly 100 other chemicals, 75 plants, 40 herbs, 60 pharmaceutical drugs, and 25 "smart drugs." In a separate section are 202 Blue Mystic testimonials with titles ranging from "The Best Thing EVER" to "Oh My God, We've Really Fucked Up," along with three detailed stories of "2C-T-7 Related Deaths."

A guy who calls himself Mitra and puts his body weight at 175 pounds wrote a 2001 post about combining Ecstasy and 2C-T-7 that is titled "Aliens Reprogrammed My Brain." It is typical, if any of them can be. Two and a half hours after taking a "very strong" MDMA pill, his

> roll is tapering off and I feel very grumpy that I do not have another pill or any acid to bring me back up. I find I usually don't get the most interesting part of the roll until I bump. I remember that I have some 2CT7 in the closet. I had previously done a small quantity of it and had not been very impressed. Then some of friends did some of my 2CT7 and they all puked and complained so I had never tried it again. Temporarily forgetting about the negative parts of my friends experiences, I went to the closet and retrieved a premeasured 20–25 mg (not exactly sure) bundle. I snort roughly half of it (~10 mg).

Mitra goes on to describe a trip filled with greater hallucinations than he has ever experienced before, and the reader gets the idea that he has had some pretty great ones. His night over, he assumes, he goes to bed at around seven the next morning.

> [T]his is when the interesting part starts. I am getting some neat very brightly colored closed eye visuals and then something organizes them into some alien combination lock. I realize that it is the password protection machanism too [sic] my mind and something is trying to hack the code.

Said something is very good at this and the pieces start falling into place. As each piece falls into place, I feel something shift and open in my mind and a coresponding [*sic*]physical shift and opening in my body. When something finishes dialing in the correct combination, everything unlocks and opens up like some sort of puzzle box and I am in hyperspace. . . . I reach back to another place that I remember used to exist and I run a command there called "open the eyes" this works and I snap back into my body and open my eyes.

Such an overabundance of drug information may fairly be called the product of a "Just say no" upbringing. Childhood friends, Fire and Earth both graduated from high school in 1987 and wound up at the famously liberal New College of Florida. The school was at the forefront of the national upswing in Ecstasy and acid use, but the Erowids "kept to the sidelines," recalled Fire. "The combination of anti-drug scare stories and a lack of solid, accessible information made it difficult to come to any sort of rational conclusion about these substances." Earth remembers it the same way. "I couldn't find anything useful. Everything was one extreme or the other," he told me.

So the Erowids set out to collect as much reliable information on psychedelic drugs as they could. At the start, they did so mainly for themselves. Over the next few years, their collected knowledge "pil[ed] up in unorganized electronic stacks in the form of scattered e-mails, URLs, books, and journal references," Fire recalled. When the pair moved to the Midwest after graduation and Fire took up Web programming as a hobby, the data made for good material to play around with.

In late 1994, the Erowids moved to San Francisco, where psychedelic drugs and the Internet were both exploding. The couple soon joined a group known as the Rhythm Society, which celebrated the spirituality of dancing all night, sometimes aided by psychedelics. The group was a presence on the burgeoning rave scene, where it tried to press turntablism and tab-taking into the service of, as its mission statement puts it, "balanc[ing] our individual desires with the goal of harmony among ourselves, our neighbors, and the world."

Such visionary aspirations were in the air. The year before, as Fire put it, the Web had been "navigable largely through hierophantic ASCII interfaces that only a computer geek could love." In San Francisco, they found that text-only sites were fading out, opening up greater possibilities for creative networking. A site called the Hyperreal Drug Archives was then the most popular online resource for psychonautical investigations, but Fire and Earth wanted to do something different with their data collection: provide an objective, accurate, and highly specific catalog of drug information, not an overview of psychedelic culture as a whole.

In early 1995, Fire came up with the name Erowid, and the site went live. Four years later, Erowid moved onto Hyperreal's servers and incorporated the earlier site's information into its own archive. In 2007, it won the right to call itself a 501(c)3 organization. Fire and Earth are careful to keep their personal politics away from the site, but their mission statement does betray their idealism: "Truth, accuracy, and integrity in publishing information about psychoactives will lead to healthier and more balanced choices, behavior, and policies around all psychoactive medications, entheogens, herbs, and recreational drugs."

Until then, the site provides a warning that any drug warrior would approve of: "It is not recommended that any of the activities described actually be carried out. These files are provided FOR EDUCATION and INFORMATION ONLY." At Burning Man in 1996, the couple watched a friend take way too much GHB by confusing the dosage between two sources, so that he "consumed from one (more potent) source but dosed according to the correct dosage for the second (less potent) source," said Fire. After watching their friend go into convulsions, they began putting more and more cautionary information online.

Today, those assembling at Erowid.org include everyone from casual users to medical professionals. Traffic has grown steadily and now hovers at around 1.5 million unique visitors a month, with somewhat lower numbers when colleges are on break. (To put that in perspective, the *New York Times* Web site averages between 10 and 20 million unique visitors a month.)

Use of the site is "very widespread" among her peers, said Kristen Kent, a toxicologist at the University of Massachusetts Memorial

Medical Center. "I haven't found any errors. If I did, I'd just write them and tell them." For medical professionals, the site has lifesaving potential. "I haven't been a teenager for a number of years," said Kent, by way of explaining that Erowid is most useful when somebody comes into the ER under the influence of a drug she hasn't heard of. The Erowids were even invited to speak at a national toxicology conference in 2006. According to Kent, they "were very well received."

Schedule I—drugs that the DEA considers to be the most dangerous and have the least medical value—is something of a tribute to Alexander Shulgin. A former Dow Chemical Company chemist, Shulgin, now in his eighties, is a legend in the psychedelic world, having synthesized MDMA in the fifties after stumbling across a discarded recipe. He went on to invent the overwhelming majority of Schedule I drugs, making him the godfather of all research chemicals. At Erowid.org, he and his wife and collaborator, Ann Shulgin, each have a "vault," a collection of resources that includes a brief biography, interviews, and audio transcriptions. One of the site's membership gifts is a signed set of photographs of Shulgin's lab, a shed behind his Lafayette, California, home. The donation required to get one currently starts at $750.

Shulgin's work doesn't exactly fly in the face of the law, but it does test it. As long as he can show that he's engaged in legitimate research—say, looking for the next Paxil—it is legal for him to create chemical compounds that have never before existed. It's also legal for him to test the drug on himself or on others, assuming consent. If he "accidentally" creates a drug that is mind-altering instead of mood-altering—the litmus test of legality in the United States—he records the recipe online and moves on. Often, the DEA will then classify the new compound as illegal.

Shulgin first collected his research in 1991 in the book *Phenethylamines I Have Known and Loved: A Chemical Love Story*, coauthored with Ann and known as PiHKAL. Shortly thereafter, his cooperative relationship with the DEA—he had a license to work with Schedule I drugs and in exchange gave expert testimony for the feds in court—came to an end. The DEA raided his lab, discovered record-keeping irregularities, and revoked his license. Shulgin was undeterred, and in 1997, he and Ann self-published *Tryptamines I Have Known and Loved: The Continuation*, or TiHKAL. The two books combined are nearly two thousand pages long and include detailed recipes for the production of hundreds of drugs. PiHKAL has sold more than fifty thousand copies and TiHKAL is in its second printing, with well over twenty thousand copies in circulation, says Shulgin. They've both been translated into Spanish and Russian, and both are available in online versions through Erowid.

PiHKAL and TiHKAL don't stop at recipes. They also suggest some of the nearly limitless variations that could be made to each compound to slightly alter the experience it induces, and they include a personal account of drug experimentation. In the entry for 5-methoxy-diisopropyltryptamine, aka Foxy, Shulgin writes that while he was taking the drug, everything "was shaded with eroticism. Sex was explosive. . . . Colors on the edges of the wiggles of the eye, a sort of Jessie Allen running design with color contrasts and sparkle. . . . This is a definite sense-distorter. I am not completely sure I like it." In his summary, he concluded that the altered state that he and his coexperimenters entered "was one that they simply couldn't use. They couldn't make intuitive leaps. They were wasting their time."

As long as a chemist can demonstrate that he isn't trying to make something illegal, the discovery process isn't covered by the Analogue Act. Indeed, some designer drugs were first synthesized with a more conventional purpose in mind—say, mood stabilizers made by pharmaceutical companies. The potent psychedelic AMT— 5-methoxy-α-methyltryptamine—is one such substance, developed as an antidepressant in the sixties and banned for its hallucinogenic effects in 2004. AET, or α-ethyltryptamine, is another vintage creation, first sold by Upjohn as an antidepressant in 1961. It was soon shelved owing to concerns that it might cause severe white-blood-cell reduction, but a couple of decades later, street dealers became aware of another, more marketable effect: a convincing simulation of an Ecstasy high. Thirty-two years later, AET was placed on Schedule I.

Until Shulgin tries one of his chemicals, he argues, he can't be sure whether it's psychedelic. That strategy creates risks beyond mere criminality. "There's nothing but danger in taking a large dose the first time. You're asking for trouble," he told me, describing a drug trial that didn't go well. "The question attached to a new chemical that's never been tried is, How much do you take? I start at the microgram level and move up. When I got to 1.5 micrograms, I found myself running out the back door and vomiting. So I backed off and tried again a few days later with 1.5 micrograms. I vomited again. It was toxic. It may have been amazing and hypnotic at 10 micrograms, but I was never going to get there. I abandoned that line of synthetic exploration."

For Shulgin, exploration is something of an end unto itself. "I don't feel responsible for having created something that some people find interesting and some find useful and others find awful," he said. "I compare it to painting."

It's not surprising that the Web-savvy and the drug-savvy have come together at Erowid. Psychedelic drugs have influenced some of America's foremost computer scientists. The history of this connection is well documented in a number of books, the best probably being *What the Dormouse Said: How the 60s Counterculture Shaped the Personal Computer*, by *New York Times* technology reporter John Markoff.

Psychedelic drugs, Markoff argues, pushed the computer and Internet revolutions forward by showing folks that reality can be profoundly altered through unconventional, highly intuitive thinking. Douglas Engelbart is one example of a psychonaut who did just that: he helped invent the mouse. Apple's Steve Jobs has said that Microsoft's Bill Gates would "be a broader guy if he had dropped acid once." (In a 1994 interview with *Playboy*, however, Gates coyly didn't deny having dosed as a young man.) Markoff writes that Jobs told him that his own LSD experience was "one of the two or three most important things he has done in his life."

After LSD inventor Albert Hofmann died, in early 2008, Multidisciplinary Association for Psychedelic Studies founder Rick Doblin gave me a letter that Hofmann had written to Jobs suggesting that if acid had been so important to him, he ought to consider donating money to psychedelic research. The previously undisclosed letter led to a thirty-minute phone conversation between Jobs and Doblin but no contribution. "He was still thinking, 'Let's put it in the water supply and turn everybody on,'" recalled a disappointed Doblin.

Thinking differently—or thinking different, as one Apple slogan had it—is a hallmark of the acid experience. "When I'm on LSD and hearing something that's pure rhythm, it takes me to another world and into another brain state where I've stopped thinking and started knowing," Kevin Herbert told *Wired* magazine at a symposium commemorating Hofmann's one hundredth birthday. Herbert, an early employee of Cisco Systems who successfully banned drug testing of technologists at the company, reportedly "solved his toughest technical problems while tripping to drum solos by the Grateful Dead." "It must be changing something about the internal communication in my brain," said Herbert. "Whatever my inner process is that lets me solve problems, it works differently, or maybe different parts of my brain are used."

Burning Man, founded in 1986 by San Francisco techies, has always been an attempt to make a large number of people use different parts of their brains toward some nonspecific but ostensibly enlightening and communally beneficial end. The event was quickly moved to the desert of Nevada as it became too big for the city. Today, it's more likely to be attended by a software engineer than a dropped-out hippie. Larry Page and Sergey Brin, the founders of Google, are longtime Burners, and the influence of San Francisco and Seattle tech culture is everywhere in the camps and exhibits built for the eight-day festival. Its Web site suggests, in fluent acidese, that "[t]rying to explain what Burning Man is to someone who has never been to the event is a bit like trying to explain what a particular color looks like to someone who is blind."

At the 2007 event, I set up my tent at Camp Shift—as in "Shift your consciousness"—next to four RVs rented by Alexander and Ann Shulgin and their septua- and octogenarian friends from northern California. The honored elders, the spiritual mothers and fathers of Burning Man, they spent the nights sitting on plastic chairs and giggling until sunrise. Near us, a guy I knew from the Eastern Shore— an elected county official, actually—had set up a nine-and-half-hole miniature golf course. Why nine and a half? "Because it's Burning

Man," he explained. Our camp featured lectures on psychedelics and a "ride" called "Dance, Dance, Immolation." Players would don a flame-retardant suit and try to dance to the flashing lights. Make a mistake, and you would be engulfed in flames. The first entry on the FAQ sign read, "Is this safe? A: Probably not."

John Gilmore was the fifth employee at Sun Microsystems and registered the domain name Toad.com in 1987. A Burner and well-known psychonaut, he's certainly one of the mind-blown rich. Today a civil-liberties activist, he's perhaps best known for Gilmore's Law, his observation that "[t]he Net interprets censorship as damage and routes around it." He told me that most of his colleagues in the sixties and seventies used psychedelic drugs. "What psychedelics taught me is that life is not rational. IBM was a very rational company," he said, explaining why the corporate behemoth was overtaken by upstarts such as Apple. Mark Pesce, the coinventor of virtual reality's coding language, VRML, and a dedicated Burner, agreed that there's some relationship between chemical mind expansion and advances in computer technology: "To a man and a woman, the people behind [virtual reality] were acidheads," he said.

Gilmore doubts, however, that a strict cause-and-effect relation-ship between drugs and the Internet can be proved. The type of person who's inspired by the possibility of creating new ways of stor-ing and sharing knowledge, he said, is often the same kind interested in consciousness exploration. At a basic level, both endeavors are a search for something outside of everyday reality—but so are many creative and spiritual undertakings, many of them strictly drug-free. But it's true, Gilmore noted, that people do come to conclusions and experience revelations while tripping. Perhaps some of those revela-tions have turned up in programming code.

And perhaps in other scientific areas, too. According to Gilmore, the maverick surfer/chemist Kary Mullis, a well-known LSD enthu-siast, told him that acid helped him develop the polymerase chain reaction, a crucial breakthrough for biochemistry. The advance won him the Nobel Prize in 1993. And according to reporter Alun Reese, Francis Crick, who discovered DNA along with James Watson, told friends that he first saw the double-helix structure while tripping on LSD.

It's no secret that Crick took acid; he also publicly advocated the legalization of marijuana. Reese, who reported the story for a British wire service after Crick's death, said that when he spoke with Crick about what he'd heard from the scientist's friends, he "listened with rapt, amused attention" and "gave no intimation of surprise. When I had finished, he said, 'Print a word of it and I'll sue.'"

Spending time with Alexander and Ann Shulgin, you get the sense that the federal government would have a hard time finding a jury to convict him. With bushy silver hair and a long beard, he exudes softness and kindness. His wife, meanwhile, is everyone's perfect grandmother—sassy, warm, and proud. Both possess an earthy sense of humor. "When Sasha feels like he's being worshiped too much, he'll fart," joked Ann, a therapist who's researched the therapeutic potential of MDMA and other drugs.

The Shulgins have become media darlings, granting interviews to all who call and quickly winning over reporters. Exhibit A is a 2005 *New York Times* magazine cover story, "Dr. Ecstasy," a deeply sympathetic portrait published at a time when the prevailing national attitude had soured on MDMA. Although Shulgin has been raided twice, neither time led to jail. The incidents were serious enough, however, that he now hangs a sign on his shed informing any visiting agents that his work is within the law.

"As far as the illegality, that's the DEA's concern," he told me. "I can say I'm making antihistamines or antidepressants. If it's psychedelic, I'll publish it and get rid of it." There's no evidence that Shulgin has profited from his inventions, other than his having been rewarded with speaking gigs all over the world. But his published recipes have allowed the growth of a vast gray market in which others are definitely making some money.

There seems to be no shortage of chemists following Shulgin's lead. He said that in early 2007 he was asked by a colleague to share his working notes on a drug far down the line in the T family, a sulfur-based group of chemicals that gives the user a feeling somewhere between those induced by Ecstasy and mescaline. ("T7 is my favorite of the T family," Shulgin noted.) Shulgin sent him his working recipe, and the chemist, without asking his permission, posted it online. The chemist had a change of heart and pulled the recipe down a week later, apologizing to Shulgin for the breach of trust. But the chemical cat was out of the bag. Within three weeks, a Chinese chemist had duplicated Shulgin's substance, reposted the results, and made the new drug available for distribution.

Shulgin continues to allow his detailed drug recipes and reflections to be posted on Erowid.org. He has also acted as an in-house consultant for those who might be conducting their own chemical research. Want to know why a certain compound turned brown while separating at 50 degrees Fahrenheit? Until recently, users could just click through to a link that asked Shulgin directly. With the chemist now on sabbatical and that link inactive, the social-networking possibilities of Erowid have been pretty much exhausted.

Earth said that the primary reason to keep the site free of socializing is to protect readers. He doesn't want Erowid to be used by law enforcement to entrap those who are looking for accurate information about drugs. Another reason he doesn't allow users to post directly to the site is the supreme importance of providing accurate information. A mix-up of grams and milligrams, for instance, could turn an experience into something very unpleasant, if not fatal. Information submitted by hundreds of users is fact-checked by dozens of volunteers, all of whom have been trained and approved by the Erowids. The info is then rechecked and, finally, posted.

Thus visitors to Erowid.org are confronted by one Seattle contributor's thoroughly vetted "Dangerous Overdose" entry on Shulgin's Blue Mystic: "At about 4 am I came to my senses. I was standing in front of some bank doorway, without my jacket and sweatshirt, wearing only a t-shirt in 30 degree weather[,] a quarter-sized abrasion on my left eyebrow and blood down to my chin. Right knee badly scraped and sore, bump on the back of my head with some scabbing, abrasion on left shoulder. My wallet was gone."

The site also recounts the story of seventeen-year-old Joshua Robbins, who, Memphis, Tennessee, media reported in 2001, died as a result of taking Ecstasy. Erowid investigated and posted an account pieced together from the recollections of various witnesses, including one who had driven Robbins to the hospital. According to the Erowid version, he had indeed taken Ecstasy, but the substance that probably killed him was 2C-T-7. "He spent the last minutes of his life screaming at the top of his lungs, 'I dont want to die! this is stupid!' and I have a feeling that he was still violent when the people put him into my car and said that he had 'calmed down,'" one of Robbins's friends recalled. The post concludes with a note signed by the Erowids: "Recreational use of research chemicals can kill."

A similar warning from the DEA or the White House would be laughed off. Coming from Erowid.org, it sends shivers through the psychedelic community. The Erowids have even earned the grudging respect of the National Institute on Drug Abuse (NIDA), which in 2002 invited them to address a conference the organization hosted.

I asked NIDA several times about the invite and was repeatedly told that it wouldn't comment on an outside drug resource. Eventually, though, a NIDA spokeswoman, Dorie Hightower, said that Fire and Earth were invited to speak because Erowid is regularly mentioned in meetings on drug use and abuse.

Nevertheless, other arms of the government deem Erowid a threat. In 2004, after Earth wrote the DEA to correct inaccuracies on the agency's Web site, he received this note in reply: "With all due respect, you will appreciate that it is highly inappropriate for us to establish any sort of dialogue. We are on opposite sides of a very high fence. Please do not contact me again. Thank you."

As a result of the Internet's ability to bring together large groups of like-minded people, it's becoming increasingly difficult for a single actor—say, the state—to crush any given activity, even one that hovers at the edge of legality. "The balance of power has shifted decisively into the hands of the networked public," said VRML coder Mark Pesce. His upcoming book, *The Human Network*, will describe the ways in which centralized power fails to oppose decentralized, networked power. One chapter, he told me, will explain Gilmore's Law, the tendency of the Internet to defy efforts to censor it.

The feds, in announcing the Operation Web Tryp bust, indicated that it wasn't their Web sleuthing that led to the bust, but dumb luck. They had infiltrated a "rave-style party" at Hampton Roads

Naval Base in Virginia, and the sailors confessed they'd gotten their exotic drugs online. "This is the beginning of this operation, it's not the end," promised Ed Childress, a special agent for the DEA, to the *Mohave Daily News*. "There's more to come."

There wasn't. Five years later, that five-company sting remains the biggest research-chemical takedown in cyberhistory. Demand for research chemicals has always been small relative to that for other drugs, but producers and consumers are still out there. They've simply moved into less conspicuous corners. Adventurous psycho-nauts now have to work harder—especially to avoid online scams.

Today, offshore dealers use small closed networks, advertise qui-etly, and make sure to disguise their identities and locations. One psychonaut I know who's used such a network—which depends on the tight-lipped loyalty of its patrons to avoid detection—told me that product quality is assured by the necessarily close community of users. Some private sites even allow for customer ratings and reviews, he said.

When word of the Web Tryp bust broke, I e-mailed another designer-drug connoisseur with the news and got an immediate response: "Noooooooooooooo!!!!" I e-mailed him nearly five years later to ask if he was still buying research chemicals online. He was skeptical of the closed networks my other source described, and suggested that many might not be all that professionally run. It "sounds like the old days," he wrote. "I know i would never order anything now. . . . I prefer to have my weird research chemicals come with COA's (Certificates of Analysis). I could get those before—I don't think your local underground psychedelics men are going to provide 3rd party verification on what they are selling you."

He's not despairing, though. Instead, he takes the long view. "I'd say the days of getting your hands on things that will not be good street drugs but may have other interesting effects is down for the count for this round," he said. "But this is a battle as old as history itself, and just like the modern revival of shamanism and alchemy the day will come again when we win back these tools."

In the meantime, he doesn't need any LSD substitutes. The real thing is back.

CHAPTER 14

Acid Redux

T he guy in the Cat-in-the-Hat headgear was shirtless, with
his shorts around his ankles and his arms out wide, getting a blow job on a pedestal fifteen feet in the air. It was
a moment before I realized what I was seeing, and I quickly looked
away. After all, there was plenty else to see.

It was the middle of the night in Black Rock City, Nevada, the site
of the annual Burning Man get-together, and the playa—the festival's town square of sorts—was filled with tens of thousands of mostly
young, successful, and attractive white folks, the majority of them
from San Francisco and parts north. The playa sparkled with Day-
Glo colors adorning bodies and bicycles and "art cars." Some of the
last were Mack trucks converted into roving double-decker raves,
complete with bars and DJs. It was a spectacle of consumption,
hedonism, and philanthropy that was as multifaceted and American a
phenomenon as you could imagine, but I was there with just one real
purpose: looking, again, for LSD.

When acid disappeared earlier in the decade, its near total
absence at Burning Man was the example given by heads to demonstrate the profundity of the loss. "There was no acid at Burning Man!"
said astonished longtime Burner Mark Pesce when I asked him about
the drought a couple of years before.

When I first wrote about acid's disappearance, in 2004, I relied on
published data, some cultural musing, and a lot of personal observation

in the form of interviews with dozens of people who ought to know whatever there was to know about LSD. At the end of that story, I cautioned that despite what appeared to be a fairly complete vanishing of the drug, you should never bet against a comeback. By the time I got to Burning Man four years later, cultural musing and personal observation had convinced me that acid was on its way back, though I had no data to back that speculation up.

It made sense, however, given one of the long-standing facts of the drug trade: no matter how major a producer a government takes down, it can't totally rid the world of the two things needed to keep producing and distributing a drug: the will and the way. By taking out Leonard Pickard, the feds may have struck a blow against the way, but surveys and the scene on the playa showed that the will to trip was still very much alive. And where there's a will, well, there's a way.

Drug producers and distributors have always found ways to adapt to interdiction and other pressures against their products. When U.S. meth makers saw the bottom of the boot in the 1970s, Mexicans stepped in to keep the nation tweaking. When the feds brought the dragnet down to Miami and the Caribbean in the 1980s, the cocaine trade similarly moved elsewhere. When U.S. forces pushed hard against Afghan poppy-growers, farmers switched to marijuana. Users, too, know how to adapt. When religious figures turned public opinion against alcohol in the nineteenth century, Americans discovered their love of opium. When LSD fell off the map in the twenty-first century, acidheads turned to substitutes such as research chemicals, ayahuasca, and salvia. One of the few sustained declines of a drug's use in America in which there's been no obvious substitution strategy at work involves something perfectly legal: tobacco. Following aggressive efforts to card kids who try to buy tobacco products and to educate adults about the health hazards of smoking, cigarette use has plummeted—and without a single seller or user being dragged off to prison.

But that's in the legal market. In the illegal market, of course, someone's going to get arrested. That threat helps keep the interrelationships of drug makers, distributors, and users and their various products and proclivities hidden to some degree or other. Cause and effect can be hard to discern, and it's usually only in hindsight that we can hope to be even remotely accurate about them. Survey numbers take ages to come out, and they often show only slight movements from year to year. I was able to prove the LSD collapse only because it had happened several years earlier, allowing time for the National Survey on Drug Use and Health and the emergency-room survey from the Drug Abuse Warning Network (DAWN) to be published.

Rick Doblin, the founder of the Multidisciplinary Association for Psychedelic Studies, had told me that there were at least three major acid producers up and running in the United States by the time I visited Black Rock City, in the summer of 2007. In conversations throughout my week at Burning Man, festivalgoers generally told me that they'd heard that LSD was making a resurgence, or even that they'd tripped at some point in the last year. But they also insisted that the drug was by no means prevalent.

Nonetheless, a random guy walking through our campsite on the event's last night handed me two hits on blotter paper. The problem for a reporter is that there's no sniff test for LSD. Sure, a chemist could analyze it and tell me what it's made of, but that would require driving with it, flying with it, and otherwise putting myself at legal risks I would rather avoid. At the same time, I didn't want to try it. It had been years since the last time I'd tripped, and my twenty-nine-year-old mind was much less interested in having its doors blown off than my college one had been. "The young mind can deal with certain kinds of gooping around that I don't think at this age I could," Bill Gates told *Playboy* in 1994 when asked about his youthful dosing.

I popped the drug in anyway. An hour later, it was clear the guy was for some unknown reason handing out free fake LSD. I was relieved. But I took another deep breath and, half hoping for the same reaction, ate a presumably dosed sugar cube that a friend had given me earlier in the week. I climbed into the passenger seat of our rented car as we pulled into the giant traffic jam of departing Burners. This acid was real.

The feeling that came over me as we crawled along was a deeply familiar one. The trip brought me back instantly to high school and college, and the scene around us added to the hallucinatory effect. Picture thousands of people piling whatever bizarre artwork they didn't burn into the backs of, or onto the tops of, colorful vehicles and then lining up for miles in the desert. Even without the drugs, it would have been an unmistakably psychedelic sight. This was the counterculture—or, at this point, subculture—that acid had inspired. It was comforting to know that the two had been reunited after only a brief separation.

Or it was until we came across another, less Utopian vision of psychedelic America a few minutes later: a brightly painted hippie bus, overturned by the side of the road, some of its passengers still trapped inside.

Because of the slow pace of the research, as I write, the most recent data available from the feds date back to 2007; DAWN's most recent emergency-room data are three years old—from 2005. (By the time this book is published, new numbers will be available, and I'll post them at YourCountryOnDrugs.com.)

A look at the data available now gives a hint of the reversal that's perceptible on the ground at hippie festivals. The percentage of young adults who claim to have used acid in the past year had been falling steadily in both the federal survey and in the *Monitoring the Future* report, which is produced by the University of Michigan and tracks drug use among teens. In 2005, the numbers for acid began to reverse, rising in both studies for the first time in years. The increase wasn't huge, because the numbers are so small, but it was a bump nonetheless. In the Michigan survey, which has more up-to-date numbers for high schoolers, the number has continued upward, bouncing from 1.7 percent in 2006 to 2.7 percent in 2008 among twelfth-graders. The numbers for twelfth-grade use in the past thirty days showed an even sharper move, from 0.6 percent in 2006 and 2007 to 1.1 percent in 2008—a rise the researchers deemed highly statistically significant at the 99 percent confidence level. (Most year-to-year moves are too small to be statistically significant even at a lower confidence level.)

The DAWN numbers show a bounce, too, although because the study's methodology was changed, the data from the second half of 2003 onward cannot be directly compared to the data before it. DAWN, run by the Department of Health and Human Services, isn't a scientific survey; it merely records the "mentions" of drugs by patients entering emergency rooms. (For instance, if you visited the ER with a broken finger, doctors asked if you were on drugs, and you said, "Yes, LSD," you'd go down in the LSD column, even if you were fibbing or the acid had nothing to do with your injury.) But DAWN data are still a good rough measure of drug trends. Between 1995 and 2000, mentions of LSD by emergency-room patients remained relatively stable, hovering at around 2,500 for each six-month period. But in the second half of 2001, LSD mentions dropped below 1,000 for the first time. In the next six-month period, they fell below 500.

Using the new methodology, DAWN found 656 mentions in the second half of 2003. That jumped to 1,953 over all of 2004, roughly a 50 percent spike. The next year saw 1,864 mentions.

There's evidence that attitudes could be changing about LSD among even the youngest of teens. The Michigan survey shows a steady decline in the number of eighth graders who see "great risk" in using LSD once or twice. Around 40 percent thought that the drug was high risk in the early nineties; only 20 percent thought so by 2008, with much of the decline coming after LSD vanished. "Disapproval" of acid—a metric taken separately from risk perception—has also tumbled, falling from nearly 80 percent in the early nineties to close to 50 percent in 2008.

Few have spent as much time measuring and thinking about such numbers than the University of Michigan's Lloyd Johnston, lead researcher on *Monitoring the Future*. I had last talked to him in 2004, when I was writing about acid's disappearance. This time, I called before the 2008 numbers were available and told him that the drug seemed to be making a return. He immediately pointed to the perceived-risk numbers.

"Perceived risk," he said, "is it." After decades of going over the data, Johnston said, he has become convinced that the leading indicator of a coming "epidemic" is almost always a change in the perception of the risk inherent in the use of a given drug. When we'd spoken a few years before, he'd told me how surprised he'd been to see LSD use drop off so sharply, because there was no corresponding rise in perceived risk. Rarely, if ever, had he seen such a phenomenon, leading him to conclude that the decline must have been due to a supply shortage, as I had argued in my *Slate* piece.

During acid's absence, the risk that teens associated with it continued to fall. "What I have seen is a portion of kids who are perceiving much less risk in LSD. That means that they're more susceptible to having a new epidemic," Johnston said. He also wasn't surprised that the decrease in perceived risk occurred primarily among the youngest kids the survey addresses.

"The eighth graders are often the first to show movement up or down," he said. "They don't have established sets of attitudes yet, so they're more susceptible to changes in the environment and more responsive to that in the short term. Most of them weren't around when there was the last LSD epidemic." Because the initial collapse of acid was due to economic rather than cultural reasons, and because youthful attitudes have become increasingly tolerant toward the drug, LSD seems poised for a comeback.

"There's a reemergence of new suppliers. I have no doubt that's in the process of changing," Johnston said. "I think we may be seeing a swing of the pendulum soon, and maybe you're getting an early indication of where it's coming from."

On May 13, 2008, Dr. Peter Gasser, a Swiss psychiatrist, gave a dose of LSD to a patient. He did so legally, launching the first LSD-assisted psychotherapy study in more than thirty-six years. Gasser, funded by Doblin's Multidisciplinary Association for Psychedelic Studies and approved by the Swiss government, enrolled twelve patients who'd recently been diagnosed with a terminal illness and were having difficulty coping. Acid aficionados consider LSD to be a "transitional" drug—that is, it can be beneficial during transitional periods in your life, not only the coming-of-age years examined by the Michigan survey, but also the slide into death that each of Gasser's patients was facing. Acid inventor Albert Hofmann, before his own passing in April 2008, personally raised money for Gasser's study.

The scientific world, at least, is undergoing something of a psychedelic renaissance. Since 2001, fourteen studies involving such drugs as DMT, Ecstasy, ayahuasca, peyote, and mescaline, many of them paid for by the Multidisciplinary Association for Psychedelic Studies (MAPS), have begun or been approved in the United States. Dr. John

Halpern at the Harvard Medical School has a study in development that looks at LSD's ability to alleviate cluster headaches. Halpern, who was a good friend of Pickard's before his arrest, published results of a similar, though less clinical study, in the journal *Neurology* in 2006. Halpern and two other researchers interviewed fifty-three people who'd used magic mushrooms or LSD to try to combat their "suicide headaches"—excruciating ordeals often likened to being stuck in the eye with a hot poker or having a stake driven through the top of your skull. 'Shrooms worked for 25 of 48 users, and acid worked in 7 of 8.

Researchers in Switzerland, the United States, Spain, and Israel are all studying the use of MDMA for posttraumatic stress disorder. With thousands of soldiers returning from war, there's no shortage of subjects. Psychiatrist Michael Mithoefer is leading one such project in South Carolina, in which a therapist walks a patient through his or her most traumatic experiences under the influence of Ecstasy. Charles Grob at UCLA's Harbor Medical Center, meanwhile, has nearly completed research into 'shrooming's impact on end-of-life anxiety. And in 2001, the FDA approved research by the University of Arizona, Tucson's Francisco Moreno into psilocybin's effect on nine patients with obsessive-compulsive disorder, after published case studies showed that people who'd 'shroomed on their own had found an improvement in their condition.

No matter how rigorous such studies might be, America has shown just about zero capacity to learn from its long and complicated history with drugs. Show me a quotation celebrating cocaine and playing down its dangers, and I couldn't tell you whether it's from 1980 or 1890. If technology continues to quicken the pace of drug trends, coke's next honeymoon could be right around the corner.

It takes about seven years, say drug-policy experts, for folks to realize what's wrong with any given drug. It slips away, only to return again as if it were new. Using drugs responsibly requires an educated understanding of the risk you're taking. It requires knowledge of the downsides, because the upsides make themselves known pretty damn quickly. While getting high might be fun, getting addicted isn't. Getting fired or arrested isn't. Getting your kids taken away isn't. After reading several rooms full of books, surveys, and memoirs about drugs and drug use and talking with recreational users, addicts, and nonusers alike, I've realized that when we're talking about the decision of whether to alter one's mind, we're talking very basically about what it means to be human, about the meaning of life, about hopes, dreams, fears, and all of that—stuff that, as Barack Obama might say, is above my pay grade.

Will kids start taking acid again? Sooner or later, yes. And the return of Phish for a three-day concert in March 2009 will surely whet the appetite. Will adults start bingeing on coke again? Barring an impossible victory in the U.S. drug war abroad, the answer is the same. To do so is human, and we live in a country that's always considered itself a grand human experiment. Whether Americans are more inclined to use drugs than other people depends on which type of American you mean. On one hand is the can-do idealist with a passionate faith in either religion or the republic who abhors intemperance. On the other is the libertarian individualist who wants not to be trodden on and believes that drug use is an expression of freedom. The vast middle, naturally, has always been a muddle of both. Sometimes one extreme takes over for a while; sometimes the other.

The past few years have seen a slight recession in antidrug attitudes. In every election season since the early nineties, we've moved farther from personal drug use being an issue for presidential candidates. Al Gore, John Kerry, and George Bush, the three major candidates to run in 2000 and 2004, all admitted to getting high; Bush is widely alleged to have also used coke during his party-boy days. Obama wrote about snorting "a little blow" in his first book, 1995's *Dreams from My Father: A Story of Race and Inheritance*, and when he was asked if he inhaled, said, "That was the point." In 2008, John McCain's denial of having ever done drugs was almost apologetic; he reminded audiences that he missed Woodstock because he was "tied up." Even McCain's hard-line evangelical running mate, Alaska governor Sarah Palin, confessed to having smoked pot.

Some slivers of recent pop culture have dealt with American drug use in a more realistic way, too. In August 2005, the cable channel Showtime introduced the series *Weeds*, which follows the tribulations of a widowed suburban California housewife who, in need of a career, decides to sell marijuana. A critical success and breakout hit, the show was described by the *New York Times* as "transforming for Showtime." As of this writing, the series has been renewed for at least four more seasons and drew 1.3 million viewers to its season 4 premiere. AMC subsequently launched the copycat *Breaking Bad*, about a high-school chemistry teacher diagnosed with cancer who becomes a meth dealer. HBO's critically celebrated *The Wire* preceded both series in its humanization of those involved with the drug trade and refusal to moralize on whether it should exist. All three shows treat drugs as something that's simply there. It's not much of an insight, perhaps, but it's something.

And it's something the U.S. government still refuses to acknowledge. No matter how entertaining the drug war might be on cable television, in the real world it remains grim business. In 2007, the United States set a record for marijuana arrests, collaring 872,720 potheads. A full 775,138 were busted for possession, which far exceeds the number of people arrested for all violent crimes combined.

Even as LSD receded and the Grateful Dead and Phish retired, the hippie-fest circuit continued to grow. Today, an energetic fan of jam bands could catch a festival pretty much every weekend somewhere in the United States from spring through fall. The All Good Music Festival & Camp Out, launched in 1996 at the height of the last acid boom, is modestly sized. It draws around twenty-five thousand people, and at the twelfth annual version of the event, held in the summer of 2008 in the hills outside Morgantown, West Virginia, about half of the attendees appeared to be college students.

One night was headlined by Phil Lesh & Friends, a group that plays mostly Grateful Dead songs led by a former bassist with that band. The next night brought Widespread Panic, still touring, followed by a 2 A.M. show by the Dark Star Orchestra, a Dead cover band that plays entire concerts start to finish, complete with the original dialogue between songs. Even the mistakes are repeated.

At Phish's final show, in Coventry, Vermont, back in 2004, a friend had said to me, as we waded through knee-deep mud to go from our tent to the stage, "I'm glad they're quitting so we don't have to do this anymore." At that show, only a few folks were wandering around offering "Doses, doses." Four years later, at All Good, it seemed as if every tenth person was offering it up. Later that summer, the Drug Enforcement Administration arrested Vanessa Marie Griffee, a thirty-one-year-old woman in Eugene, Oregon, and charged her with LSD distribution. The feds had busted a man in North Carolina who told them that Griffee would mail sheets of acid to "post offices that were located near music festivals and hippie gatherings," including to a P.O. box near that summer's Rainbow Gathering in Wyoming.

The first dealer who stopped by our campsite at All Good showed us a stack of sheets of blotter paper and another bag filled with sheets of the gel tabs that had been popular in the nineties. He said that a friend had recently arrived from the West Coast and brought "tens of thousands" of hits with him. ("This place is flooded," he lamented of All Good.) A friend bought a strip of ten hits for thirty dollars, significantly less than the ten or twenty dollars per hit that had become the norm post-2001. The dealer told me that he was having no problem unloading his wares at that price. A couple of our campmates were happy to sample them, and they stayed up until ten the next morning.

The next guy through also displayed dozens of sheets of acid. He was asking a similar price, but he said that his product wasn't moving as quickly as he'd like. "Either you want to trip or you don't," he said. I asked him about the LSD shortage in the early years of this century, and he said that he'd met Leonard Pickard in the Lot in the late nineties, but had assumed that the acid kingpin was another typical old Deadhead. Later, someone showed him a *Rolling Stone* story about Pickard's bust and trial, and he put two and two together.

The dealer mentioned that at the same time Pickard was taken down, another member of a different Family was put out of commission when someone gave him a massive dose of LSD. Because the Family member was diabetic, he was killed by the very drug that he had helped to manufacture. The story is the kind of legend that's common in the drug world—and close to impossible to verify. "I saw the funeral notice," the dose-man argued.

A more entrepreneurial dealer, a man from Indianapolis who called himself Rino, said that few people at All Good had asked him for acid. "You have to push LSD," he observed. But once he let people know that he had it, he said, he was able to move it fairly quickly. He'd also heard of the diabetic Family member who ate a huge dose and died. Following that and following Pickard's arrest, he recalled, LSD had doubled in price virtually overnight.

He scoffed, though, when I suggested that it had disappeared for a time. "I could always find it," said Rino, before charging us thirty dollars for ten hits of fake acid.

ACKNOWLEDGMENTS

Without the help of Leonard Roberge in shaping and editing this book, it would be little more than a few half-baked ideas and three hundred pages of data. Leonard helped cull out the parts you would have skipped over and ridiculed me whenever I tried to get away with not thinking an argument through or grappling with counterexamples. Before moving into book editing, Leonard was an editor at the *Washington City Paper*, where I was a reporter. The *City Paper*'s loss was my gain. His former boss, Erik Wemple, taught me pretty much everything I know about writing and reporting.

Eric Nelson, my editor at Wiley, deserves a giant chunk of the blame/credit for this work, too. I can't count the times I rejected his advice only to realize months later that he'd been right all along. And there's no doubt the book wouldn't exist were it not for my agent, Howard Yoon, suggesting the idea and helping to guide it to completion. He even came up with the clever title.

Slate's Jack Shafer took a chance on my first article about LSD way back when. A trend watcher's greatest nightmare, he has helped me resist the urge to make sweeping claims that aren't backed up by reality.

My longtime friend Jamal Wilson built the Web site Your CountryOnDrugs.com and was always looking to chip in some of the psychonautic tidbits that make the subculture so vibrant. (Check out Exodus 16:13, man.) I owe Harold Tripplehorn a huge debt for checking out books from the Library of Congress that had long gone out of print. Jeff Hild, too, helped with research both in the field and in the library. James Sappington was an able research assistant on many field excursions, as was my brother, Greg, the member of the family with the writer's gene. My mother, Cindy Quinn; father, George Grim; and stepmother, Melissa Grim, deserve credit for not disowning me when I began writing and reporting about drugs and in fact encouraged me the entire way.

Lisa Burstiner produced the book, and with her sharp eye caught a number of embarrassing typos and mistakes. Jim VandeHei and John Harris, my old bosses at *Politico*, were kind enough to let me take a significant amount of leave to write this book, however nervous they may have privately been as to what I'd come up with during that time.

Dave Jamieson and Rebecca Sinderbrand read portions of the book and gave thoughtful, and free, feedback, which was most appreciated. Christian Parenti talked me into joining him in Bolivia, convinced (correctly) that there would soon be an uprising and that we'd be among the only journalists there to cover it. He generously shared his driver, fixer, and translator.

Elements of this book have appeared in *Harper's*, *Slate*, *Salon*, *Mother Jones*, the *American Prospect*, *In These Times*, and *Politico*. The editors there helped shape my thinking, and I thank them for that. *Reason* magazine's Radley Balko opened up space on his must-read blog, TheAgitator.com, for me to post large chunks of this book while it was in rough form. His talented and (thankfully) critical readers caught errors of fact and reasoning in the early drafts, and the book is better because of it. Call it crowd-editing, I suppose.

Jon Hanna, who organizes the annual Mind States Conference, was always willing to do what he could to help me find sources that might be able to move this book forward—and he puts on a great conference, too. You should check it out. Some of the people I met there, too, have given generously of their time and knowledge, including Mark Pesce, Coco Conn, and Josh Wakefield. Alexander and Ann Shulgin are quite possibly the two kindest people I've had the privilege of meeting, and both were a great help.

Troy Dayton, Tom Angell, Aaron Houston, Bruce Mirken, and Paul Armentano routinely shared what they knew with me. Eric Sterling has a wealth of information and lent it to me willingly. Rick Doblin is one of the best resources a writer on drug policy and drug culture could ask for. His organization, the Multidisciplinary Association for Psychedelic Studies (maps.org), is doing great work in this world and is in need of support. If you make one contribution to a drug policy organization this year, I'd suggest considering his. Or consider erowid.org, the amazingly thorough online store of objective information on drug use. The site's founders, Fire and Earth Erowid, were immensely helpful in the writing of this book. They often found errors in the sections I shared with them, and for that I'm grateful. Any errors that remain are my own.

Leonard Pickard has kept up a correspondence with me for close to five years now, and I hope we can one day continue the conversation in a freer environment.

I had a great deal of help crafting this book every step of the way from researchers and writers who have come before me and continue their work today; I've named them either in the text itself or in the notes on sources.

And my wife, Elizan Garcia, put up with the loss of more than a year of evenings and weekends. It must have seemed to her—as it did to me—that I was trying to fill up a landfill with a spoon, but somehow I finished and couldn't have done it without her love and support. Thank you.

NOTES

Wherever it didn't totally wreck the flow, I put sourcing directly into the text. But that wasn't always possible.

In chapter 1, the scene of the chase and arrest of Leonard Pickard was pieced together from interviews with and letters from Pickard; interviews with a lead DEA agent on the case, Carl Nichols; and court testimony.

I rely on drug statistics throughout the book, many of them dependent on the honesty of drug users, which makes them necessarily suspect. But they should be just as suspect today as they were in 1975, which should allow the numbers to be used, at the very least, to describe trends. I most heavily used two surveys: the National Survey on Drug Use and Health and the University of Michigan's *Monitoring the Future* survey. The former I often refer to in shorthand as "a federal survey," because it is conducted by the Substance Abuse and Mental Health Services Administration. The latter I often refer to as "the Michigan survey"; it has questioned middle- and high-school students since 1975, and shortly after its inception, it expanded its scope to include older people, too.

I also refer to a reliable survey conducted by the Drug Abuse Warning Network, which measures the number of times a drug is mentioned by patients admitted to emergency rooms. Note that a drug doesn't need to have caused the trip to the hospital to be included in the survey; the patient merely had to have used it at some recent time before the injury. The global survey on drug use I reference in chapter 1 was conducted in 2008 by the World Health Organization. In helping me parse and understand these piles of numbers, I'm grateful to Peter Reuter and Lloyd Johnston, two of the most knowledgeable academics studying drug trends. Johnston has been running the Michigan survey for decades and knows the numbers cold.

In chapter 2, the story of the founding of the Woman's Christian Temperance Union comes from the group's own literature, bolstered by contemporaneous news accounts. Historian David Musto's collection, *Drugs in America: A Documentary History* (New York: New York University Press, 2002), compiles primary sources stretching back to the European discovery of the continent; it was of invaluable use in researching the eighteenth and nineteenth centuries.

Two other works of research were also useful to both chapters 2 and 3: David Courtwright's *Dark Paradise: Opiate Addiction in America Before 1940* (Cambridge, MA: Harvard University Press, 1982) and *Forces of Habit: Drugs and the Making of the Modern World* (Cambridge, MA: Harvard University Press, 2002). My opium-importation statistics, for example, come from *Dark Paradise*. The accounts of New York City police commissioner Theodore Bingham and other law enforcement officers' reaction to drugs in the early twentieth century also come from Courtwright, as do the reports by two Chicago doctors who studied more than five thousand narcotics addicts between 1904 and 1924. Much of the rest of the history is drawn from the *Congressional Record* or contemporaneous news reports. The cannabis-extract numbers come from congressional testimony.

Angela Valdez helped with the research for chapter 4. She won a 2007 AltWeekly Award for media criticism of flawed meth reporting, so there are few reporters out there who could have been a bigger help.

The numbers on Washington, D.C.'s and the nation's number of heroin addicts in the late sixties and early seventies, along with the story of President Richard Nixon's attempts at implementing treatment programs, come from Michael Massing's book *The Fix* (Berkeley: University of California Press, 2000). The DEA's budget and numbers of agents employed throughout its history are available on the Department of Justice's Web site (www.usdoj.gov), as are the agency's estimates of drug imports, seizures, prices, and purity cited in chapter 5.

Elsewhere in chapter 5, the story of Mountain Girl's position as a gourmet-pot pioneer and the tale of the FBI's attempt to set up Jerry Brown using Timothy Leary's wife both come from Martin Torgoff's 2004 book *Can't Find My Way Home: America in the Great Stoned Age, 1945–2000* (New York: Simon & Schuster, 2005). The data about Miami's coke-boom economy and customs seizures come from *Time* magazine as well as other contemporaneous reports mentioned in the chapter. The congressional testimony of the Medellín cartel's top accountant, Ramon Milian Rodriguez, appeared in 1999 in Alexander Cockburn and Jeffrey St. Clair's *Whiteout: The CIA, Drugs, and the Press* (Brooklyn, NY: Verso, 1999). The background on club owner Peter Gatien comes from Frank Owen's *Clubland: The Fabulous Rise and Murderous Fall of Club Culture* (New York: Broadway Books, 2003). The murder and crime figures come from the Department of Justice.

The record-sales numbers in chapter 6 come from the Recording Industry Association of America's Web site (www.riaa.com). The rest of the chapter and much of chapter 7 rest on the stack of journal articles cited in the text. The prescription-drug studies referenced include the 2008 Pew Internet & American Life Project's "Prescription Drugs Online" and the National Center on Addiction and Substance Abuse's 2008 study "You've Got Drugs!: Prescription Drug Pushers on the Internet."

The numbers on salvia mentions in the media in chapter 8 come from a May 2008 *Slate* piece by Jack Shafer, "Salvia Divinorum Hysteria: The Press Helps Fuel the Next 'Drug Menace.'"

The NAFTA/drug-smuggling connection described in chapter 9 was first made in Cockburn and St. Clair's *Whiteout*. The White House report that shows an increase in drug smuggling in the mid- to late nineties was done by the Office of National Drug Control Policy and is called "Estimation of Cocaine Availability: 1996–1999." It includes data dating back to 1991. The prison-population numbers are from the 2008 Pew Center on the States report. The drug-court numbers come from a 2006 Department of Justice special report produced by the National Institute of Justice. The cost-benefit numbers come from James L. Nolan Jr.'s *Reinventing Justice: The American Drug Court Movement* (Princeton, NJ: Princeton University Press, 2001).

The summary of Peter Reuter's analysis of black markets in chapter 10 is drawn from his book *Disorganized Crime: The Economics of the Visible Hand* (Cambridge, MA: MIT Press, 1983) and from interviews with him. His other relevant works include *Drug War Heresies: Learning from Other Places, Times, and Vices* (Cambridge, UK: Cambridge University Press, 2001), which he coauthored with Robert J. MacCoun; and *Chasing Dirty Money: The Fight against Money Laundering* (Washington, DC: Peterson Institute (2008), which he coauthored with Edwin Truman.

I couldn't have written chapter 12 without the help of Amanda Reiman, a lecturer at the University of California, Berkeley's School of Social Welfare. The author of an in-depth study of California's medical marijuana clinics, "Cannabis Care: Medical Cannabis Facilities as Health Service Providers," she generously gave me a tour of Bay Area dispensaries. Her introductions made club owners comfortable enough to share with me the details and history of their businesses. Our mutual friend Abby Bair, formerly of Americans for Safe Access, made the connection. Betty Yee, chairwoman of the State Board of Equalization, which collects taxes for the state of California, helped immensely as I tried to divine the tax revenue that the state takes in from its pot clubs.

Chapter 13 benefited greatly from the cooperation of Earth and Fire Erowid, the tireless founders of erowid.org, a must-read Web site for anyone looking for accurate information on drugs. I'm also grateful to Ann and Sasha Shulgin for sharing their wisdom with me regarding the creation of and experimentation with new kinds of drugs. Rebecca Snowden introduced me to the Brooklyn warehouse owner who hosts ayahuasca ceremonies.

Rick Doblin's organization, the Multidisciplinary Association for Psychedelic Studies (MAPS), compiled the information on current and past psychedelic studies, and Doblin himself was always helpful making connections and giving background information.

For more specific sourcing, check out YourCountryOnDrugs .com, where I'll post links to all of the relevant information that's available online. If something's still unclear, write to me at ryangrim@gmail.com, and I'll dig up the source for you.

INDEX